The Amish Struggle with Modernity

The Amish Struggle with Modernity

EDITED BY

Donald B. Kraybill

AND

Marc A. Olshan

University Press of New England

HANOVER AND LONDON

University Press of New England
Hanover, NH 03755

Printed in the United States of America
5 4 3 2 1
CIP data appear at the end of the book

CONTENTS

PART III
Occupational Changes

PART IV
Theoretical Perspectives

EDITORS' PREFACE

Many members of modern society embrace social change with delight—viewing each new gadget as a welcome sign of the upward spiral of progress that leads to a brighter tomorrow. Unlike such moderns the Amish have been skeptical about the fruits of scientific advance even though they have enjoyed some of them. Indeed, the Amish have often met the press of progress with stubborn resistance. Their battle with modernity has been a struggle to save their cultural souls.

In fact, we might say that the Amish struggle with modernity has been a war against progress, or at least the spirit of progress. They certainly are not opposed to everything new, and as the following essays show, they have acquiesced to modernity in many ways. But the Amish are engaged in a war against the spirit of progress—against arrogance, against progress as a goal, and against the social fragmentation and alienation that often accompany some forms of "progress."

It might seem odd to portray the pacifist Amish as engaged in warfare, even at the level of metaphor. But, in fact, the Amish see themselves as constantly fighting against the influence of worldly institutions. As one Amishman put it: "The Christian life is a warfare." The Amish war against progress, however, is not expressed in a blind resistance to all change. The chapters in this volume underscore the substantial degree of adaptation and compromise that has inevitably accompanied Amish survival.

Their battle has been against a particular concept of progress—one that has been enthusiastically embraced by much of the rest of the world since the Enlightenment. This notion of progress rests on the perfectibility of human institutions. It is founded on the confidence that reason and its handmaiden, technology, will eventually eradicate war, hunger, poverty, and all other evils that plague human beings. For the Amish such a view of progress is only one more expression of arrogance. To reject this view in all of its forms requires a constant struggle, a continual "warfare." This war is waged with faith rather than firepower and with self-effacement instead of smart bombs. But it is a war nonetheless, requiring courage, tenacity, and at times the tactic of compromise and even retreat.

The essays in this collection trace the Amish struggle with modernity in selective areas of their life. Their battle with the spirit of modernity focuses not only on the larger society but also within their own communities, on such matters as gender roles, the development of institutions, the appropriate use of technology, and the proper place of work as well as education and schooling. In their struggle with modernity the Amish have resisted change but they have also changed themselves. Many times they have had to change in order to resist the changes thrust upon them from the outside world. The authors of this volume profile the gains and losses in the Amish war against the spirit of progress in the twentieth century.

The stubborn resistance of the Amish has led them to reject the ownership of automobiles, high school, higher education, Sunday school, bureaucracy, and the use of electricity from public utility lines. Although friendly, they are in many ways an exclusive group that rejects many of the charms of modernity—inclusivity, diversity, scientific analysis, critical thinking, individual rights, and the venting of emotional reaction.

But the Amish have not stopped the clock of progress. Modernization has not by-passed their communities. Indeed, it has often pushed them toward the same patterns of social organization that virtually all other groups have been forced to adopt. That the Amish have not been pushed as far or as fast as others is a tribute more to their self-conscious resistance to modernization than to their immunity from it.

The contributors to this volume use the analytical power of their respective academic disciplines to better understand the Amish struggle with modernity. Of equal importance, the authors bring to their analyses decades of living and working in Amish communities. Their participation in haying, quilting, worshipping, socializing, and in Amish friendships hopefully corrects any tendency to treat the Amish as an ethnographic oddity. By understanding Amish responses to the universal pressures of modernity, perhaps we put ourselves in a better position to understand not only the Amish but also the limitations and potentials of our own encounter with modernity.

The following chapters trace the Amish struggle with modernity across many of their communities in North America. After noting the considerable diversity from settlement to settlement, several chapters provide descriptive portraits of social change. Three authors offer historical accounts of the Amish struggle with education, telephones, and tourism. The following section is devoted to the significant occupational changes that are underway in the Amish communities of North America. Theoretical considerations are then explored in three chapters dealing with fundamental assumptions of Amish society, with bureaucracy, and with the role of women. Finally, we ponder the question—"What Good Are the Amish?" The appendix provides a helpful discussion of migration patterns and growth over two decades as well as a listing of all the Amish settlements in North America.

Our debt of gratitude for assistance in completing the project is sizeable. We are especially grateful to Gertrude Enders Huntington, David Luthy, Thomas J. Meyers, Steven M. Nolt, Kimberly D. Schmidt, and Diane Zimmerman Umble, who have contributed essays to the volume. Anne Weidner provided able editorial assistance and guidance throughout the full spectrum of the project. Brenda Troutman in her always pleasant style coordinated many of the details and performed the bulk of the word processing. Erin Keefe and Sherry L. Troutman aided our editorial work in a splendid fashion. The Young Center for the Study of Anabaptist and Pietist Groups at Elizabethtown College provided ample support in many ways. We also thank Michael Lowenthal with the University Press of New England for his encouragement and unwavering support, and the staff of Herrick Memorial Library at Alfred University for their professional assistance. And we thank each other for the satisfaction of a pleasant partnership. Above all we thank the many Old Order Amish who have freely shared their homes, thoughts, and encouragement throughout the project.

DONALD B. KRAYBILL
MARC A. OLSHAN

The Amish Struggle with Modernity

A woman drives the horses that pull a modern haybaler. Although struggling to separate themselves from the larger culture, all Amish communities to some extent have accepted various aspects of modern technology. (Photograph by Lucian Niemeyer).

1

Introduction: The Struggle to Be Separate

DONALD B. KRAYBILL

In this introductory chapter Donald B. Kraybill offers an overview of Amish society. From their origins as dissident Anabaptists in sixteenth-century Europe to their present status as a religious minority in North American society, the Amish have struggled to maintain a distinctive subculture. After charting key features of Amish life and social organization, Kraybill shows how the decline of farming and emergent conflict with the state have brought significant changes in recent years to the Amish struggle to remain a separate people.

A Legacy of Dissent

Describing Amish attempts to establish their own schools in the face of stiff public opposition, Amishman Noah Hershberger called the conflict *A Struggle to be Separate*.[1] The Amish are a people of separation. Indeed their entire history can be called a struggle to be separate. They are one of several Anabaptist groups that trace their origins to the Radical Reformation of sixteenth-century Europe. Displeased with the slow pace of the Protestant Reformation and insisting that the church should be free from state control, a small group of dissidents sparked the beginnings of the Anabaptist movement in 1525 in Zurich, Switzerland. Insisting on adult baptism as the public sign of Christian faith, they were soon dubbed "Anabaptists," or "rebaptizers," by their opponents because they were twice baptized—first as infants in the Catholic church and now a second time as adults.

The Anabaptists stressed a double separation: the separation of church and state as well as the separation of the church from the evils of the larger culture.[2] In many ways it was a single separation because church and society were very much the same in the sixteenth century. In any event, the Anabaptists called for an unconditional adult commitment to a church that was free from the dictates of the state and separate from the values of the larger society that stood "outside the perfection of Christ." The Anabaptist movement soon spread into surrounding countries and encountered severe persecution. The claim of a free church, autonomous from the state, threatened to rupture the very fabric of society, the *corpus christianum* that had woven church and state into a seamless cloth over the centuries. Thousands of Anabaptists were soon tortured and killed as both civil and religious authorities sought to repress the new movement.[3]

Many of the Anabaptists eventually became known as Mennonites, owing to the influence of Menno Simons, one of their prominent leaders. Present-day Mennonites, Hutterites, and Amish trace their religious lineage to the Anabaptist movement.[4] The Amish emerged as a distinct group in about 1693 under the leadership of Jacob Ammann in the Alsace region of present-day France. Ammann, an Anabaptist leader, proposed some innovative practices in congregational life that included among other things social avoidance—the social shunning of persons who had been excommunicated from the church. This deviation from Swiss Anabaptist practice triggered a schism and the subsequent formation of the Amish church.[5] Ammann also advocated other practices that drew sharper lines of separation between the church and the larger world.

After the division the Amish and Mennonites maintained separate organizational identities but shared of course a common Anabaptist religious heritage. Both groups began migrating to the new world in the eighteenth century and often settled in the same geographical areas. Old Order Mennonite groups emphasizing strict separation from the world emerged as a conservative subgroup in the late nineteenth century when growing modernization led to schism and division in the Mennonite church. Today the Old Order Mennonites share many similarities and interests with the Old Order Amish including horse and buggy travel, plain dress, a conservative lifestyle, and the use of one-room parochial schools.[6]

Organizational Patterns

Unlike the Hutterites, who live in communal groups, the Amish own private property and live interspersed with their non-Amish neighbors in more than 230 settlements scattered across 22 states and the Canadian province of Ontario.[7] Amish society is informally organized along three levels or tiers—*settlement*, *district*, and *affiliation*. A settlement encompasses the general geographical area where Amish families live in proximity. Settlements vary considerably in size. A new settlement may consist of only one congregation whereas a large, established one such as the Lancaster, Pennsylvania, settlement may have over 100 congregations or church districts.

Some 25 to 35 families make up a typical church district—the basic social unit within the settlement. All members who live within the geographic boundaries of the district must participate in its social and religious life. About 150 persons, adults and children, live in an average church district.[8] The size of the district of course varies with its age. Older districts tend to be larger numerically, but often smaller geographically. Families living within the district worship together in each other's homes every other Sunday and they also share many neighborly activities. When the number of families grows too large to hold services in a home, the congregation branches into two smaller districts. The church district is the primary social and religious unit of Amish society—parish, precinct, tribe, and club all wrapped into a single social package.

Church districts that are "in fellowship" with each other constitute an affiliation. The congregations that are related within a particular affiliation share similar church practices and are able to exchange ministers in their worship services. Affiliations may stretch across several states. Moreover, several different affiliations may exist side by side in the same geographical settlement. The conservative Swartzentruber affiliation, for instance, has congregations in several states, but it also co-exists with a handful of other Amish affiliations in the Holmes County area of Ohio.

Leadership responsibilities in a church district are divided into three roles. The bishop is the senior official charged with exercising oversight of the spiritual welfare of the district. He officiates at worship services, communions, baptisms, weddings, confessions, and funerals. Typically each district also has two ministers and a deacon. The ministers are responsible for preaching in the Sunday worship services as well as for giving spiritual leadership to the life of the community. In addition to specific duties in the worship service, the deacon cares for the poor and needy in time of emergency and also works closely with the bishop to enforce the rules and discipline of the church. The ordained leaders, whose title in German (*Diener*) means "servant," team together to provide leadership for the congregation.

Selected by a congregational process known as the "lot," they serve for their lifetime without formal training or pay.[9]

In some settlements the ordained leaders meet once or twice a year to discuss problems of common concern. In other settlements they only meet if a special issue arises. Although the districts within a common affiliation try as much as possible to uphold the same rules and discipline, there may be some variation in practice from district to district. Each congregation or district, under the leadership of its bishop, has considerable autonomy. Both districts and affiliations are loosely linked together in a floating federation of personal ties but they do not have a central office, centralized leadership, or an annual conference. Senior bishops in a settlement typically receive deferential respect and are a source of wisdom and counsel, but all things considered the organizational structure is rather loose and flat. Its amorphous character sometimes frustrates outsiders who want quick and simple answers about "Amish policy" from a chief executive officer in a national office.

The congregational autonomy and loosely coupled affiliation structure also breed diversity. Among the nine hundred plus Amish congregations in North America, there is enormous variation in everyday practice. One bishop may permit the use of bicycles but a neighboring bishop may not. Telephones may be installed in a shop in one district but not in another. Artificial insemination of dairy cattle may be routine in one congregation but rejected in another. The biggest source of diversity, however, is between affiliations. The many differences within and between affiliations are often camouflaged by public symbols of Amish identity that provide a common public front and draw a sharp line of separation from the outside world.

These common badges of Amish identity include the Pennsylvania German dialect, the use of horse-drawn transportation, the rejection of electricity from public utility lines, the use of homes for worship, plain dress, beards for men, a prayer cap for women, an eighth-grade education, and the use of horses for field work. There are of course many other distinctive markers of Amish lifestyles but these public symbols of identity are shared by most Amish groups across North America. What is remarkable, yes astonishing, is that the Amish have been able to preserve these common badges of separation without a centralized national structure to link the more than 900 congregations across more than 230 different geographic settlements in North America.

Order and Separation

To maintain a strict separation from the larger culture requires a well-defined moral order. The orderliness of Amish life emerges from the implicit authority of the *Ordnung*—the understandings that prescribe the expectations of Amish life. The Ordnung is a religious harness that guides the community in the paths of faithfulness. Typically unwritten, the Ordnung embodies the dos and don'ts of Amish life by articulating the guidelines of Amish practice. The Ordnung includes both prescriptives (obey your teacher, wear traditional dress, use a horse and carriage) as well as proscriptives (do not drive a car, attend high school, or join the Rotary club).

The ways of the Ordnung are absorbed by children as the taken-for-granted assumptions of what it means to be Amish. The Ordnung stretches over many aspects of Amish life—from the technology used for farming to household decorations, from leisure activities to the proper accessories for the carriage. From time to time church leaders, with the endorsement of their congregations, will revise an aspect of the Ordnung to adapt to new changes in the environment. However, once "an understanding" becomes inscribed in the Ordnung it becomes quite difficult to revise it, at least for several years. "Our church Ordnung does not replace the Bible," said one Amishman, "It interprets the Bible as the church feels it applies to life today" ("Beyond" 1980:8).

Adult baptism is the singular event in Amish life when members not only make a public commitment to the Christian faith but also vow to uphold the teachings of the Ordnung for the rest of their lives. Although children learn the ways of the Ordnung from birth, they do not formally promise to comply with its expectations until they are baptized in their late teens or early twenties. Because of this, many parents and church officials are somewhat tolerant, although certainly not endorsing, of rebellious teenage behavior. Those who stray from the flock and are never baptized into the Amish church do not face excommunication or shunning.

Standing solidly in the Anabaptist tradition, the Amish place supreme importance on the baptismal decision. Those who pledge allegiance to the church in their baptismal vow are expected to faithfully uphold their commitment for life. Deviants who have taken the baptismal vow and then spurn the teachings of the church face excommunication and social avoidance (*Meidung*). Based on biblical teaching, shunning is a powerful form of social control that is intended to help maintain the purity of the church. The back door of the church always stands ajar. Those who repent of their mistakes and publicly confess their failures are welcome to return to the fellowship of the church and be reinstated. The experience of shunning, however, is always a painful one. An excommunicated person with considerable bitterness said, "You suddenly lose all your security and you become a goat and among the Amish you're treated like a piece of dirt."

The harness of the Ordnung is designed to prevent members from straying into the pitfalls and cesspools of worldliness. Separation from the world is a cardinal tenet of Amish faith. The severe persecution of their Anabaptist forebears in Europe inscribed into Amish consciousness a cautiousness toward the outside world that lingers today. The kingdoms of this world based on coercion, greed, and fame clash with the virtues of humility, simplicity, and nonresistance that form the heart of Amish faith. "The world hates nonconformity," said an Amish farmer as he summarized the tension the Amish feel between the church and the world.

Separation from the world is based on biblical texts such as Romans 12:2, which admonishes, "Be not conformed to this world," and II Corinthians 6:17, "wherefor come out from among them and be ye separate, saith the Lord. . . ."[10] The struggle to be a separate people is translated into many areas of life—dress, transportation, marriage to outsiders, the use of mass media, membership in public organizations, and public officeholding, to name a few. This religious belief, affirmed by biblical teaching and echoing the testimony of Anabaptist martyrs, marks the contours of this sectarian subculture's relationship with the larger society.

Amish leaders fear that a gradual drift toward worldliness will undermine the very integrity and identity of the Amish church. Consequently the church is in a constant struggle with the forces of worldliness, hoping to avert absorption into mainstream cultural values. "There is only one way to remain different from the world, and that is to be *separate*," wrote an Amish leader. "There is no way we can mingle freely and unrestrictedly with people who hold different values, and not be influenced by that mingling" ("Beyond" 1980:8).

Preparing for Eternity

In many ways the lovely quilts crafted by Amish women symbolize the patchwork of Amish beliefs and values. Stitched together over time, these deeply held values shape the religious outlook of Amish life. Describing the quiltwork of Amish values, one leader said, "Our whole way of life is interwoven. One part cannot be understood apart from the whole" ("Beyond" 1980:7). He then went on to describe the religious underpinnings of Amish culture, "We are not here to have a good time, or to make a lot of money or become famous. Instead we are here to do the will of God, love our fellow men, and prepare for eternity." Prayers before and after meals as well as daily scripture readings embroider each day with a sense of reverence.

The Amish believe that faithful religious lives can best be nurtured in the womb of strong families living together in rural areas. One leader spelled out in eloquent but simple terms the social ideals that shape the Amish worldview. "We put a lot of importance on home, family, church, and community. We believe God wants his people to live in love with each other in a close-knit brotherhood of believers. We stress the virtues of purity, devotion, honesty, and faithfulness. Our desire is to live quiet, humble lives, raising our children in the fear of God and helping to build the church" ("Beyond" 1980:7).

Amish society is pervaded by communal values. The collective welfare and common good transcend claims of individual rights, personal achievement, and selfish ambition. Indeed self-denial, humility, meekness, and obedience are considered four of "the most important Christian duties" in Amish life (*Questions* 1992:82). These virtues would likely skid to the bottom of modern society's ladder of values. While moderns assume that happiness rises as individual freedom expands, the Amish argue that genuine satisfaction comes not from an unbridled individualism but from giving oneself up in the service of an orderly community.[11] True happiness is discovered not in the unfettered exercise of individual rights but in yielding to the desires of a larger community. It is only in the ordered routines of a religious community, the Amish contend, that one can find true identity, eternal meaning, and secure belonging.

Early Anabaptists sometimes used the German word *Gelassenheit* to signify the yielding of oneself to higher authorities—to God and the Christian community. Gelassenheit, the bedrock value of Amish culture, entails self-surrender, self-denial, contentment, and a quiet spirit. Those who cloak themselves in the spirit of humility are eager to yield the right of way to others. They are willing to forgo ambition and the pursuit of individual goals for the sake of the larger community. "Who are the most devoted, sincere, and useful Christians?" asks an Amish catechism book. The straightforward response, "They who practice self-denial" (*Questions* 1992:77).

Pride is the enemy of Gelassenheit. Vanity, arrogance, and deceit lead to self-adulation that clamors after jewelry, fashionable clothing, and public recognition—all the things that moderns consider essential for healthy self-esteem. Ideal Amish values are embodied in a quietness of spirit and an unadorned gentleness—a sense of reserve that is not always seeking to control things. In the face of conflict, and even insult, many Amish prefer silence, suffering, or patient resignation.

Moderns cringe at the thought of not expressing every thought, protecting every right, and asserting every wish in the face of interpersonal competition. But to the Amish person an orderly religious community can only be built on the bedrock of Gelassenheit—which requires the death of self and a full surrender to God and community. An Amish admonition to humility ends with the words of a hymn,

> Oh, to be emptier, lowlier,
> Mean, unnoticed, and unknown,
> And to God a vessel holier,
> Filled with Christ, and Christ alone! (*Questions* 1992:81)

Pride and disobedience threaten to disrupt the harmony of an orderly community. Individuals who call attention to themselves and insist on having their own way wreak havoc in community life. Consequently Amish leaders must diligently be on the lookout for arrogant, self-seeking behavior that elevates the individual and mocks a full surrender to the ways of community. The taboo on jewelry and personal photographs is one way of curbing expressions of individualism. Distinctive costume in Amish society not only serves as a collective name tag but it also hampers the use of dress as a tool of individualism. In all of these ways members are expected to forgo the self and pledge their support to the larger community.

Growth and Retention

The Amish have enjoyed remarkable growth in the twentieth century. Despite their emphasis on separation and penchant for traditional ways, they have thrived in the midst of the social and technological upheavals that have accompanied the twentieth century. From a paltry band of 5,000 at the turn of the century, the Amish have grown to more than 140,000 today. Because they are reluctant to count their flock for fear of pride, it is difficult to obtain precise numbers of members. Accurate records of the number of congregations, however,

TABLE 1.1.
Amish Population Growth, North America 1900–1992

Year	*Church Districts*	*Estimated Population*
1900	32	4,800
1910	57	8,550
1920	83	12,450
1930	110	16,500
1941	154	23,100
1951	202	30,300
1961	269	40,350
1971	367	55,050
1981	569	85,350
1991	898	134,700
1992	930	139,500

Note: these population estimates assume 150 persons per district.
Sources: Raber (1993), Luthy (1992), *The Mennonite Yearbook,* and various informants.

permit a reasonable estimate of the number of children and adults who claim the Amish name. In recent years their population has been doubling about every twenty years. In the ten-year period from 1981 to 1991 the population jumped from about 85,000 to nearly 135,000 as shown in table 1.1. This represents an increase of 329 church districts—about 33 per year in the decade. David Luthy describes the population growth and migration patterns in detail in appendix I.

Several factors have produced the robust growth rate. Groups can only grow by making babies or making converts. The Amish have grown largely through natural reproduction rather than through evangelism. They average about six or seven children per family.[12] Throughout the twentieth century the Amish have gradually increased their use of modern medicine and tapped the services of trained physicians, thus reducing infant mortality and helping families to flourish. Children are typically viewed as an economic asset in agrarian societies and in Amish eyes they are seen as a blessing from the Lord.

But making babies is not enough. Children must be persuaded to pledge their allegiance to the community. The rise of Amish parochial schools in many states in the last half of the twentieth century undoubtedly has contributed to the church's persuasive pull. Retention rates vary of course by settlement and affiliation as well as by historical periods depending on the particular mix of economic, social, and religious circumstances of the time. In the three largest settlements the retention of children is typically 80 percent or higher. In the Elkhart-Lagrange settlement in northern Indiana about 81 percent of the adult children affiliate with the church. The Lancaster settlement retains at least 85 percent of its youth.[13]

In the Holmes County area of Ohio the retention rates vary by affiliation. The large Old Order affiliation persuades about 86 percent of its youth to stay with the church. The more conservative "Andy Weaver" group in the same settlement holds about 95 percent of its youth. On the other hand, the more progressive New Order churches are only able to retain about 57 percent of their youth.[14] The relationship between affiliation and retention is discussed in more detail in chapter 4.

In any event the evidence suggests that on the average at least four out of five Amish youth will join the church of their birth. The vigorous population growth in the twentieth century has been bolstered by large families, the growing use of modern medicines, the rise of Amish parochial schools, and the ability of the church to retain over 80 percent of it progeny. Although the Amish have prospered numerically in the twentieth century, they have also experienced major changes as they have struggled to remain a separate people. Two significant areas of change involve their occupations and their relations with the state. The following two sections trace the contours of change in these two areas.

The Demise of a Legacy

The dramatic shift in Amish occupations from farming to microenterprises and in some cases to factory work will undoubtedly have a long-term impact on the nature and character of Amish life. For three hundred years, since their European origin, Amish life has been rooted in the soil. Their agrarian way of life has provided a cradle for their families, bestowed stability on the church, cultivated their distinctive identity, and in many ways shielded them from the outside world. But in recent years their agrarian legacy has been eroded by the swift currents of modernity.

Amish attachments to the soil remained firm until the middle of the twentieth century when they began to unravel. The rising cost of prime farmland, encroaching suburbanization, growing tourism, and the burgeoning Amish population have all contributed to the decline of farming. Changes in farming technology and government regulations—especially those related to milk production—have made it difficult for some farmers to earn a living. All of these factors have gradually steered the Amish in the older, larger settlements away from the farm. These same forces have also encouraged other Amish families to establish new settlements in more rural areas where they can purchase cheaper farmland.

The exodus from the farm has grown steadily in the past thirty years in the larger established settlements. In the Elkhart-Lagrange settlement of Indiana, Meyers (1991b:315) reports a steady drop in the percentage of men involved in farming, from 61 percent in 1970 to 37 percent by 1988. Concomitant with this shift was a rise in factory employment, especially in recreational vehicle factories. This trend, which increased from 26 percent in 1970 to 43 percent by 1988, is described in detail by Meyers in chapter 10.[15] The Elkhart-Lagrange settlement is distinctive for the large number of persons who have taken up employment in factories.

The number of farmers in the Amish settlement in Geauga and Trumbull Counties in northeastern Ohio had dipped to nearly 30 percent by 1977. And already by that time 27 percent were employed in factories.[16] In the largest Amish settlement in North America, in Holmes County, Ohio, farming has also dwindled. In 1965 about 72 percent of male household heads were farming but today the number tilling the soil has dipped to 43 percent.[17] The percentage who are farming in the Holmes County settlement varies considerably by affiliation. Among the more conservative Swartzentruber group more than three-fourths are on farms, but among the progressive New Orders the number drops to nearly 35 percent. Those who have left their plows behind are involved in hundreds of small microenterprises as well as factory work, but the rate of factory employment is lower than in Indiana's Elkhart-Lagrange settlement. A recent inventory of the Holmes County area lists over seven hundred Amish-owned and -operated microenterprises. Table 1.2 displays the various types of small businesses that have grown up in this settlement.

A similar occupational pattern has emerged in the Lancaster settlement in Pennsylvania. As early as 1977 about two-thirds of the men were farming. In recent years the number on farms has dropped to about 50 percent.[18] Unlike some of the other settlements, Lancaster has strongly discouraged persons from working in factories. Those who have deserted their plows and cows have established nearly one

TABLE 1.2.
Distribution of Amish Enterprises in the Holmes County, Ohio, Settlement (in Percentages)

Cabinet and woodworking shops	21.5
Carriage shops	6.8
Pallet lumber shops	6.8
Carpentry crews	6.6
Harness shops	6.6
Repair shops	6.4
Blacksmith shops	4.3
Engine shops	2.7
Bulk food stores	1.9
Quilting, sewing, weaving	1.9
Upholstery shops	1.9
Greenhouses	1.7
Painters	1.7
Hickory rocker shops	1.6
Masonry work	1.6
Concrete finishing	1.4
Sharpening service	1.3
Archery and gun supplies	1.1
Bakeries	1.1
Country stores	1.1
Dry goods	1.1
Plumbing and well drilling	1.1
Gas appliances	1.0
Orchard and produce	1.0
Tarp shops	1.0
Excavating	0.9
Bike shops	0.7

TABLE 1.2.
Continued

Metal work	0.7
Roofing	0.7
Shoes	0.7
Used furniture and clothing	0.7
Miscellaneous enterprises	10.3
Total $N = 701$	Percent = 100

Source: Address and Business Directory of Holmes County and Vicinity [Amish] (1993).

thousand cottage industries and small businesses—the bulk of them since 1980. The story of their phenomenal growth is told in chapter 9.

The mythic stereotype portrays Amish families living self-sufficiently on pleasant farms. But the reality behind the myth has crumbled in the last decades of the twentieth century. In several of the larger settlements less than half of the families are farming and in some cases less than a third. This rather dramatic shift in occupations will surely change the character of Amish life and culture over the generations. The rise of cottage industries and small businesses has preserved many of the traditional values of Amish culture. Nevertheless, the exodus from the farm will undoubtedly have an impact on family size, revise child rearing practices, alter attitudes toward both work and leisure, increase interaction with the outside world, and introduce greater variations in wealth and status within the community. It promises, in short, to be one of the most consequential changes that has touched the Amish community in the last half of the twentieth century and will surely shape their destiny in many ways.

Separation from the State

In their struggle to be a separate people the Amish have frequently clashed with the designs of an ever-expanding state in the twentieth century. The desires of the state, based ultimately on brute force, have collided inevitably with the gentle but stubborn spirit of Amish Gelassenheit. The spirit of religious freedom, however, has hovered over the Amish despite dozens of legal struggles and sometimes bitter disputes at various levels of government (Kraybill 1993a). Some

Amishmen have been fined and others have sat in prison for disobeying laws that they felt infringed upon their religious convictions. Three legal disputes were reviewed by the U.S. Supreme Court between 1972 and 1990.[19] But despite all the legal wrangling, the Amish have fared rather well. For the most part they have been able to practice their religious faith not only without state interference but often with its protection. Indeed, the prosperity that the Amish have enjoyed in the twentieth century has partly flowed from the tolerable, even accommodating political conditions they have experienced in North America.

Encountering a happier fate than that of their religious forebears in Europe, no North American Amish have been executed for their faith and few have chosen to migrate for religious reasons. Indeed the ironies of history have brought tourists by the millions to gawk and gaze at Amish ways in some of the larger settlements. So, by a strange twist of fate, those who were once hunted and burned at the stake have become the object of public curiosity if not outright admiration and respect. Despite such public esteem and sometimes sympathetic support, Amish clashes with the state have intensified in the twentieth century. Indeed, in the sixty-year period between 1930 and 1990 they have experienced more conflict with the state than in any other time in their three-hundred-year history except for the violent suppression of their European forebears.

At least seven factors have contributed to the spiraling conflict with the state. First, the expanding Amish population and subsequent migrations have led them to new regions where government officials were often unfamiliar with and sometimes intolerant of Amish beliefs and customs. Second, the movement into new areas has sometimes posed an economic threat or at least a perceived one to their new neighbors. An influx of Amish settlers sometimes boosted land prices, contributed to a decline in farm equipment sales, and shrank per capita subsidies for public schools—not to mention the chopped-up roads from horseshoes and a decline in gasoline sales.

A third and major source of conflict has resulted from the growing tentacles of the state welfare system, ever expanding since the depression of the thirties. The ever-encroaching net of government programs—Social Security, Workers' Compensation, unemployment insurance, Medicare, Medicaid, and a host of agricultural subsidy programs—has threatened to strangle Amish values of mutual aid and separation from the world. Amish involvement in such programs would lead to the demise of spontaneous mutual aid within their community as well as to an erosion in separation from the world.

The regulatory apparatus of the state, increasing in scope and intensity during the mid-twentieth century, has provided a fourth source of the growing legal battles. The rolls of red tape were intended to protect the environment, prevent disease, and assure the safety of employees and consumers alike, as well as to regulate zoning practices to assure the orderly development of land. Based for the most part on good intentions, the regulatory arm of the state has often frustrated the Amish, who simply wanted to follow age-old customs handed down from former generations without any government interference.

Fifth, conflicts have also flared because of the wide variety of laws and their multiple interpretations by the many layers of government officials: local, county, regional, state, and national. Educational expectations and regulations for slow-moving vehicles vary from state to state. Zoning regulations typically vary from township to township even within the same county. The growing maze of laws and regulations often baffle and frustrate Amish persons who are unfamiliar with the ways of bureaucracy.

A sixth factor that has added to conflict and misunderstanding with the state is the decentralized, amorphous nature of Amish society. Without a central headquarters or national structure, and with over nine hundred local congregations aligned with different Amish affiliations in more than two hundred settlements, there has been no official "Amish" policy or common view on most issues. Indeed it was the growing wave of legal conflicts that prompted the emergence of the National Amish Steering Committee so that the Amish could begin to speak to the government with a somewhat unified voice. Marc A. Olshan describes the evolution of this organization in chapter 12. Although the emergence of the National Steering Committee provides a national forum for discussing disputes with the government, it is not a highly centralized bureaucratic response.

Perhaps the most significant factor stirring confrontations with the state in the twentieth century has been the growing gap between Amish practice and the technological pace of modern life. Horses and carriages seem downright dangerous on high-speed roadways, at least from the modern point of view. But in the words of one Amishman, "It's the car that kills, not the carriage." Gas lanterns sitting around in barns and homes seem to be literally playing with fire. And who but the Amish would dare to challenge the modern assumption that more and more education is the primary ticket to happiness? The growing chasm between Amish ways and modern values has exacerbated the spate of legal conflicts in the twentieth century.

These seven factors have spurred legal clashes over education, midwifery, the use of hard hats at construction sites, Social Security, Workers' Compensation, the use of slow-moving vehicle signs, land use, sanitation, zoning regulations, and health care. The list goes on and on.

The On-Going Struggle

On three particular issues the state has acquiesced to Amish convictions in ways that have bolstered their well-being and preservation. Longtime conscientious objectors, the Amish along with other religious objectors have enjoyed the option of performing alternative service rather than joining the armed forces. Many Amish have been able to receive farm deferments during times of military draft, but others have served in various alternate service projects during World War II as well as in the fifties and sixties. Without this provision many Amish would have likely considered migrating to countries more hospitable to their pacifist convictions.

The Amish have always insisted that the church should care for the material needs of its members. When asked to cooperate with Social Security they refused because in their eyes the program was an "insurance" that would erode their mutual aid commitment to the church. Amish convictions collided with the Internal Revenue Service in 1955 when the Social Security program was extended to cover self-employed farmers. The dispute continued for a decade until Congress in 1965 exempted self-employed workers if they were members of a recognized religious sect that opposed accepting public retirement and disability benefits. The exemption was expanded in 1988 when new congressional legislation stretched it to Amish persons who work for Amish employers. Although non-Amish employers of the Amish must withhold Social Security, most Amish employees do not tap its benefits. Exclusion from Social Security was indeed a major victory for the Amish.

Their most significant win, however, came in 1972 when the U.S. Supreme Court ruled in their favor in the landmark *Wisconsin v. Yoder*. This decision sanctioned the Amish school system and permitted Amish youth to end their formal education after eight grades. In a culmination of the legal skirmishes, fines, jail sentences, and bitter disputes that had begun as early as 1914, the Supreme Court verdict freed the Amish from the fingers of public education and boosted the growth of one-room Amish schools, which today number more than eight hundred. This critical juncture in Amish-state relations has helped the Amish to propagate their own values, insulate their young from alien views, as well as monitor the social relations of Amish youth with the outside world. The schools, in short, have contributed in a significant way to the preservation of the culture of separation.

The outcomes of other legal disputes are mixed. All but the most conservative of Amish groups have agreed to display slow-moving vehicle signs on their carriages as well as battery-operated lights. Those living in more congested areas have complied, but sometimes grudgingly, with zoning and sanitation requirements. Shop owners have been forced to conform with zoning and fire codes in the construction of their businesses. And many Amish, but not all, have cooperated with public health officials in the immunization of children. Farmers wanting to ship milk to Grade A markets have been forced to store their milk in large tanks and follow chilling and sanitation standards. In all of these ways and many more, the state has modified Amish practices in the twentieth century.

Despite their desire to be separate from the world, the Amish have become entangled with the larger society in many ways. The occupational shift toward microenterprises has directly tied them into the economic structure of the outside world. The many changes in the welfare and regulatory scope of the state have clashed with Amish hopes to be a separate people. Struggling to remain a free church in the face of such economic and legal entanglements has tested the steely character of Amish convictions. But in their struggle to be separate the Amish have enjoyed the tolerance of a political order resting on a constitutional commitment to uphold religious liberty for cultural minorities. Because of this commitment by the host society, the Amish struggle to remain a separate people has for the most part been successful, at least for the moment.

Part I

Social Change and Adaptations

After fire gutted a woodworking shop the community rallies to clean up debris and rebuild. A uni-loader on rubber tires is permitted by the Ordnung of Lancaster County because it is rented and not owned by a church member. (Photograph by Dennis Hughes).

2

The Amish Encounter with Modernity

DONALD B. KRAYBILL

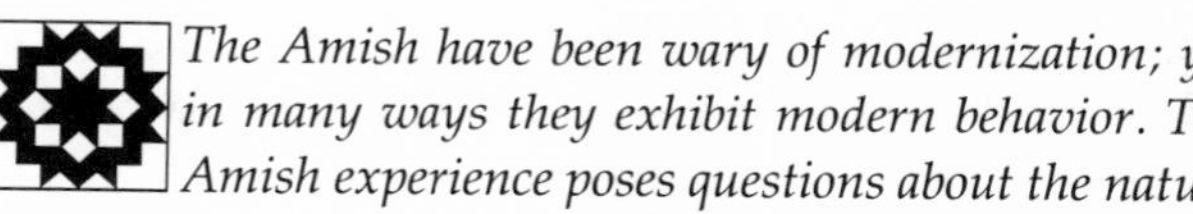

The Amish have been wary of modernization; yet in many ways they exhibit modern behavior. The Amish experience poses questions about the nature of modernity. In this chapter, Donald B. Kraybill identifies some features of the elusive concept of modernity and then profiles the extent of Amish adaptations at both cultural and structural levels. Kraybill concludes by arguing that modernity is a process of social separation that fragments and differentiates. Thus the Amish, in order to maintain cohesive communities, have tried to remain separate from modernity, the Great Separator.

Modern Amish?

Booming machine shops in some Amish settlements hold sophisticated manufacturing equipment powered by air and hydraulic pressure. Some Amish craftsmen use the latest fiberglass techniques to manufacture horse-drawn carriages. Hundreds of Amish-owned microenterprises place entrepreneurs in direct relation with the outside world on a daily basis. Successful Amish dairy farms in the more progressive settlements are efficient operations that use feed supplements, vitamins, fertilizers, insecticides, chemical preservatives, artificial insemination, and state-of-the-art veterinary practices. Professional farm consultants advise Amish farmers in some settlements about their use of pesticides, fertilizers, and seed selection. New Amish homes in the more progressive settlements tout up-to-date bathroom facilities, modern kitchens with lovely cabinets, formica, vinyl floor coverings, and the latest gas stoves and refrigerators. In spite of cherished stereotypes, some Amish are embracing certain aspects of modernity.

Modernization, however, varies considerably from settlement to settlement across North America. Among the more conservative Amish groups, refrigerators and indoor bathrooms are taboo. Cows are milked by hand and hay balers are not pulled in fields. It is reasonable to hypothesize that Amish adaptation to modern life directly varies with the population density of non-Amish who live in the same geographical area. In other words, innovative Amish behavior appears highly correlated with urbanization. Amish settlements in more isolated rural areas are, generally speaking, more resistant to modernizing influences.[1] Settlements such as the one near Lancaster, Pennsylvania, situated in the midst of a rapidly urbanizing region, are quite progressive in their use of technology and openess to the outside world.

The Amish do indeed cling to older customs in their church services, in their attitudes toward education, and in their rejection of individualism. The lack of electricity in their homes blocks the door to microwave ovens, air conditioners, toasters, doorbells, televisions, clothes dryers, and blow dryers. But does a rejection of high school education, cars, and public-utility-line electricity mean that the Amish are a premodern folk society? The unusual mixture of progress and tradition abounding in Amish society poses interesting questions about the meaning of modernization. How have the Amish responded to the pressures of modernity? What strategies have they employed to cope with modern life in the twentieth century? They have drifted along with the stream of progress in some areas of their culture but have staunchly and successfully resisted it in others.

The Process of Modernization

Modernization, modernity, and modern are elusive concepts. Their conceptual attraction lies in their ability to link vast and diverse elements of social life into a common interpretative framework. But their glory is also their gloom. The sweeping analytical scope of the concept of modernization, for example, threatens to render it meaningless because its elasticity stretches over virtually all aspects of society. The present moment is somehow always a "modern" one. Nevertheless, the notion of modernization provides a conceptual perspective from which to read and interpret social change.

Modernization is a social *process;* whereas modernity refers to the social *features* of modern societies. Typical use of the concept of modernization reveals several salient characteristics. Modernization is comprehensive, longitudinal, and societal in scope. Modernization denotes macro-level, *massive* changes that occur *over time* throughout an *entire* society. The typical practice of juxtaposing modern societies against "traditional" ones is an example of what Levy (1986) calls the "fallacy of misplaced dichotomies," for it erroneously implies that modern societies lack traditions. All societies including modern ones develop traditions of one sort or another. Levy argues that it is more accurate to think of the differences that arise between modern and nonmodern societies.

The conceptual waters are often muddied as cognate terms—progress, industrialization, urbanization, development, and westernization—float alongside modernization in common parlance. These terms have more specific meanings than modernization although the concept of modernization is often used to encompass many of them. What is the driving force that fuels the engine of modernization?

Social theorists are in general agreement that the application of technology (industrialization) to virtually all aspects of social life is the prime catalyst in the modernizing process. However, operational definitions of modernization are innumerable and vary considerably by analyst. For Lerner (1968:386) it is "the process of social change whereby less developed societies acquire characteristics common to more developed societies . . . the process of social change in which development is the economic component." With a more succinct formula that focuses explicitly on technology, Levy (1972, 1986:3) argues that modernization is simply the ratio of inanimate to animate sources of power. Berger et al. (1973:9) define modernization as "the institutional concomitants of technologically induced economic growth." Berger also contends that perceived choice—the shift from fate to options—is the hallmark of modernity. The exercise of control over the physical and human environment is paramount in a modern society.[2] While the definitions of modernization vary in focus and nuance, they typically underscore the role of technology in stimulating social change.

The development of machine power, technological production, the factory system, and a rationalized economy, all in their own way have contributed to the rise of the modern era. This does not presume a technological determinism, for certain values or attitudes may indeed be required in the social seedbed before technological innovations are able to germinate. Thus, while technology drives modernization, technology itself is of course shaped by human ideas in a reciprocal process. For instance, a certain world view may encourage technological invention—the development of a computer. The new form of technology, the computer in this case, may in time act back upon and alter the way humans think and organize themselves. The Amish, whose religious values steered them away from large factories to small shops, will likely discover over the years that their own miniaturized factories are in fact changing the very values that sent them to the shops in the first place. Thus, while technological innovation propels modernization forward, there is always a dynamic circularity between human ideas and material technology.

At the outset, several assumptions about modernization deserve clarification. First, modernity should not be equated with progress. Modern life in sociological perspective is not necessarily either better or worse than nonmodern life. Modernity, like any other form of social organization and epoch of history, can be objectively analyzed. Its costs and benefits can be assessed; but we ought not to confer an a priori superiority on modern life. In some ways it is, and in other ways it surely isn't, superior to nonmodern life. Second, societies are not completely modern or nonmodern; that is, there are degrees of modernity. Many aspects of nonmodern life permeate even modern societies. A given society may be rather highly modernized on some dimensions while exhibiting minimal modernization on others.

Third, modernization can be conceptualized on two levels of social reality: *structure* and *consciousness* (Berger et al. 1973). Modernization thus not only revamps the social organization or social architecture of an entire society, it also penetrates human consciousness and alters our ways of thinking. An ever-increasing division of labor reflects the structural encroachment of modernity while a growing embrace of the importance of individual rights echoes such change at the level of consciousness. The dimensions of modernity enumerated in this essay will be identified and analyzed at both structural and ideological levels. Under normal conditions, we might expect a direct relationship between the modernization of structures and the modernization of consciousness. That is, without making causal assumptions, the two dimensions of modernization can be expected under normal social conditions to rise and fall together. Under certain conditions, however, they may function independently of one another. In terms of the Amish we can ask to what extent the modern world has transformed their organizational patterns as well as penetrated their collective consciousness—their values and ways of thinking.

Fourth, *individual* and *collective* units of analysis must be distinguished. In chapter 11 Olshan argues that the Amish exhibit modern traits because they make deliberate choices. They have made collective decisions, for example, to reject certain forms of technology and accept others. They have decided to establish their own schools, have chosen to permit riding in cars but not ownership, and have agreed to use tractors at the barn but not in fields. Indeed, in all these ways the Amish have made deliberate choices—have acted in modern ways at the *collective* level. However, the consequences of many of these collective decisions limit and restrict choices for *individuals*. Members are not free to dress as they please, buy a car, enter certain occupations, or pursue higher education. Thus, while the community acts in a modern fashion *collectively* by making choices, it nevertheless on the individual level has restricted personal behavior by deterring *individuals* from acting in a modern mode—exercising all the rights and freedoms of unfettered individualism.

Dimensions of Modernity

To what extent have the features of modernity penetrated Amish life—their organizational structure as well as their cultural consciousness? The facets of modernity identified by social analysts are legion. The following, somewhat arbitrarily selected dimensions of modernity are not exhaustive nor do they follow a causal sequence.[3] Typically underscored by sociologists, these factors do, however, distinguish modern worlds from nonmodern ones. After a brief discussion of each dimension, we will explore the ways in which the Amish have grappled with it.

Modern societies by and large are highly *specialized*. In nonmodern societies social functions from cradle to grave—birth, work, play, education, worship, friendship, and death—revolve around the home. They often, in fact, occur in the home. In advanced societies such social activities "grow up" and leave home, and as they depart, they split into specialized spheres. These cradle-to-grave functions eventually become lodged in specialized institutions—birthing centers, fitness spas, day care centers, schools, grooming salons, factories, hospitals, golf courses, hospices, and funeral homes. It is in these sharply differentiated settings that experts deliver their highly specialized services. The automobile and mass transit enable modern folks to spend their days shuttling from site to site to both deliver and receive such services. The imprint of structural differentiation and functional specialization is thus stamped across the face of modern life.

The degree to which specialization has shaped Amish life varies of course among Amish settlements, but without exception the Amish world is clearly less differentiated than modern society. The rejection of high school and the primacy given to agriculture have minimized occupational specialization. As Amish families move from farms to microenterprises as well as into factory work in some settlements, the degree of occupational specialization will likely increase. It will undoubtedly remain low as long as high school and college remain taboo. Terminating education at eighth grade effectively deters members from pursuing professional jobs. The relatively low degree of occupational specialization has also minimized social class differences and contributed to the relative homogeneity of the Amish social structure. The rising numbers of Amish microenterprises in some settlements may over time encourage the emergence of a three-tier class structure consisting of farm owners, business entrepreneurs, and day laborers.

Institutional specialization is also notably nil. Schools, shops, and several libraries are the primary institutional expressions beyond the home that have physical structures and permanent locations. Schools and shops are frequently located in the immediate locale—nearby at least, if not at home. There is a growing differentiation in the type and scale of Amish manufacturing shops and retail stores. The formation of the Amish National Steering Committee and the organized programs of mutual aid, discussed by Olshan in chapter 12, suggest emergent trends toward bureaucratization.[4] But nevertheless highly specialized institutions—retirement centers, denominational agencies, health care facilities, colleges, and mission agencies—remain absent from Amish life.

At the level of consciousness Amish culture lacks the specialized vocabulary that typifies professional life. Technical jargon is of course one of the dubious by-products of higher education. In a distinctively nonmodern fashion, Amish talk is concrete and specific. The bulk of social life—birth, play, worship, work, education, and death—remains nearby home and relatively undifferentiated.

Second, the pervasive force of specialization cultivates a *pluralistic* ethos in modern life. Dicing social functions into narrow specialties forces moderns to deal with a complicated network of social agencies ranging from pet shops to investment brokerages, from health care providers to travel agencies. Modern societies, with their many institutions, are a complex social web. In contrast to peasant societies where common values, similar sentiments, and shared traditions bind members together, economic interdependence holds mass societies intact. Diversity rather than commonality is the norm in the modern world. Modern societies are in many ways glued together by their diversities, whereas the solidarity of nonmodern ones rests on their commonalities. This of course is a long-standing observation made by Durkheim (1984) in his classic book *The Division of Labor in Society*, first published in 1893.

The pluralism of modern life means that individuals face many views of reality—a bewildering array of beliefs and opinions. The common sentiments of traditional cultures dissolve in the streams of pluralism. The wide assortment of ideas and clashing lifestyles focuses the stark relativity of modernity since "it all depends" on who you are, on where you're from, and on your point of view. The religious beliefs of individuals become especially fragile and vulnerable to change as discrepant world views collide in the public media of mass society.

At both structural and cultural levels the Amish have remained aloof from the pluralism of modern life. Their theological stance of separation from the world has in many ways insulated them from the forces of diversity afoot in the modern world. The Amish community does interact with the surrounding society, tapping the use of professional services—medicine, dentistry, and law. Moreover, they are frequently buying and selling supplies and services for personal use as well as for business purposes. The practice of endogamy, the use of the dialect, the prohibition on membership in public organizations, the taboo on political involvement, and the rejection of mass media are among many of the factors that help to preserve the cultural boundaries that separate the Amish from the winds of pluralism. All of these factors impede structural assimilation and preserve the homogeneity of Amish life.

More importantly, Amish parochial schools bridle interaction with outsiders—both peers and teachers—and restrict consciousness. Amish children do not study science or critical thinking, nor are they exposed to the relativity and diversity so pervasive in higher education today. The Amish rejection of mass media, especially television, severely limits their exposure to the smorgasbord of modern values. The tight plausibility structure embodied in the Amish community thus helps to hold the forces of pluralism at bay.

Third, modern life is characterized by *discontinuity*. Job specialization and rapid transportation induce mobility, which in turn weakens social bonds as individuals move from job to job, home to home, and marriage to marriage across the country. Hence, social ties in modern life are temporary and transitory. In a rural society, where social networks of family, tribe, and neighborhood overlap, an individual relates to a small number of persons for a long time. Modern citizens, on the other hand, interact with a multitude of persons in different locales—most of whom are strangers to each other. Thus, the social ligaments in modern societies are by nature, loose, mobile, and transitory. The ratio of secondary to primary relationships rises in modern life. The durable, stable, and predictable social couplings typical of rural society are endangered by the shifting, portable social networks that accompany modernity.

In contrast to the discontinuities of modern culture, Amish societies exude continuity. Social relationships are more likely to be primary, local, enduring, and stable. The rejection of automobile ownership, bicycles, and air travel places limits on Amish mobility. To be sure, the Amish do travel in hired motor vehicles and in public busses and trains, but, all things considered, the amount of mobility is relatively low. The rejection of college and consequently of professional work enables young adults to live in their childhood communities, which increases the longevity of social ties with family, neighborhood, and place. Parents teach occupational skills to their children.

Amish schools are a supreme example of continuity. Children often walk to school, where they may have the same teacher for all eight grades. The teacher, responsible for some thirty students, may relate to only a dozen households, since many families have several children in attendance. Such continuity contrasts starkly with modern education, where children may have dozens of teachers in a few years and teachers relate to hundreds of families.

To cite another example of continuity, grandchildren and grandparents frequently work and play together because grandparents live in an apartment adjacent to one of their children rather than in a distant retirement village. The overlay of dense social networks in Amish life means that social interaction is limited to fewer persons in more roles, which enhances the stability of primary social ties. Everyone tends to do everything with everyone else in these dense overlapping networks. The relatively low occupational mobility between generations also contributes to the continuity of Amish life—grandchildren understand the lives and occupations of their grandparents.

A fourth mark of modernity is *rationalization*. The calculating mentality of modern minds sets goals and selects the most efficient means to obtain them. Planning and preparation for the future are sure signs of modern thinking. On the personal level, family planning and career planning betray a futuristic posture. Organizations and governments, as well, engage in long-range scenarios and strategic planning. Bureaucracy, the institutional embodiment of control, order, efficiency, and planning, is, according to Max Weber (1968), the organizational expression of rationalization in modern life.

The Amish commitment to a rational mentality that calculates means and ends has grown as their farming enterprises expand and as they enter the larger world of commerce via cottage industries. Although Amish entrepreneurs engage in planning to keep their businesses afloat, there is, however, decidedly less planning activity among the Amish than typically found in modern life. The absence of artificial means of family planning, career planning, and time management reflects a less rationalized approach to life—a greater willingness to yield to nature and destiny. The rejection of science and critical thinking in Amish schools, the taboo on theological training for ordained leaders, and the lack of a formal theology attenuate the level of rationality in the collective consciousness.

The tentacles of bureaucracy have barely touched Amish society. Their social architecture is remarkably decentralized, small, and informal. A central national office, with an executive director and professional staff have never developed. Church districts are organized as a loose federation in each settlement, and there is little centralized or formal coordination between settlements. The decentralized character of Amish society fosters diversity in the struggle with modernity. Different settlements and different church districts even within affiliations adapt at different paces and in different directions. The *Ordnung*, the body of policies regulating the life of the community, is generally not written down but is a fluid, dynamic set of understandings. The hierarchial, formal, rationalized structure of modern bureaucracy has simply not developed in Amish society.

Olshan (1993) has charted the embryonic evolution of bureaucracy in the Old Order Amish Steering Committee, which began in 1966. This national committee, with traces of bureaucracy, emerged as the Amish grappled with legal issues that were foisted upon them by the State—military conscription, Social Security, and government regulations. Some publishing ventures and microenterprises as well as committees for medical, fire, and liability insurance also show slight imprints of bureaucracy as noted by Olshan in chapter 12, but, all things considered, rationalized expressions of social organization are remarkably few.

The foregoing traits of modernity encourage *individuation*—the widely heralded triumph of modern culture. The modernizing process unhooks individuals from the confining grip of custom and encourages individualism to flourish. In traditional societies, individuals for the most part are under the tight thumb of kin, tribe, and village. Modern culture with its ideology of individual rights, liberties, privileges, and freedoms celebrates the individual as the supreme social reality. To question the rights of an individual has become a cardinal and unforgivable sin. The personal résumé is, of course, the ultimate document of individuation, and one that is missing in Amish files. Modern individuals are free to pursue careers and seek personal fulfillment, but they also carry the responsibility to succeed—"to make it"—a responsibility that entails the fear of failure.

The subordination of the individual to the community is the fundamental key that unlocks many of the riddles and puzzles of Amish life and sharply distinguishes their culture from modern ways. *Gelassenheit*, submitting and yielding to higher authorities—parents, teachers, leaders, and God—structures Amish values, symbols, personality, rituals, and social organization. Personal submission clashes with modern individualism and its concomitants of self-achievement, self-expression, and self-fulfillment. By contrast, the Amish vocabulary of obedience, simplicity, humility, and the posture of kneeling—for baptism, prayer, confession, and ordination—reflect a premodern understanding of the individual. Clothing, for instance, is used in modern life as a tool of self-expression. In Amish life, uniform dress serves as a badge of group identity and loyalty as well as a symbol of self-surrender to community priorities. The taboo on photography, publicity, jewelry, and other forms of personal adornment bridles an individualism that otherwise might foster pride and arrogance. The Amish rejection of individualism—that supremely cherished value of modern culture—reflects the heartbeat of a counterculture that has not absorbed modern ways.

In the sixth place, *abstraction* permeates modernity from language to corporate structures. Modern things are large. From theoretical words to multinational corporations, modernization separates individuals from their immediate social context. Modernization in essence decontextualizes. Moderns are often separated by distance, experience, and values from the very institutions that shape their everyday lives. Television programs, legal codes, personnel policies, fast-food menus, federal regulations, and designer fads are concocted in and administered from abstract, far-away headquarters. The vocabulary of modern talk is filled with jargon, technical terms, abstractions, and generalizations that are anchored only loosely, if at all, in specific, concrete settings.

The rejection of higher education and the embrace of manual labor have screened abstract jargon and philosophical terminology from

Amish vocabulary. Amish affairs are rooted in practical experiences shaped by local settings. Philosophical speculation and a specialized vocabulary are missing from this high context culture where individuals are tied to a specific and concrete geographical locale. Social organization revolves around the local church district—the geographical unit where each person has an emotional niche among some twenty-five to thirty-five families. Small-scale social organization—small church districts, small shops, small farms—all stand in remarkable contrast to the large, global, corporate structures that grid the modern world. Small-scale organization assures the individual of an emotional home, increases informality, spreads power, and inhibits bureaucracy.

Finally, the modern social fabric is branded with *choice*. In fact, Peter Berger contends that one of the chief functions of traditional groups is to free their members from the burden of choice. The transition to the modern era is a shift from fate to choice, from destiny to decision. A complex society imposes choices on all of its members so that even groups like the Amish, who prefer fate, are forced to choose not to be modern. Like it or not, moderns have been condemned to choices. The multiplicity of choices that stare individuals and organizations in the face each day means that modernity is unusually open-ended; it is uncertain. The predictability that undergirds traditional cultures, which are regulated by seasonal routines, customary norms, and fatalistic views, evaporates in the face of modern life. Thus, the texture of modernity is filled with uncertainties ranging from nuclear terrorism to job insecurity. Tomorrow is no longer dependable.

As Olshan contends in chapter 11, the Amish have made collective choices. But many of these decisions have been reactive responses to choices imposed on them by modern life. The Amish have been less likely to be proactive—deliberately initiating choices, for such initiatives parallel the modern impulse to plan, order, and control one's environment. The Amish have made collective choices not to be modern. They have rejected higher education. But in many other cases they have surely conceded to modernity by accepting the use of modern forms of technology.

Their collective decisions, however, have restricted individual choice. Individuals are not free to wear what they want, to aspire to professional occupations, to own a car, or to buy a television set. This does not necessarily mean that Amish folks are dour and unhappy. A variety of evidence suggests that they are as happy and satisfied, if not more so, than many "homeless" moderns. The range of occupational options and lifestyle choices available to the individual in Amish society is of course quite narrow. And although a restricted range of choices may suffocate the modern spirit of freedom, it also removes the burden of incessant decision making with its concomitant guilt, stress, and anxiety from the shoulders of many Amish persons.

The Great Separator

Throughout the twentieth century the Amish have tenaciously sought to preserve their traditional community life in the wake of the sweeping tide of modernization. While they have also been tantalized by the lure of progress and have obviously benefited from the by-products of industrialization, the Amish have remained skeptical of the long-term consequences of technological advancement. They feared that a treacherous undercurrent beneath the smooth surface of modernity would, in time, break up their cohesive community.

The Amish suspicion that fragmentation might follow in the wake of modernization was not an idle one. Indeed, some analysts argue that social separation accompanies virtually all of the changes induced by industrialization.[5] Social separation occurs on many levels and in numerous ways. The history of the factory system is a tale of the separation of work into smaller and smaller component tasks. Removing work from home and scattering social functions—education, work, worship, leisure, and grooming—into specialized institutions at different locations pulls families apart. Social and geographical mobility isolates family and friends and also severs long-term ties with physical places.

Rationalization separates ends from means in the human mind. Abstract thought allows individuals to separate themselves from their immediate environment at least mentally—if not physically. Large corporate structures remove the throttles of power from the immediate control of local people. In contrast to traditional peoples, moderns are often "freed" from the constraints of caste, neighborhood, and family. Discontinuity, mobility, and individuation loosen social ties, making it easier to sever relationships when convenient—divorce being the most obvious example. Even the modern personality is diced up and separated into multiple selves that must perform on different social stages throughout a day—or a lifetime, for that matter, to different audiences—often separated from each other in time and space.

To be sure, the electronic age, with instantaneous communication and high-speed travel, has multiplied the number of possible connections an individual might have with others around the globe. But, for the most part, modernization separates and partitions whole systems—psychological, social, and organizational ones—into smaller parts in the name of efficiency and productivity. The systemic ties that bind modern systems together are for the most part abstract, complicated, and separated from the individual's immediate context. The fragmentation of modern life is sometimes experienced on the personal level as alienation—when meaningful ties to purpose, friends, work, and neighborhood are ruptured.

The hallmark of Amish culture has been its highly integrated community where all the bits and pieces of social life, from birth to death, are gathered into a single system. To avoid the fragmentation that accompanies modernity, the Amish have separated themselves from the modern world. In order to stay whole, to preserve their community, they have separated themselves from modernity—the greatest separator of all. The Amish impulse to remain separate from the great separator has become a significant strategy in their cultural survival.

Seen in this light it is not surprising that a fundamental tenet of Amish religion is separation from the world—a belief that sprouted in the seedbed of European persecution and is legitimated today with references to the scriptures. This linkage between the fragmentation of modern life and the integration of Amish society unlocks many of the Amish riddles. For only by being a separate people are they able to preserve the integrity of their tightly knit community. Many of the seemingly odd Amish practices that often perplex outside observers are in fact social devices that shield their subculture from the divisive pressures of modernity that threaten to tear their corporate life asunder.

A Honda gasoline engine powers a cake mixer in a pastry shop operated by three single women. Alternate forms of power are often used in shops, barns, and homes because of the taboo on electricity from public utility lines. (Photograph by Lucian Niemeyer).

3

War Against Progress: Coping with Social Change

DONALD B. KRAYBILL

Amish resistance to modernity in many ways is a war against the spirit of progress. The cultural battle waged by the Amish involves the drawing and redrawing of social lines to maintain their identity and preserve their culture. Donald B. Kraybill explores the external and internal sources of social change in Amish life and discusses the process by which new practices are rejected or gradually accepted. He identifies some of the social throttles that influence the adoption of innovations and discusses the cultural mixing of old and new that sometimes produces the baffling hybrids of Amish life.

Arenas of Conflict

"I don't want to push the line too much," said the owner of an Amish manufacturing shop when asked why he didn't hook up a copy machine to his generator. A few miles down the road the head of an Amish lumber company, a member of a New Order Amish group, has already stepped across the line. He uses a portable gasoline engine to operate a generator that runs the copy machine in his office. The bishop of the cautious shop owner had not placed a formal taboo on copy machines, but the owner respected the de facto line that had been drawn and didn't want to "make any trouble." Moreover, with his productive enterprise there might be more important lines to press against someday if he did choose to challenge the *Ordnung* of the church. The process of social change in Amish society can be viewed as a war against progress—a battle that requires the drawing and redrawing of the lines of cultural engagement.[1]

Human communities etch lines of distinction into the consciousness of their members to mark off ideological and behavioral turf. These socially constructed lines separate good from evil, sacred from profane, status from stigma, dirt from dignity, and vice from virtue, as well as health from illness. The never-ending drawing of lines confers order, predictability, and stability to fragile social worlds that otherwise would fall into chaos.

The Amish war against progress entails a continual struggle to draw appropriate lines in order to protect their communities from absorption into the larger society while still permitting a modicum of social change. Lines are drawn, erased, and redrawn in a continual process of negotiation—trying to strike compromises between the forces of tradition that fear any change and the reckless voices of progress that hanker after every novelty.

Several arenas of social change have been especially contentious in the Amish bout with the spirit of progress in the twentieth century. Although telephones remain banned from homes except in some New Order districts, they have steadily inched closer to home in many settlements and have indeed been installed in some outbuildings and shops. The use or "borrowing" of phones, in both public settings and from non-Amish neighbors, has also increased.[2] The taboo against tapping 110 volt electricity from public power lines has been a long-standing tradition in Amish life. And although the taboo persists, the use of some forms of electricity is on the rise. Batteries that provide 12 volt DC current are routinely used in most settlements, but knowing where to draw the appropriate line on electrical usage has not been easy. In some settlements 12 volt electric motors are used to power small equipment in shops and barns. Some affiliations permit the use of generators to power electric welders in shops and portable electrical tools at construction sites. Moreover, inverters that create "homemade" 110 volt electricity from 12 volt batteries are also being used in some communities.[3]

The use of motor vehicles has also become an arena of conflict. The Amish had uniformly spurned car ownership in the first quarter of the twentieth century. However, over the years expanding settlements, business pressures, and more tolerant attitudes have led to widespread hiring of cars, vans, and trucks. This practice is on the rise in almost every settlement, and in a few cases leasing vehicles has also become a temptation. Communities struggle with where to draw the line on the hiring of vehicles. Can they be hired on Sunday for hospital visitation? What about their use for leisure trips that hardly pass for business purposes?

The use of tractors has also stirred controversy. Fearing that the widespread use of tractors, especially those with rubber tires, might over time lead to the use of the car, the Amish have tethered their tractors at the barn. In some New Order church districts tractors, equipped with pneumatic tires, are taken to the field and sometimes even driven on the road—a practice that blurs historic lines and confirms traditionalist fears that road use will surely lead to the car. Drawing lines between the use of pneumatic, hard rubber, and steel wheels has varied from settlement to settlement on the various battlefronts in the war against progress.

The use of new types of farm equipment has provided another arena of struggle. Some communities have mounted gasoline engines on field equipment designed for tractors but adapted by Amish mechanics for use by horses. Some of the most difficult battles have flared in the milk house as Amish leaders struggled to decide if bulk cooling tanks and automatic milkers unnecessarily blurred the line of separation from the world. The use of bulk tanks and the means of chilling and stirring the milk became a major issue in many settlements because it meant the difference between higher-priced Grade A milk markets and shipping milk in cans to cheese plants for lower prices. The use of bulk tanks not only increased the price of milk but also enabled farmers to expand the size of their dairy operations. Settlements that have adopted bulk tanks and automatic milkers often show many traces of economic prosperity.

New battle lines have been drawn and redrawn in Amish homes as well. Virtually all Amish settlements have adopted mechanical washing machines powered by gasoline engines or in some cases by air and hydraulic pressure.[4] Although electrical appliances have been kept at bay, gas stoves and refrigerators as well as indoor bathrooms and modern-looking kitchens have appeared in some settlements. Others still use outhouses. Commercially prepared foods and synthetic fabrics are also on the rise. Professional landscaping beautifies Amish homes in the more progressive settlements—another sign that they may be losing the war against progress.

In all of these areas the Amish have struggled with the forces of modernity, trying to remain faithful to their heritage while ever adapting to new forces, both internal and external, that have pressed for change. The Amish have waged the most successful war against progress in the preservation of their ritual and ceremonial activities related to church services and community life. Worship services and church rituals have changed little over the years. With the shift to parochial schools, described by Huntington in chapter 5, the Amish educational program has also remained fairly stable. The most tumultuous areas of battle have involved the introduction of new technology as well as shifts in occupational patterns.

External Prods

The war against progress intensified as five external factors produced social change among the Amish in the twentieth century. These outside forces have knocked on Amish doors in various ways in the different settlements. Sometimes they have received a cool reception or outright rejection and in other cases a grudging embrace. In any event they have triggered Amish cultural wars that, in areas such as education and Social Security, have led to extended campaigns stretching over several decades.

1. *Economic Incentives.* Daily pressures to make a living, and sometimes a comfortable one, have shaped many of the changes in Amish life. Virtually all of the technological changes on the farm can be traced to attempts to improve productivity and efficiency without jeopardizing Amish identity. An Amish entrepreneur describing the purchase of a state-of-the-art forklift for his machine shop said, "we simply had to buy it because of the competition." The adoption of bulk milk tanks and mechanical milking machines in some settlements has boosted family incomes in rather dramatic ways. The installation of automated hog and broiler operations as well as the adoption of mechanized field equipment were also responses to economic prods that promised a better and more stable standard of living. Greater use of telephones, hiring more and more vehicles, as well as expanding the use of air and hydraulic power in Amish shops have all been induced by economic forces. Some more conservatively inclined settlements have steadfastly resisted these newer technologies, often at considerable economic peril. In any event many of the significant changes related to wider use of technology have been prompted by economic stimuli.

2. *Legal Factors.* Numerous changes have been foisted upon the Amish by governmental agencies at the local, state, and federal level.[5] Slow-moving vehicle emblems and flashing lights on buggies are required by law in some states. Although most Amish have grudgingly

accepted these in the interests of highway safety, the extremely conservative Swartzentruber group has resisted the use of slow-moving vehicle signs despite a series of legal challenges including a review by the U.S. Supreme Court.[6] In settlements located near growing urban regions, zoning considerations have also had an impact on the Amish in many ways—regulating the size of their shop buildings, the number of employees, the use of sewage systems, conformity to fire codes, and the arrangement of "dawdy houses"—retirement apartments for grandparents. In all of these ways and dozens of others the legal apparatus of the state has steered many of the social changes in Amish society.

3. Structural Shifts. Structural changes in the larger society have also nudged and sometimes shoved the Amish in new directions. The development of large consolidated schools was the catalyst for the formation of hundreds of one-room Amish elementary schools. Prior to 1950 the overwhelming majority of Amish children attended rural public schools, but after midcentury and especially after the historic *Wisconsin v. Yoder* decision by the U.S. Supreme Court in 1972, Amish parochial schools have flourished. The story of this growth is told by Huntington in chapter 5.

The rise of tourism in American life, made possible by widespread automobile ownership and a growing network of interstate highways, has also touched many Amish who live in the larger settlements. The influx of tourists has provided a market for Amish products and increased interaction with the outside world, bolstering both Amish self-consciousness and their collective self-esteem. Urban encroachment around several Amish settlements has pushed some farmers off the land and into microenterprises and in some cases into factory work, as described by Meyers in chapter 10. In other settings it has spawned new ripples of migration. All of these structural changes in American society have induced changes in Amish ways as well.

4. Social Ties. Increased interaction with the outside world in many Amish settlements has accelerated social change in virtually every aspect of Amish life. The experience of working in nonfarm jobs, meeting tourists, traveling, and using outside professionals has increased the exposure of Amish persons to the dominant culture and provided a conduit for new ideas and new products. Growing use of doctors, dentists, lawyers, accountants, veterinarians, and other agricultural specialists has funneled new practices into Amish life. In one settlement an agronomic consultant has dozens of Amish farmers as clients. He advises them on a regular basis about the use of fertilizers, weed control, seed selection, and crop rotation. Nonfarm work in factories, small businesses, motels, restaurants, and private homes as well as roadside stands has exposed the Amish to a whole array of new habits, some of which they have adopted. Increased contact with physicians and midwives has introduced immunization and vaccination of children.

5. *Technological Changes.* The selective adoption of new technology by the Amish fluctuates of course directly with its availability in the larger society. The Amish remain resolute in their refusal to tap certain technologies—dishwashers, air conditioners, television, self-propelled combines—the list goes on endlessly. But they have welcomed some innovations. Detergents, instant pudding, weedeaters, gas grills for barbecuing, haybalers, and automatic milkers, to name a few, are some of the many new gadgets that have been accepted in some Amish settlements. The use of new technology is certainly cautious and selective, but the Amish are not using nineteenth-century technology. Their adoption of new tools, however, is prodded by their availability outside the Amish fold. In all of these ways external forces have provided an impetus for change in Amish life.

Internal Initiatives

The impetus for social change is not entirely spurred by changes in the outside world. Some of the initiatives for change come from within the Amish community itself. These internal forces, added to the external ones, have produced a wide array of changes in Amish life in the twentieth century.

1. *Convenience and Comfort.* The Amish are people who, like their neighbors, prefer comfort over pain, convenience over obstruction. Their European history is filled with suffering and martyrdom, but they are not social masochists who believe that suffering is desirable or even necessary in order to gain rewards hereafter. They do fret that too much convenience and creature comfort will lead to sloth and ingratitude. Although wary of convenience, they will accept some technological changes that increase comfort, but not too many. Each generation of Americans draws new lines between luxury and convenience and so it is with the Amish. In each settlement certain persons

press for greater conveniences that in the next generation become necessities.

Indoor bathrooms have replaced outdoor privies in many Amish homes but not in all of them. In some settlements motorized washing machines have replaced hand washers, gas stoves have superseded wood stoves, refrigerators have replaced iceboxes, and synthetic materials have pushed cotton fabrics aside. The shift from old ways to more convenient ones is endless. Harnessed by the Ordnung of the particular affiliation, and not without struggles, these new changes often creep into practice because they simply offer greater convenience.

2. *Idealism.* All human cultures cope with gaps between ideal values and actual practice. Various members of the community may seek new ways to be faithful to the teachings of the scripture, new ways to revitalize the ideals of their heritage. Indeed Jacob Ammann's attempts at revitalization first led to the formation of the Amish in 1693. Olshan (1992) has noted that Amish efforts to live in the world but not be of it will inevitably lead to frustration, which "historically has led to charges of backsliding, to new interpretations of scripture, to new guidelines for community life—in short, to social change."

The social changes accompanying the formation of the New Order groups in some settlements sometimes reflect a refurbished idealism that hopes to recover the original vision of the faith and practice it more consistently. More conservative interpreters might argue that such high hopes are simply being used to mask greater individual freedom or borrow more freely from modern ways. Internal struggles to find new avenues of faithfulness to scripture and the Amish heritage have brought some changes in Amish practice, and at times have triggered new schisms—new attempts to recreate the heavenly city.

3. *Population Growth.* Another internal source of change is the natural diversity produced by population growth. As reported in chapter 1, the Amish have enjoyed a rather robust rate of growth in the twentieth century. Size breeds differentiation and diversity in social organization. Amish population growth also promotes migration, which in its own way leads to greater diversity. Larger settlements tend to have more diversity and are able to absorb it more easily—to some extent—without resorting to schism. New settlements in more isolated areas are free to create their own Ordnung. Sometimes these new settlements are composed of conservatively

minded folks who are fleeing the larger and more progressive settlements such as those in Geauga County, Ohio, or Lancaster County, Pennsylvania. In any event, the growing size of the Amish community in North America, as described by Luthy in appendix I, has also contributed to social change.

4. Authority Structure. The leadership structure of Amish society is remarkably decentralized, and this in its own way fosters social change. Without a national office or annual convention, let alone a common book of rules and discipline, the authority structure is pliable and ultimately rooted in the local congregation. Some nine hundred local congregations, each enjoying considerable autonomy, provide a fertile seedbed for social change. Moreover, weak and inept leaders in some settlements have carelessly and at times nonchalantly overlooked changes that have crept into practice, making it difficult for other more conscientious leaders to hold the line on social change. The diffused authority structure has in some ways encouraged social change.

It is tempting to identify these nine external and internal factors as discrete sources of change in Amish life. Real life, however, is not so neatly organized. Many of these factors are entangled in complex and reciprocal relationships. Placing engines on field equipment, for example, fortifies the economic base and enhances convenience, but it can only happen as the technology becomes available. The press of urbanization has pushed many Amish persons into microenterprises, heightening interaction with outsiders and exposing members to new ideas and new products. This circularity of influence makes it difficult to tease out discrete reasons for change, for as one Amish writer observed: "Our whole way of life is interwoven. One part cannot be understood apart from the whole" ("Beyond" 1980:7).

Tracing Social Change

New practices may slip into place in a variety of ways. In many cases changes are processed in a thoughtful and deliberate fashion, but at other times the use of a new product spreads into practice haphazardly. Describing the process of change, an Amish entrepreneur said, "We do not object to technology. When something new comes along we look at it, analyze it, and try to decide if it's good, neutral, or bad for our way of life and our goals. Then we decide if we want it or not based on that." The Amish have not created a formal process to monitor change, and despite the entrepreneur's hope, some of the decision making, in his own words, "is simply politics."

Surprising to many outsiders, many of the forbidden practices are not regarded as "sinful" in and of themselves, but are rejected because they might lead, over time, to unrighteous behavior or harm the life of the community. An Amish bishop noted that "a car is not sinful in and of itself, but it's the harm that it might bring to future generations that's the problem." Despite the Amish concern for long-term consequences, the decision-making process that regulates social change is for the most part informal, somewhat unpredictable, and, like any human community, subject to the quirks of personality and the entanglements of interpersonal networks.

The fate of a new practice may follow several tracks. Something that is clearly outside the moral boundaries of Amish behavior may be dealt with and banished by leaders in the local church district. Plugging a video recorder into an electric inverter would surely meet this fate if its use became public knowledge. On the other hand, a new gadget—a gas grill for barbecuing—that does not threaten Amish ways might be viewed as a "friendly" change and gradually slip into practice by default without any formal discussion or decision making.

In the case of a questionable practice—the installation of phones in shops—the innovation will likely provoke discussion and controversy as it gradually creeps into use in some districts. At this point the new practice may face three possible responses. First, church leaders may frown on the practice and grumble about it but not take any action—thus permitting its use by default. This may happen if the practice is rather widespread and impossible to eradicate by the time it becomes a public "issue," or if it is not deemed a serious threat. A second response might be that some bishops would take a firm stand against the innovation and reject it in their congregations or require wayward members to "put it away" or face excommunication. Other bishops might tolerate the same practice, thus creating a "ragged" pattern of social change. For example, electronic cash registers may appear in shops in certain bishop districts but not others. Finally, a third response might be that ordained leaders would meet as a group and reach a consensus that something is clearly intolerable, and then they would work in concert to banish it. This was the case in 1986 when ordained officials in the Lancaster settlement prohibited the ownership of personal computers for fear that they would lead to the use of televisions.

The Throttles of Change

Several social throttles govern the speed of change in Amish communities. These factors that regulate the acceptance of new practices are, once again, interrelated with each other in the decision-making process. The four throttles identified below may function simultaneously to shape the acceptance or rejection of new practices.

1. *Separation from the World.* As noted in chapter 1, separation from the world is an enduring theme in Amish culture. Based on religious teaching, the church seeks to maintain a separate identity from the larger society. "We are different," said one Amishman, "That's our goal."

The term "worldly" is a somewhat slippery, but convenient word to tag new ventures that may threaten the harmony and stability of the community. Consequently, innovative practices, such as eating out in restaurants, that might blur the lines of separation from the world may encounter resistance.[7] New patterns of behavior that do not erode ethnic boundaries will likely receive a warmer welcome. Changes that are not public or easily visible are more likely to slip into acceptance than more obvious ones. It is easier, for example, to change from the use of wood to fiberglass in the construction of carriages than to drop the more obvious traditional colors and styles.

Amish farmers typically do not use pipeline milkers to pump milk directly from the cows to cooling tanks via glass pipelines. However, oil pumped under high pressure in hoses, is widely used to power hydraulic machinery in Amish shops. When asked about the difference between milk in a pipeline and oil in a hose, a shop owner made this distinction. "By using hydraulic," he said, "we are not like the English shop owners, who use electricity, and so the nonconformity or separation from the world is preserved. But if an Amish farmer uses a pipeline milker, he is just like an English farmer and the separation would be lost, that's the difference." The principal of separation from the world throttles many of the decisions regarding social change. This fundamental religious value perpetuates and protects Amish identity and any compromises that inch the community closer to the world threaten the very essence of Amish identity.

2. *Relationship to the Ordnung.* The Ordnung of a particular Amish community also regulates the process of social change. The Ordnung

is the social blueprint, the oral policy manual so to speak, that spells out the "understandings" of acceptable and unacceptable Amish conduct. The Amish are reluctant to make hasty decisions to accept or reject new practices, for once a taboo is woven into the Ordnung it is difficult to rescind. Thus innovations that infringe on traditional understandings of the Ordnung, such as those related to dress, carriages, cars, electricity, telephones, and tractors, will undoubtedly meet resistance and stir controversy.

Two factors have created a somewhat ragged pattern of social change at times. In some cases a zig-zag pattern develops because the Ordnung might have forbidden a particular tool at one time but then later accepts a newer product that becomes available. This happened when power lawn mowers were rejected in the fifties in some settlements, but weedeaters were accepted in the eighties. Thus in the nineties some families push hand-mowers across their lawn and also use power weedeaters to trim around its edges.

A second detour pattern emerges occasionally when "fence jumpers" try to circumvent the Ordnung in an ingenious fashion. Leaders may permit changes that do not violate the literal meaning of the Ordnung even though they bypass its spirit. The use of inverters to make "homemade" 110 volt current illustrates this pattern. Over the years the Amish have developed a firm distinction between the use of 12 volt current from batteries and 110 volt electricity from public utility lines. This demarcation effectively eliminated the use of electrical gadgets and appliances as they became available in the twentieth century. Electrical inverters, however, now transform 12 volt current from batteries into 110 volt current, suitable for operating electric typewriters, copy machines, and cash registers. The inverter upholds the letter of the Ordnung because it taps current from batteries and thus preserves the public utility line taboo. But this circumvention now permits the use of small electrical gadgets that were historically beyond the pale of Amish life. Although inverters are used in some of the more progressive Amish settlements, they are forbidden in many others.

A similar detour developed in the Lancaster settlement when the church forbade mechanical gutter cleaners to clear manure out of cow stables. Some farmers obeyed the ruling to the letter, but later they installed liquid manure pits under their barns. This permitted them to flush water through the gutters to clean them and drain the runoff into the pits beneath the barn. Thus cleaning operations became automated and it became easier to expand the size of dairy herds. The tenacious influence of the Ordnung, the growing pressures for convenience, as well as human ingenuity all contribute to what at times appears as a zig-zag pattern of change.

3. Social Impact. The screening of new behaviors and products often involves an assessment of their long-term impact on the Amish community. Changes that erode loyalty to the community, create undue temptations, foster inequality, and encourage individualism are suspect. "Bigness," remarked an Amish carpenter, "ruins everything." Apart from family size the Amish have a clear preference for small-scale operations in farms, schools, businesses, and church districts. One Amish writer ("Beyond" 1980:9) put the bias this way, "We don't farm with modern machinery because then we tend toward bigger and bigger operations, and toward less and less working together with our neighbors."

An Amish farmer in Ohio lamented that one of his New Order neighbors remarked, "We put all our oats into hay this year so we don't have to waste time helping the neighbors to thresh." Threshing and silo filling have traditionally pulled neighbors together in cooperative work crews. Larger and more modern machinery enables farmers to work more independently and thus tends to undercut the role of communal work groups. Large shops with more than a half-dozen employees concentrate wealth and power in a few hands and thus are also discouraged. Social changes that increase interaction with the world, fragment the community, and accent individual achievement typically receive a cold shoulder from church leaders. Automobile ownership, for instance, would promote all of these trends—mobility, speed, status, individuality, and the fragmentation of community. Technical innovations that entail so many widespread and long-term consequences thus receive skeptical reviews if not outright rejection.

4. Intergroup Relations. A final throttle that may temper the speed of social change is the nature of intergroup ties with other Amish and related groups. This factor is particularly decisive in settlements with historic schisms where two or more affiliations live side by side. After a division the more conservative group may make special efforts to lag "behind" the more progressive group. Thus the presence of a nearby progressive group may brake the speed of change in a more traditional affiliation. Greater use of telephones and tractors by a more progressive group may make traditionalist neighbors decry their use in order to protect group boundaries and identity.

In Holmes County, Ohio, some farmers in the Old Order affiliation were pleading with church leaders to permit mechanical milkers and bulk tanks in the summers of 1992 and 1993. The more progressive New Order group, which had formed some twenty years earlier, had long used mechanical milkers and bulk milk tanks. This made it difficult for the Old Order leaders to acquiesce to the pleas for new equipment because such acceptance would have blurred the group boundaries—producing an embarrassing loss of face for the Old Orders. Indeed one Old Order farmer told a New Order minister, "If we get bulk tanks and milkers, then you guys will be able to do anything"—meaning that in order to keep group identities intact, the New Orders would have to forge ahead in some other areas. Maintaining social face and preserving the proper social distance between groups is an additional factor that modulates the pace of social change in some settings.

Amish Hybrids

In their struggle to harness the relentless press of progress the Amish have often negotiated delicate compromises that enabled them to preserve their traditional identity while at the same time tapping the fruits of progress. Such social hybrids illustrate the intensity of the Amish war against progress. And while these mixtures of tradition and modernity reflect an earnest search for flexibility without selling out their souls to the merchants of modernity, the cultural marriages are often misunderstood. Outsiders, including some scholars, are fond of calling the hybrids "problems," "inconsistencies," or even "hypocrisies," suggesting that they somehow reflect moral lapses that tarnish Amish life.

Rather than hypocritical backsliding, the blending of old and new represents an astute attempt to draw fine lines whose deeper meaning escapes the gaze of touristic observers. There is real deviance in Amish communities. Some members disobey the church's teaching—sometimes openly and other times in secret. Such departures from the faith are real and sad inconsistencies. The community-wide compromises, however, that have been endorsed by the church in formal and de facto ways are hardly moral inconsistencies despite their puzzling appearance to outsiders. Moreover, many of the negotiated bargains have become symbols of Amish identity.

For conceptual purposes we can distinguish at least four types of social hybrids that have emerged in the Amish struggle with modernity: communal, economic, convenience, and temporal. These mixtures of old and new represent ways of drawing cultural lines of resistance to preserve the integrity of Amish life and arrest the speed of change. The hybrids described below vary from settlement to settlement and from affiliation to affiliation.

1. *Communal Hybrids.* A widely misunderstood compromise that the Amish have negotiated with modernity is their distinction between the use and ownership of certain forms of technology. Members are sometimes permitted to use technology but not to own it. Appearing hypocritical to outsiders, this rather shrewd arrangement recognizes the positive contribution that technology can make if it is selectively controlled by the community rather than left to individual discretion.

Permitting individuals to own cars would increase mobility and dramatically alter the tight social networks in the local community that are held together by horse and buggy travel. But the selective use of vehicles, especially for long-distance travel and business purposes, can also serve the interests of the community if properly controlled. Thus vehicles may be hired but not owned.

The Amish have also developed distinctions between the use and ownership of other forms of technology as well. Telephones may be used in public settings or in a neighbor's home but not installed in a private Amish home. Amish persons employed in a non-Amish office may use computers in their work, but may not purchase them for personal use or for their business. Electrical power tools, hooked to public utility lines, may be used at construction sites because the property is not Amish owned. The Amish contractor however in all likelihood may not use the tools at his own home. An Amish family renting a non-Amish farm before purchasing one of its own may be permitted to use electricity in the barn because they don't own the property.

In some settlements an Amish person may operate a small riding mower at his place of employment but not own one at home. In other situations, rented tools may be used for special occasions at home but not on a regular basis. A rented front end loader might be used to landscape a new home. All of these compromises distinguish between use and ownership and permit the selective use of technology but nevertheless keep it under communal control and scrutiny. It would be virtually impossible to regulate the use and spread of technology if individual ownership were permitted.

2. *Economic Hybrids.* Many of the social hybrids that have emerged in Amish life reflect the struggle to have a reasonable standard of living while not caving in to the forces of assimilation. The communal

hybrids discussed above are obviously shaped by economic forces, but in many other cases private ownership is permitted with certain stipulations. Modern haybalers, which increase the storage capacity of feed for dairy herds, are used in many settlements but they are powered by gasoline engines and pulled by horses. A variety of other farm implements are also powered by engines but pulled by horses in some settlements. Bulk tanks are used to store and chill milk to obtain higher milk prices but their agitators are spun by 12 volt current from batteries. In many Amish shops electric motors are stripped off modern machinery and replaced with air and hydraulic motors—preserving the historic taboo on electricity but also boosting productivity. All of these blends of modern and traditional ways are clearly driven by economic forces.

3. Convenience Hybrids. Other Amish hybrids are driven more by convenience than by economic concerns. The cultural lines are redrawn in the direction of convenience, but not too far. Air tires in some settlements may be permitted on the front tire of a tractor to ease turning but not on the large rear wheels, which would permit easy use of the tractor as a road vehicle. Scooters provide a convenient halfway mode between walking and bicycles for young people. In one affiliation, a continuous hot water supply in homes is considered too convenient and thus not permitted, but water may be heated by a gas furnace each time hot water is needed.

4. Temporal Hybrids. The pressures of modernity have also produced some temporal negotiations that provide a way of adapting to the pressures of change while still holding on to traditional practices. One way of adapting to change—a way of negotiating with modernity—is to permit the encroachment of modern ways during the week but to restrict traditional practices to sacred times—on Sunday. A historic practice may thus be retained, but only on Sunday, permitting the community to adapt to modern ways but converting the everyday practice, in essence, into a ceremonial sabbath ritual. As the hiring of vehicles grew for business purposes and intercommunity visitation, restrictions were placed on hiring vehicles on Sunday. Sunday hiring was only permitted in the case of "emergencies" such as hospital visitation. Moreover, members were strongly discouraged from hiring vehicles to travel to Sunday services. Despite the wide latitude given during the week for hiring vehicles, the Sunday taboo effectively ritualizes and almost sacralizes the use of horse and carriage as key symbols of Amish identity.

The dramatic occupational shift in some settlements that pushed

Amish entrepreneurs into hundreds of small businesses has decorated miles of back country roadways with "No Sunday Sales" signs—a virtual announcement of the presence of an Amish business. In this negotiated hybrid entrepreneurs said, "yes, we will leave the farm and enter the market place, but not on Sunday." In settlements that have installed bulk milk tanks, milk companies are not permitted to pick milk up on Sundays as they do on non-Amish farms. The Amish in essence said, "yes, we'll accept bulk tanks," but "no we won't acquiesce to Sunday pickups."

Clothing provides another example of the growing secular/sacred differentiation. Buttons, typically eschewed in Amish costume, are now being worn on "work" clothes in some communities. The traditional hook and eye fasteners, however, are still required for Sunday clothing, thus preserving Amish identity while permitting flexibility during the week. This trend of shrinking traditional, everyday practices into only Sunday use increases the sacred/secular compartmentalization of Amish culture. The shrinkage preserves key symbols of Amish identity and practice while at the same time opening the doors of change throughout the week.

In assessing the war against progress it cannot be overemphasized that the Amish are a human community, laced with the typical foibles and political vagaries of any other human community. Despite noble attempts to filter the intrusion of new products through the screen of ideal values the community decision-making process sometimes becomes entangled in personality conflicts and interpersonal squabbles. Although sincere in seeking to practice their religious convictions, the Amish, like other peoples, are not immune to the political struggles that haunt any process of social change.

In any event, the Amish struggle to draw the battle lines at fitting places in order to preserve the faith, and to arrest assimilation—all the while being open to constructive changes that knock on their door. One Amishman said, "We all agree we need to be separate in order to maintain a Scriptural difference from the world. But how different? Where shall we draw the line? How much exposure to the world can we permit until the influence of the world becomes greater than the influence of the church?" ("Beyond" 1980:9). Drawing lines involves the delicate art of balancing the forces of tradition against the press of productivity, and it makes all the difference, because the battle lines ultimately determine the victor in the war against progress.

A family works together loading hay bales near the village of Charm in Holmes County, Ohio. (Photograph by Doyle Yoder).

4

Plotting Social Change Across Four Affiliations

DONALD B. KRAYBILL

The Amish response to modernity has not been uniform. Different affiliations of Amish in various settlements have developed a diversity of lifestyle practices. Donald B. Kraybill compares four affiliations that live side by side in the largest Amish settlement of North America in the Holmes County area of Ohio. The four major groups in this geographical setting have drawn the battle lines in different places in their struggle with modernity. Kraybill explores the relationship between the retention of youth and the use of technology and suggests that both reflect an underlying shift in consciousness among the more progressive groups.[1]

The Holmes County Spectrum

The Amish settlement in the vicinity of Holmes County, Ohio, hosts not only the largest concentration of Amish in the world but also one of the more interesting and complex. Some twenty different Amish and Mennonite groups have branched out from the original Amish settlement that took root in Holmes County in 1809. The settlement has enjoyed robust growth in the twentieth century despite a steady dribble of members to more progressive Mennonite churches and other evangelical groups. The various Amish groups grew from some 55 church districts in 1965 to more than 160 by 1993.[2] Averaging about

145 persons per congregation, the settlement is likely populated by more than 23,000 persons.

Some nine Amish groups live side by side in the same region but maintain distinctive practices. This cultural diversity, flowing from a common historical root, and yet seeking to be obedient to particular understandings of the faith, provides a rich laboratory for reflecting on the Amish struggle with modernity. Each group has drawn different lines in the endless battle with the forces of assimilation. The lines not only mark off boundaries with the outside world, they also stake out intergroup fences that give symbolic identity and integrity to each of the subgroups that claim the Amish name.[3]

Over 90 percent of the Amish are affiliated with four major groups: Swartzentruber, Andy Weaver, Old Order, and New Order. The four groups stretch across a spectrum of traditionalism ranging from the very conservative Swartzentrubers to the progressively minded New Orders. Although they share a common Amish identity, the four clusters function rather independently. Each group has its own *Ordnung* and distinctive practices. The visual impact of these differences is striking even to the casual observer. Swartzentruber farmsteads with their dirt lanes, flowerless gardens, and paint-peeled buildings embody the lack of concern for aesthetics and other worldly standards that typifies this "low" church. In contrast the often immaculately maintained gardens and buildings of New Order families with neatly graveled and flower-lined lanes more closely resemble popular expectations of Amish homesteads.

Since the four groups are not "in fellowship" with each other they do not exchange ministers or permit their members to attend the communion services of the other groups. The Old Orders represent the historic mainstream of the Amish community, and with nearly one hundred congregations they dwarf the smaller groups, of about twenty congregations each, which broke off from the main trunk. The Swartzentrubers and the Andy Weaver group were conservative departures from the Old Order mainstream in 1913 and 1952 respectively. By contrast the New Orders charted a more progressive path that diverged from the Old Order road in 1968.

The four groups share historic Amish beliefs—separation from the world, an emphasis on humility and simplicity, and the shunning of excommunicated members, as well as many other historic practices. All four affiliations use horses for field work, travel by horse and carriage, expect men to wear beards and women to wear a head covering, worship in homes or barns, and reject the use of electricity from public utility lines. Despite these common commitments, other practices vary considerably from the conservative Swartzentrubers to the more tolerant New Orders.

Conservative Branches

The Old Order label emerged in the 1860s as some progressively minded groups in Holmes County left the main body of Amish and eventually merged with Mennonite groups. Those holding to the historic practices became known as the Old Order Amish about 1860–1862.[4] Thus the Old Order represented the mainstream of conservative Amish sentiments until 1913, when the Swartzentruber division yielded a more conservative stream of thinking. Bishop Sam Yoder argued that the ban on excommunicated persons should be lifted only if the persons returned to the church that baptized them and made an appropriate confession. Old Order leaders did not support such a "strict shunning" or severe interpretation of the *Meidung*. Consequently Sam Yoder and his followers formed a conservative faction, which became known as the Swartzentrubers—a name that was associated with later leaders S. J. Swartzentruber and Levi Swartzentruber.[5]

The Swartzentrubers have become legendary for their stubborn traditionalism. Of all the major Amish affiliations in North America they are the most reluctant to accept new changes in technology. Trying to freeze history whenever possible, they have successfully rejected many of the technological innovations of the twentieth century. Unmoved by pleas for safety, they have stubbornly refused to place slow-moving vehicle emblems and battery-operated lights on their carriages (Zook 1993). Technological adaptations such as indoor bathrooms and the use of tractors around barns—widely accepted by many Amish groups across North America—have been stridently forbidden by the Swartzentrubers.

About midcentury another dispute among the Amish of Holmes County led to a second conservative schism. Once again the apparent issue was "strict shunning." Andy Weaver, a young and articulate bishop, argued that Amish members who joined a more progressive nonresistant church—a Mennonite group—should be shunned. Old Order leaders were more tolerant and willing to relax the shunning if the wayward member joined another nonresistant church such as the Mennonites. Strict shunning, Old Order leaders contended, should be reserved for those who join mainstream Protestant churches or commit a serious moral offense.

Unable to resolve the dispute, Andy Weaver and his followers formed a second stream of conservative Amish in Holmes County in 1952. At this time some Amish boys were driving cars before they were baptized into church membership—a practice the Old Order leaders tolerated in the hope that the rebels would eventually join the church. Weaver's new group, however, decreed that if unbaptized young people purchased a car and continued to live at home, their parents would be "set back" and not permitted to take communion.[6] This and other conservative practices helped the Andy Weaver church establish a conservative identity for itself midway between the Swartzentrubers and the Old Orders.[7]

New Order Amish

The third split from the Old Order mainstream branched off in a more progressive direction in the late sixties. Already in the late forties and throughout the fifties progressive thought was stirring in pockets of Holmes County Amish. Hoping to help young people better understand their convictions as conscientious objectors, some ministers organized meetings to teach nonresistance. Some of the meetings emerged into a regular "youth meeting" on Wednesday evenings that functioned much like a prayer meeting or Sunday school. Revivalist style preaching by out-of-state evangelists in the fifties also fanned the fires of progressivist thinking.[8] Such preaching encouraged individual interpretations of scripture, accented personal salvation, promoted mission work, and belittled the importance of "works" (dress and distinctive practices) for salvation.

The revivalist sentiments swirling in the fifties led some Amish families to form a Beachy Fellowship in Holmes County in 1958.[9] This group, which readily began using cars, telephones, and electricity from public power lines, emphasized a more personal and evangelical theology. After leaving the Amish fold, these congregations eventually affiliated with the Beachey Amish Mennonite Fellowship—midway between the Amish and mainstream Mennonites.

The New Order Amish included in this study emerged in 1968, but their roots were forming at least a decade earlier.[10] In this third major splinter from the Old Order vanguard—this time in a progressive direction—the issue was not strict shunning as in the earlier divisions. The New Orders strongly opposed "bed courtship" practices common among Old Order youth.[11] The renewal movement also preached against the use of tobacco and encouraged Bible studies and youth

TABLE 4.1.
Profile of the Four Major Affiliations in the Holmes County Settlement

	Affiliation			
	Swartzentruber	*Andy Weaver*	*Old Order*	*New Order*
Traditionalism	extreme	high	moderate	low
Date of origin	1913	1952	1809	1968
Number of church districts[a]	15	19	99	19
Estimated population[b]	2,500	2,750	14,400	2,750
Percent of males farming[c]	80	46	36	35
Average number of children[c]	—	5.9	5.1	4.9

[a] *Source: Address and Business Directory of Holmes County and Vicinity* [Amish] (1993); 1991 Supplement to the 1988 *Ohio Amish Directory, Holmes County and Vicinity;* Raber's (1993) *Almanac,* and local informants.

[b] Population estimates are based on the assumption of 145 persons (members and dependents) per church district, which was the average reported in the 1988 *Ohio Amish Directory of Holmes County and Vicinity.* Informants estimate a higher number of persons per district among the Swartzentrubers. An estimate of 165 was used to project their population estimate.

[c] Based on occupations reported in the 1988 *Ohio Amish Directory, Holmes County and Vicinity.* The Swartzentruber percentage of farmers was estimated by local informants. Family size was obtained from the 1988 *Directory.* The family size of the Swartzentrubers is generally larger than that of the three other groups.

meetings. The New Orders reflected a more progressive theological development emphasizing personal Bible study, the assurance of salvation, personal conversion, and "understanding what you believe." In short, it was a more rational and individualistic understanding of Christian faith.

All of this threatened Old Order leaders, and the bishops finally "put the brakes on" in 1968 by asking a minister who was leading youth meetings "to discourage them and work against them." He refused, and by 1971 about a dozen church districts had left the Amish mainstream to form the New Order group. Thus by the early seventies four sizeable affiliations stretched across the Amish spectrum in Holmes County—ranging from the extremely traditional Swartzentrubers to the Andy Weavers, the Old Orders, and the more progressive-minded New Orders as displayed in table 4.1.

Religious Change

Although the four groups share basic understandings of Amish faith, their practices nevertheless sort the groups across a continuum of traditionalism in many areas, including church services, theological beliefs, degree of individualism, separation from the world, and the use of technology. Swartzentruber worship services, for example, are four hours long compared to three hours in the less traditional groups. The speed of singing varies across the spectrum as well. Singing the "Lobelied," the traditional second song in an Amish church service, takes twenty-five to thirty minutes among the Swartzentrubers, about twenty minutes among the Old Orders, but only twelve to fifteen minutes in New Order services. The Swartzentruber preachers tend to preach and pray in a distinctive chant-like fashion. More typical preaching replaces chanting as one moves toward the progressive pole of the continuum. The more traditional preachers tend to look above the congregation, who often sit with slightly bowed heads, in a humble posture. In the less traditional service the preachers make direct eye contact with the members, tell more stories, and give illustrations rather than only quoting scripture in a sing-song, chant-like fashion. "The New Order preacher," said an Old Order observer, "takes a more personal approach and may say the names of a couple when he marries them."

The more progressive preachers try to "explain and interpret" scriptures more than the traditionalists. This and many other signals suggest that the movement across the spectrum of faithfulness is a shift toward greater abstraction and rationalization of religious faith. The New Orders, for example, are the only group that has published an Ordnung. They also publish pamphlets and booklets explaining their beliefs—a move that is out of character with traditional Amish commitments to practice faith rather than formulate it into doctrine.[12] In the words of one Old Order person, "We don't put our beliefs down on paper."

Another trace of rationalization is the adoption of Sunday school by the New Orders. These formalized forays into religious education meet every other Sunday, on the "off Sunday" when church services are not held.[13] The Sunday schools meet in homes and the congregation divides into classes. Ministers typically teach the adult classes by reading a selected scripture passage and then explaining its meaning and leading a discussion. Historically the Amish have not engaged in formal religious education in their schools, homes, or church services.

Religious beliefs were taught informally—by casual conversation and mostly by observation. The Amish child was immersed in a tight plausibility structure where the power of a conforming community and the lack of other options were adequate and convincing forces of socialization.

The emergence of Sunday school, with its emphasis on interpreting and explaining the scriptures, reflects a more rational, verbal, and formal approach to religious education—one that deviates substantially from the informal mode that has characterized Amish practice historically. It also suggests that in the face of greater contact with the outside world the Sunday school becomes not only a formal way of teaching Amish beliefs but a means of persuading youth of the credibility of Amish ways. Olshan (1992) has observed that New Order youth are more verbal and display more assertive and gregarious body language than Old Order Amish youth.

Coupled with the greater rationalization is a growing tolerance of individualism as one approaches the progressive pole of the spectrum. More independent thinking and a greater emphasis on personal conversion and the assurance of salvation characterize New Order views. On the back of his business card one New Order bishop has printed in large type "For whosoever shall call upon the name of the Lord shall be saved" (Romans 10:13). Lay people and ministers freely talk about the personal truths they have "discovered" in the scripture. Individual Bible reading and personal interpretations are tolerated and even encouraged. The age of baptism drops to the midteens for the New Orders and becomes a prerequisite for courtship—all of which accentuates the importance of individual decision making and personal responsibility. New Order members enjoy greater freedom regarding dress and lifestyle. By contrast, the more traditional groups like the Swartzentrubers display more humility, greater simplicity, and ready obedience—in short, more *Gelassenheit*.

Separation from the World

Separation from the world declines as one nears the progressive end of the continuum. The shrinking social distance from the larger society takes on many forms. Although the New Order group practices less separation, they do, ironically, verbalize stronger convictions about separation from the world than the other groups. English, the language of the dominant society, is more widely used by the New Orders—even to some extent in their church services. Many New

Order young people work away from home in an environment where English is spoken all day and they naturally become fluent in it.[14] In one New Order congregation only one out of twenty young men planned to stay on the farm. The rest aspired to nonfarm jobs—carpentry, masonry, plumbing, electrical, drafting, small enterprises, and factory work. The overwhelming majority of Swartzentrubers, by contrast, have remained insulated from the world by remaining on the farm and avoiding factory work. The Swartzentrubers hire "taxi" service only for emergencies while some Old and New Order members will lease vehicles. New Order members are permitted to fly on airplanes, in another departure from historic Amish practice. All of these changes symbolize more amorphous boundaries with the larger society.

One minister estimates that about 75 percent of the New Order children and perhaps 20 percent of the Old Order children attend public schools, but very few if any of the Swartzentrubers do. Interest in mission activity is another gauge of social distance from the dominant society. Although the New Orders do not send out missionaries, many of them have supported an organization called Iron Curtain Ministries that ships Bibles and relief supplies to Eastern Europe.

The Amish have historically not adopted "fast" time (daylight saving time), preferring instead the traditional slow time. This not only reinforces Amish separation from the world, but also symbolizes their preference for a traditional pace that rejects what some Amish call "crazy time" and avoids "the rat race." This measure of separation from the world is also eroding. The Swartzentrubers, however, continue to reject "fast" time and the Andy Weaver group preaches against it and holds its church services on slow time, but as a result of their involvement in nonfarm work some members are following "fast" time. The Old Orders and the New Orders, with their growing entanglements in the larger society, have for all practical purposes adopted "fast" time—even for their church services.

Dress has served as one of the historic benchmarks of separation from the world for Amish communities. Although the four groups embody distinctive Amish patterns, their costume reflects shrinking separation from the world as one moves toward the New Orders. Near the progressive end of the continuum men's hair gets shorter, beards are trimmed tighter, hat brims shrink, bonnets get smaller, and brighter colors flourish. The Swartzentrubers are more likely to go barefoot in the summer and their women to wear the high-top black shoes. The Swartzentrubers prefer to use as little plastic as possible, forbidding plastic eyeglasses as well as rubber panties for babies.[15] In all of these ways and many more, the dress of the four groups signals their degree of separation from the dominant culture.

Carriage Adaptations

In Amish eyes the automobile symbolizes one of the more threatening vices of modern life with its offer of instant mobility, independence, speed, and status. The rejection of the automobile has become one of the defining characteristics of Amish identity. This in turn has bestowed upon the Amish carriage a quasi-sacred status as a symbol of Amish identity. Amish groups have given careful attention to changes in the accessories and appearance of the carriage, with the more traditional groups trying to preserve its pristine historical character, as shown in table 4.2.[16]

TABLE 4.2.
Carriage Adaptations by Affiliation

	Affiliation			
Adaptation	*Swartzentruber*	*Andy Weaver*	*Old Order*	*New Order*
Rubber tires	no	no	no	yes
Sliding doors	no	no	no	yes
Wipers	no	no	no	yes
Plush upholstery	no	no	some	yes
Windshield	no	no	yes	yes
Rearview mirror	no	no	yes	yes
Hydraulic brakes	no	no	yes	yes
Bright upholstery	no	no	yes	yes
Red safety emblem	no	yes	yes	yes
Small rear window	no	yes	yes	yes
High dashboard	no	yes	yes	yes
12 volt lights	no	yes	yes	yes

Key: No = not permitted; few = adopted in less than 10 percent of the districts; some = adopted in 10 to 50 percent of the districts; yes = no restrictions and/or used in over 50 percent of the districts.

With the exception of roller bearings for its wheels, the Swartzentruber carriage has successfully preserved an early-twentieth-century style. The Swartzentrubers have even spurned government attempts to install the slow-moving vehicle emblem on their carriages.[17] The other three groups have accepted the slow-moving vehicle symbol and have installed battery-operated lights, as well as a small rear window and a high dashboard. The Swartzentruber rejection of the small rear window symbolizes their preference for drawing sharp lines of separation from the world.

The two more progressive groups—the Old Orders and New Orders—have both installed "storm fronts" (enclosed fronts with a windshield) to protect passengers from inclement weather. These groups also permit rearview mirrors, full back seats, and hydraulic brakes, whereas the two more traditional groups use only old-fashioned block brakes that press against the wheels. The New Orders have accepted rubber tires, sliding side doors, wipers, and more plush upholstery. Brighter colors, greater use of velvet, and fancier upholstery increase across the spectrum of social change.

All four groups, however, have maintained the basic shape of the carriage as well as its black color. They have also accepted ball bearings and the use of fiberglass for carriage bodies. These distinctions and others displayed in table 4.2 mark the notches of conservatism on the sacred spectrum of carriages in the Holmes County settlement.

Household Technology

Without access to electricity, Amish homes do not have dishwashers, electric dryers, air conditioners, or microwaves. They are also void of carpeted floors, decorative drapes, and figured wallpaper. The homesteads of Holmes County do vary considerably, however, in their degree of plainness and simplicity. The Swartzentrubers of course appear the most austere. Indeed, one New Order neighbor said, "They live dirt cheap." The Swartzentrubers' Ordnung forbids indoor bathrooms, linoleum, varnished floors, window blinds, and stuffed furniture. The major household technology that has been adopted by the Swartzentrubers is the wringer washing machine powered by a gasoline engine—an appliance used by all four of the groups.[18]

The three more progressive groups have accepted stuffed furniture, varnished floors, and linoleum, as well as indoor toilets, bathtubs, and showers, as shown in table 4.3. The Old Orders and New Orders permit a continuous supply of hot water for washing and bathing.

TABLE 4.3.
Household Technology by Affiliation

Technology	*Affiliation*			
	Swartz-entruber	*Andy Weaver*	*Old Order*	*New Order*
Carpeted floors	no	no	no	no
Bottled gas appliances	no	no	no	yes
Natural gas lighting	no	no	no	yes
Gas freezer	no	no	no	yes
Rental freezers	no	no	yes	yes
Gas or kerosene refrigerator	no	no	yes	yes
Central heating	no	some	yes	yes
Window blinds	no	no	yes	yes
Continuous hot water	no	no	yes	yes
Linoleum floors	no	yes	yes	yes
Varnished floors	no	yes	yes	yes
Indoor toilet, tub, shower	no	yes	yes	yes
Sofas and stuffed chairs	no	yes	yes	yes
Washing machine	yes	yes	yes	yes

Key: No = not permitted; few = adopted in less than 10 percent of the districts; some = adopted in 10 to 50 percent of the districts; yes = no restrictions and/or used in over 50 percent of the districts.

Although the Andy Weaver church permits the use of gas to heat water, it cannot be heated on a continuous basis. Water may be heated only as needed for washing clothes or taking a bath on Saturday evenings. The two less traditional groups permit central heating, as well as gas or kerosene refrigerators and the use of rental freezers. The more traditional groups use ice boxes or ice chests for chilling food. New Order families are permitted to have gas freezers.

The Swartzentrubers burn kerosene in their lanterns because Coleman type gas lanterns, bottled gas for cooking, and natural gas are off limits. Many Amish farms in the Holmes County vicinity have natural gas wells. Swartzentrubers who have gas wells on their farms are permitted to sell the gas but cannot use it on their properties. Old Order members are not permitted to use bottled gas but may use natural gas if they have a gas well on their farm. And more recently, Old Order members have been permitted to tap natural gas from public utility lines for heating and cooking but not for lighting their homes. By contrast the New Orders use natural gas for lighting and some members have permanent "cathedral" lighting fixtures in the ceilings of their homes instead of the portable lanterns used by the other groups. All things considered, the level of convenience, the modernity of appearance, and the extent of landscaping increase as one moves toward the New Orders.

The Tractor

If the automobile symbolizes the status and individualism of modernity, the tractor represents the massive power of progress for the American farmer. "Americans," said one Amishman, "have a love affair with the car and American farmers have a love affair with the tractor." As the tractor grew in popularity among American farmers it tantalized the Amish as well. Because the Amish had already placed a taboo on car ownership, some feared that acceptance of the tractor, particularly on pneumatic tires, would in time lead to the car. Moreover, the use of tractors for field work would expand and mechanize farming operations and snatch work away from Amish youth, sending them even more quickly off to the factory.[19] "Using horses for field work," said one farmer, "is the greatest limiting factor to the size of farming operations."

The four groups have coped with the threat of the tractor in different ways as shown in table 4.4. All four groups prohibit using tractors for field work—plowing, planting, and pulling machinery. The Swartzentrubers have banned the tractor at the barn, but they do use engines pulled on a cart to chop silage and grind feed at the barn. The other three groups use tractors in selective and controlled ways, but primarily at the barn for heavy power needs such as blowing silage, grinding, and mixing feed and providing hydraulic power.

In order to discourage road use the Andy Weaver church and the Old Orders do not permit pneumatic tires on their tractors. The Andy Weaver group allows hard rubber on tractor wheels if they have "interrupted tires" with rubber cleats as a special deterrent to road use. Some Old Order districts permit air in the front tractor tires. The Andy Weavers and Old Orders permit tractors to pull farm machinery on

TABLE 4.4.
Tractor Usage by Affiliation

	Affiliation			
Usage	*Swartz-entruber*	*Andy Weaver*	*Old Order*	*New Order*
Tractor for plowing, etc.	no	no	no	no
Tractor to field	no	no	some	yes
Tractor with air tires	no	no	no	yes
Tractor as road vehicle	no	no	no	yes
Power units in field	no	no	yes	yes
Tractor used at barn	no	yes	yes	yes

Key: No = not permitted; few = adopted in less than 10 percent of the districts; some = adopted in 10 to 50 percent of the districts; yes = no restrictions and/or used in over 50 percent of the districts.

the road at slow speeds but worry that air tires will make it easier to use the tractor as a road vehicle and in time lead to the car.

By contrast, the New Orders permit pneumatic tires on their tractors. New Order farmers may also use their tractors to pull wagons loaded with fertilizer, hay, and corn between barn and field but not to pull implements in the field. In some New Order districts the tractor is used as a road vehicle to run errands, and sometimes a tractor pulls the wagon that carries the benches from house to house for Sunday services, a practice that encroaches on the horse's sacred domain and worries some New Order members. The New Orders have relaxed many of the historic restrictions on the tractor. It remains to be seen whether they will be able to restrain it over several generations—indeed one New Order district recently permitted tractors to be used for field work.

One of the negotiated midpoints between horses and tractors is the power unit—a tractor-like engine with full hydraulic power mounted on a four-wheel cart. Power units are pulled by horses but can be used much the way a tractor can to power a variety of farm implements—haybalers, mowers, corn pickers etc. This so-called "Amish tractor," which is used by Old Order and New Order alike, is a negotiated compromise that provides the virtual equivalent of tractor power while still slowing things down but without eliminating the horse—the prime symbol of Amish identity.

The Farm Equipment Maze

All four groups reject the use of self-propelled equipment—combines, harvesters, and haybines, as shown in table 4.5. A few New Order farmers have used field choppers, driven by power units, to cut and chop green corn in the field for silage. This, however, has caused some controversy and is not widely accepted. As horse-drawn equipment became more difficult to obtain, some Amish farmers began adapting tractor implements to be pulled by horses. Engines for example were mounted on haybalers that were pulled by horses. By using power units and by mounting engines on tractor equipment, Amish farmers were able to significantly increase their efficiency and productivity without relinquishing the horse.

The Swartzentrubers and Andy Weavers have generally not mechanized their field operations. They still use old-fashioned, ground-driven machinery designed for horses. Corn is picked by hand. Although they use a baler to compact dry hay into tight bales, the baler is not pulled through the field. It must be a "stationary" baler at the barn or in the field and loose hay is brought to it. The only engine-powered implement that the Swartzentrubers pull through their fields is a chemical sprayer used to control weeds and insects.[20] The Andy Weaver group is allowed to use engines on both sprayers and grain binders.

By contrast the Old Orders and New Orders use a variety of engine-powered equipment in the field—pickup balers, corn pickers, mowers, hay crimpers, and haybines to cut, crimp, and windrow hay in one operation. Hydraulic plows that force plowshares into the ground are also common. The New Orders also permit air tires on their farm equipment—a major departure from traditional Amish thinking, which feared that air tires would increase mobility, convenience, and road use, thus paving the way for the car.

Major differences also emerge in equipment utilization at the barn as seen in table 4.5. All four groups prohibit the use of pipeline milking equipment and milking parlors—a regulation that effectively limits the size of dairy operations. The New Orders have permitted bulk tanks and milking machines since their formation in the late sixties. Bulk cooling tanks and mechanical milkers are a significant change because they enable farmers to increase the size of their herds and sell their milk for drinking at much higher prices, all of which boosts farm income. The tanks and milkers, strictly forbidden by the Swartzentrubers and Andy Weavers, are a contentious issue among the Old

TABLE 4.5.
Farm Equipment Usage by Affiliation

	Affiliation			
	Swartz-entruber	*Andy Weaver*	*Old Order*	*New Order*
Field usage				
Self-propelled combines	no	no	no	no
Forage chopper	no	no	no	few
Haybine	no	no	few	yes
Hay crimper	no	no	yes	yes
Corn picker	no	no	yes	yes
Hydraulic plow	no	no	yes	yes
Mobile haybaler	no	no	yes	yes
Field sprayer	yes	yes	yes	yes
Barn usage				
Mechanical gutter cleaner	no	no	no	yes
Bulk milk tanks	no	no	few	yes
Milking machines	no	no	few	yes
Portable feed mixer	no	no	yes	yes
Forklift/front end loader	no	no	yes	yes
Automated broiler houses	no	no	yes	yes
Elevator	no	yes	yes	yes
Diesel engines	yes	yes	yes	yes

Key: No = not permitted; few = adopted in less than 10 percent of the districts; some = adopted in 10 to 50 percent of the districts; yes = no restrictions and/or used in over 50 percent of the districts.

Orders. Some Old Order farmers in a few districts have installed bulk tanks and milkers to the consternation of church officials. To adopt mechanized dairies means the Old Orders must revise their historic Ordnung—which is always difficult—but more importantly it means acquiescing to the more liberal practices of the New Orders, erasing an important boundary line between the two groups—surely an intramural embarrassment.

Diesel engines are commonly used on the farms of all four groups as a source of power in lieu of electricity from public utilities. Although diesel engines are permitted by the Swartzentrubers, some districts frown on automatic battery starters and use smaller gasoline engines. By using hydraulic and air power the Old Orders and New Orders have automated the feeding and ventilating systems in their broiler and hog operations. In fact one Old Order bishop is reported to have said that "my broiler house is so automated that I can feed my chickens wearing my *mutze*" (Sunday frock coat)—a comment that was not well received by some of his brethren.

Microenterprises

The most significant change in the Holmes County settlement in recent years has been a dramatic shift in Amish occupations. Leaving their plows behind, nearly two-thirds (61 percent) of the Amish families in the three more progressive groups earn their income from microenterprises and factory employment.[21] The percentage of Amishmen farming in the settlement dropped from 72 percent in 1965 to about 43 percent by 1988 (Kreps et al. 1992:14). A recent tally of Amish-owned enterprises in the early nineties shows over seven hundred in the Holmes County settlement.[22] Although firm numbers are not available, local informants estimate that at least three-quarters, if not more, of the Swartzentruber families are farming.

The shift from farm to microenterprises and factory work has profound long-term consequences for Amish life, including the use of technology, separation from the world, church and family life, as well as the retention of Amish youth. All things considered, the Ordnung of the church has been more flexible with new technology in Amish shops than with farming operations. This is partly due to the fact that the farm-related Ordnung has a long tradition in the Amish community and the acceptance of new technology requires changing or updating the Ordnung—a process that always meets resistance. Since shops are relatively new there is little historic Ordnung to govern them, and new forms of technology are more readily accepted as long as they don't violate a historic taboo such as using electricity from public utility lines.

Table 4.6 displays the pattern of technological adaptations in shops by affiliation. The Swartzentrubers do use gasoline engines and some

TABLE 4.6.
Shop Technology by Affiliation

Technology	*Affiliation*			
	Swartz-entruber	*Andy Weaver*	*Old Order*	*New Order*
Central electrical generator	no	no	no	some
Electric lights	no	no	no	yes
12 volt motors	no	no	some	yes
Leasing vehicles	no	no	few	yes
Portable electrical generator	no	no	yes	yes
Hydraulic power systems	no	no	yes	yes
Electric welders	no	no	yes	yes
Electrical tools at construction site	no	no	yes	yes
Acetylene torch	no	yes	yes	yes
Battery calculators	no	yes	yes	yes
Air power systems	no	yes	yes	yes
Advertising	no	yes	yes	yes
Diesel engines	yes	yes	yes	yes
Air paint sprayers	yes	yes	yes	yes

Key: No = not permitted; few = adopted in less than 10 percent of the districts; some = adopted in 10 to 50 percent of the districts; yes = no restrictions and/or used in over 50 percent of the districts.

diesels to operate shop equipment—saws, grinders, and sanders. These are operated by belt power, but not with a direct line shaft from the engine. The other three groups typically operate shop equipment directly from the power shaft of diesel engines. They also use compressed air to power a wide variety of equipment. The two most progressive groups, Old Orders and New Orders, also use hydraulic pressure to power shop tools. They also use portable generators to operate electric welders as well as electrical tools at construction sites. The New Orders are permitted to have a central generator in their shop for power tools as well as for electric lights. By replacing electric motors with air and hydraulic ones, the power of so-called "Amish electricity" has enabled entrepreneurs to create very productive and enterprising shops. Even the Swartzentrubers have been permitted to use paint sprayers, an adaptation that surprised many local observers.

The rise of enterprising shops has also pressed the historic line on Amish ownership of vehicles. Over the years the three more progressive groups have permitted shop owners to hire trucks and vans on a regular basis for business purposes. Pushing close to ownership but technically avoiding it, some shop owners in both the Old and New Order groups are now leasing vehicles for business purposes. These are often driven by Amish boys who have not yet joined the church.

General Technology

The four groups have held a tight line on members owning and driving motorized vehicles. This line is occasionally crossed by youth who are not members, but among baptized members the taboo is firm. Ironically, Old Order youth probably own more cars than New Order youth, reflecting the greater control of New Orders over their youth. The Swartzentrubers typically do not hire vehicles except for medical treatment or other emergencies. The other groups, including the Andy Weavers, hire vehicles (with a non-Amish driver) on a fairly routine basis for business and long-distance travel to funerals, weddings, and for deer hunting and fishing trips. Motorized vehicles, however, are typically not rented for Sunday services, giving the carriage a quasi-sacred status.

A variety of other new forms of technology has gradually slipped into acceptance by the three more progressive groups. As shown in table 4.7, the Swartzentrubers shun much of the technology that has been adopted by some of the other groups—especially the Old Orders and New Orders. Both of these more progressive groups have accepted bicycles as well as power mowers and weedeaters. Garden tillers, which are creeping into some Old Order church districts, are widely used by the New Orders. Artificial insemination of dairy cattle is a modern intervention into natural conception that both the New Orders and Old Orders use. The Andy Weaver group permits it only in the case of breeding problems. "And it's amazing," noted an artificial inseminator, "how many breeding problems they have!"

Knowing where to draw the line on the use of telephones and electricity has been a perplexing problem in many Amish communities. The Holmes County settlement has been no exception. The Swartzentrubers and Andy Weavers have prohibited the private ownership of telephones but members are free to use public telephones or "borrow"

TABLE 4.7.
General Technology Usage by Affiliation

	Affiliation			
Technology	*Swartz-entruber*	*Andy Weaver*	*Old Order*	*New Order*
Owning and driving vehicles	no	no	no	no
Owning computer	no	no	no	few
Electric typewriter	no	few	some	some
Air travel	no	no	few*	yes
Garden tiller	no	no	few	yes
Private telephone	no	no	some	yes
Electric inverter	no	some	yes	yes
Electric cash register	no	some	yes	yes
Artificial insemination	no	no	yes	yes
Power lawn mower	no	no	yes	yes
Power weedeater	no	no	yes	yes
Bicycles	no	no	yes	yes
Hiring vehicles	no	yes	yes	yes
Power chain saw	no	yes	yes	yes

Key: No = not permitted; few = adopted in less than 10 percent of the districts; some = adopted in 10 to 50 percent of the districts; yes = no restrictions and/or used in over 50 percent of the districts.
*Air travel is permitted in the case of certain emergencies.

the phone of a non-Amish neighbor. An Old Order businessman estimates that about one-third of the households in his affiliation have a private phone at the property line, but not inside their shop or home. The other two-thirds use public telephones. A few might have access to a phone in the garage of a non-Amish neighbor. Among the New Orders the phone has been steadily creeping into the home. A New Order minister estimates that one-third of the New Order districts have phones in the home, one-third have a private phone in an outbuilding, and the remaining third use public phones of one sort or another.

The New Orders, not surprisingly, have been the most flexible with the use of electricity as well. As noted above, the use of a central generator in New Order shops has increased their ability to use electrical tools as well as lights for business activities. Both the Old Orders and New Orders have permitted the use of inverters in recent years. The inverter generates 110 volt "homemade" electricity from 12 volt current stored in batteries. Smaller than a car battery, the inverter powers small 110 volt electrical items—cash registers, typewriters, copy machines—without tapping into public utility lines. Taboo among the Swartzentrubers and Andy Weavers, the inverters are growing in popularity among the Old Orders and New Orders. Indeed one New Order farmer said, "There are gobs of them around here." The growing use of electricity affords greater convenience around home and office and enhances productivity in microenterprises. Although none of the groups has an explicit Ordnung against computers, the rejection of 110 volt electricity has held them at bay. The growing use of inverters, however, will surely increase the temptation to use computers.

The Anabaptist Escalator

The Holmes County settlement offers a rich social setting to explore the relationship between membership retention and social change. When Amishmen, impatient with traditional ways, try to persuade their elders to permit new forms of technology they sometimes argue that greater flexibility "will help to keep young people in the church." The evidence in Holmes County raises serious doubts about the validity of that argument. The data in table 4.8 suggest an inverse or negative relationship between the retention of youth and greater acceptance of technology. In short, the evidence suggests that the more progressive the group, the more likely it is that they will lose their youth.

The retention data gathered from the 1988 *Ohio Amish Directory* show that the more conservative Andy Weaver group may retain as high as 95 percent of its young people, while among the New Orders the retention rate drops to 57 percent. The *Directory* does not provide information on the Swartzentrubers, but local observers uniformly note that the Swartzentrubers are very successful in retaining their youth—likely keeping upwards of 90 to 95 percent. In addition, those Swartzentrubers that do leave often make a radical break with their Amish tradition. In the words of one Amishman, "they go all the way" and often join a mainstream Protestant church or no church at all.[23]

Persons defecting from the more progressive groups tend to simply

TABLE 4.8.
Retention of Adult Children by Affiliation

	Swartz-entruber	*Andy Weaver*	*Old Order*	*New Order*
Traditionalism	extreme	high	moderate	low
Percent of adult children affiliated with the Amish	90	95	86	57
Percent of families retaining all their children	—	95	88	72

Source: The *Ohio Amish Directory, Holmes County and Vicinity* (1988). Local informants estimate that 90 to 95 percent of the Swartzentruber children eventually affiliate with the church.

move "up" a step on the Anabaptist escalator and join a related but more progressive Amish or Mennonite group.[24] Someone leaving the Andy Weaver group might join the Old Orders, and some defecting from the New Orders might join a conservative, but more progressive Mennonite group. A New Order farmer worries that because "our sermons emphasize what's in the heart rather than the Ordnung, we are just a seedbed for the Beachy Amish and Mennonite churches. Our young people have learned a whole new mind set that makes it easier for them to shift over later." This feeder system assures a steady flow of new and usually quite committed members to the more progressive groups as persons move up the Anabaptist escalator. One New Order minister noted regretfully, "If our church required a bishop to have all of his children in the church, many bishops wouldn't qualify."

It is tempting to assume some sort of causal relationship between the wider use of technology and the loss of young people. Such a relationship may be spurious however if both factors are propelled by a deeper underlying force such as a shift in consciousness. One observer explained that many New Order members have "changed their way of thinking and use more evangelical terms such as new birth, personal salvation, and plan of salvation, but they have kept many of the old social standards," such as no car or utility line electricity. "Thus, when young married couples leave for a more progressive group, they don't have to change their way of thinking—all they have to do is get a car and electricity." Echoing similar sentiments, a New Order member noted that "many of the young people have learned to give testimonies and tell what the Lord has done for them and use new jargon that is foreign to the Old Order, so it's rather easy for them to shift over to some sort of Mennonite group." It's relatively easy for them, in other words, to move up a step on the escalator.

The Swartzentrubers on the other hand have created a tighter and more restrictive social world—one sharply separated from the larger society, which makes it much more difficult to defect. Those who want to abandon their church must jump across a much wider cultural gulf than those in the Old Order or New Order groups. The Swartzentrubers' conservative use of technology surely reflects a more restrictive and rigid consciousness that is shaped by a high degree of social regimentation. The consciousness afloat in the more progressive groups represents a more flexible outlook. It gives greater respect to individuality, tolerates more diversity, cultivates more openness to the larger society, and appreciates ambiguity to a greater extent. This fundamental shift in consciousness, this restructuring of thinking, welcomes both the greater use of technology and also makes it easier for young people to move up a step or so on the Anabaptist escalator.

Part II

Historical Perspectives

BLACKBOARD BULLETIN

August, 1992

Enter to Learn
The Good You Can.
Leave to Serve
Your Fellow Man!

IN THIS ISSUE....

The *Blackboard Bulletin*, a monthly magazine for Amish school teachers, typically carries on its front cover maxims that capture key Amish values.

5

Persistence and Change in Amish Education

GERTRUDE ENDERS HUNTINGTON

The massive consolidation of public schools in the middle of the twentieth century endangered the traditional values of Amish education. In response, the Amish developed an extensive network of parochial schools that was endorsed by the U.S. Supreme Court in Wisconsin v. Yoder *in 1972. Gertrude Enders Huntington chronicles the Amish struggle with the powerful forces of progress that assumed that all Americans would benefit from greater and greater doses of scientific learning and critical thinking. Huntington shows how Amish education has had to change in order to maintain and preserve its commitment to traditional values.*[1]

Distinctive Values

The Old Order Amish are striving to perpetuate their community—striving to preserve their culture and their unique view of the world. To achieve this they have managed, during the past three centuries, to balance adaptability in certain behavioral areas of their culture with a steadfastness of value orientation. Through the centuries their goals have changed little, though their means for achieving these goals have been modified in response to pressures from the surrounding society.

An Amish writer succinctly expressed the difference between modifying behavior and modifying values in the title of an editorial in the *Blackboard Bulletin*, "Co-operate? Most Certainly! Compromise?

Never!"[2] The ultimate goal of the Old Order Amish is that each person born into their community achieve life everlasting. They believe this necessitates following certain prescribed, though changing, rules known as the *Ordnung*, more loosely designated as "the way we do things." Using biblical phraseology the Amish are "in the world" but "not of the world." There is constant tension between their society and the society that surrounds them. Within the boundaries of Amish culture there is remarkable homogeneity. Their holistic way of life is characterized by the integration of individual roles with cultural institutions. In the field of education the Amish explain: "Our aim is that the church, the home and the school should teach the same thing" (Miller 1988:23).

The Amish do not confuse schooling with the larger concept of what the world calls education. Although during most periods in their history they have permitted their children to be schooled by "outsiders," they have never permitted their children to be educated by the world. In the United States, when schooling encroached on education, the Old Order Amish rebelled and refused to "let their children be taken out of their hands and turned into men of the world."[3]

Anabaptist theology emphasizes the importance of a voluntary community. Adult baptism symbolizes the personal commitment of each individual initiated into this exclusive community. Amish parents cannot take a baby to the church to be baptized; the parents must raise the child to *want* to be baptized, to voluntarily request baptism when he or she has reached the age of discretion. This places a great responsibility on the parents, who are ultimately accountable for the total education of their children. Anabaptist parents have never believed themselves, or their children, to be subservient to any outside religious institution or to a civil government; they have been wary of help or intervention from the state in the rearing of their children (Schwartz 1973). Menno Simons (c. 1496–1561), an early Anabaptist leader, taught that parents were morally responsible for the condition of their children's souls. "Watch over their souls as long as they are under your care, lest you lose also your own salvation on their account" (Simons 1956:390). He considered child rearing to be the primary occupation of the Anabaptist adult, "For this is the chief and principal care of the saints, that their children may fear God, do right and be saved." Although the admonition was written about 1557, the persistence of the teaching is illustrated by the fact that it was reprinted in the Amish educational journal, the *Blackboard Bulletin*, in 1963 and again in both editions of *The Challenge of the Child* in 1964 and 1967.[4]

Anabaptist parents were admonished to instruct their children in the way of the Lord that they might "walk in all decency and discipline, [be] well-mannered, quiet, obedient to their father and mother, reverent where that is proper, after their speech honest, not loud, not stubborn, nor self-willed" (Simons 1956:950). One sixteenth-century teacher who "was greatly embittered" against the Anabaptists is quoted in the *Martyrs Mirror* as saying that "they seek to bring up their children in better discipline and fear of God, than many other people" and that in his school "their children were apter and learned more readily than any others" (Braght 1951:931). Today these traits of decency, discipline, obedience, reverence, honesty, quietness—not stubbornness or self-will—are still valued by Amish parents. Parental responsibility remains a primary concern of Amish parents, who refuse to abdicate their responsibility to specialists or to the state.

In addition to preserving parental responsibility and authority in all areas of their children's lives, the Amish maintain a degree of separation from the dominant society by living within a disciplined community. They are to be "the chosen generation, the royal priesthood, the holy nation, the peculiar people" (Simons 1956:950). A defined community is a prerequisite for this description. Anything that breaks down the community and the boundaries that define it undermines their distinctive culture. However, the Amish are sufficiently adaptable that identifying symbols can be changed and boundaries modified—as long as boundaries exist. Children must be raised within these boundaries and learn to respect the boundaries so that as young adults they will choose to become Amish.

Participation in Public Schools

Many first generation Anabaptists were educated urban dwellers, but by the time of the Amish division most of these persecuted people were farming isolated parcels of land or working as tenants on large private estates. Often living outside of villages, their children had limited access to formal schooling but received a practical education working under the tutelage of their parents. The Amish did not develop their characteristic community structure until after they came to America, where they were able to own land and live near coreligionists.

Contrary to their European experience, Amish settlers in America had equal access to schools with all other citizens. Although the Amish have always stressed education to the degree that their members could read the Bible and prayer book and could figure accounts and taxes, schooling was not emphasized. It was only in the 1960s that schooling became a significant aspect of the Amish community. This constituted a profound change. Today an Amish-administered school is almost as important for the survival of a new community as are resident clergy. Within the last thirty years the majority of Amish children have been moved from public schools to Amish-administered schools.

During the eighteenth and early part of the nineteenth century the Amish took limited advantage of whatever local elementary schooling was available—attending long enough to learn the basics of reading and writing. Sometimes the Amish were instrumental in starting local public schools. The central Ohio Amish community was founded about 1808 and the first schoolhouse in the region was built in 1815 by the Amish on an Amish farm (Glick 1933:4). An earlier school started by the Amish may have met in an abandoned cabin (Miller 1977:12–13). Amishmen regularly served on local public schoolboards until the 1950s. However, many Amish families remained suspicious of schooling and were concerned about the amount of time their children spent away from family and community—away from the real education of learning to be responsible members of the Amish community who could support themselves economically within the limitations of the Ordnung.

The small, local, public school reinforced Amish values, gave them limited contact with "the World," and taught the basic skills needed within a cohesive religious community. However, as soon as attendance became compulsory some Amish objected. In the parts of Pennsylvania inhabited by the Amish, compulsory attendance laws were not enforced until about 1895, when children age seven to twelve were required to attend. Even then, the average rural child was only in school seventy days a year (Fisher 1978:312–13). As the school year was extended and the age of required attendance increased, some individuals complained. But when the small, one-room schools were closed and pupils were bussed to consolidated schools, widespread concern and apprehension developed within the Amish community. These new schools drew students from a large area and the Amish lost most of their influence. They no longer were elected to school boards and they had no say in the hiring and firing of teachers, in what books were used, or in what activities their children engaged in while away from home.[5]

The Struggle with the State

Public school teachers who had personal contact with Amish children, even those who made no effort to understand their culture, were generally sympathetic to them, for like the sixteenth-century worldly teacher quoted in the *Martyrs Mirror,* they appreciated the Amish children's efforts to be cooperative students. In localities where rural electrification was an issue and where local farmers wanted telephone lines extended and rural roads paved during and following World War II, there was considerable hostility against the Amish. This hostility was expressed by some school administrators. The adoption of new technology such as movies and television also stimulated Amish resistance to public schools.

When movies were introduced into one village school in Ohio, Amish parents were promised that their children would not have to watch them. One-third of the students in the school were Amish and the superintendent decided all children must attend the movies. When some of the children, obeying their parents' command, refused to go to the auditorium, the superintendent forcibly and physically pushed an Amish child into the auditorium, injuring him "to the extent that he wasn't able to help chore" (Byler 1985:221). At the request of the boy's father an Amish leader went to see the superintendent. The superintendent bawled out the Amishman and asked him to leave, commenting that he was too busy to listen and furthermore his policy on movies would not be changed. A few days later the Amish parents met with the school board, who agreed to their request. Episodes like this, in addition to the problems of consolidation and school attendance beyond the age of fourteen, prompted the Amish to form their own schools.

As the age of compulsory attendance rose, the Amish became alarmed. They believed that children age fourteen and older should be under the supervision of their parents or of a community member, learning the skills necessary to succeed economically and socially within the boundaries of the Amish community. Furthermore they doubted that an "outsider" could teach Amish children these skills. "Our children should be in our homes at the age of 14 years to learn farming, housekeeping and other duties, that become us people, and to live a quiet, peaceful life in humility and meekness in Christ."[6] If too many hours are spent in school the Amish fear their children may develop "chair-mindedness" and enjoy reading more than physical labor. However, this danger is not as great as that of children being exposed to the influences of high school, where there are such harmful activities as "moving pictures, shows, bands, and other musical instruments and plays, flag saluting, etc."[7] Others decried the "gymnastic gatherings, group activities, snap studies, chair-mindedness, and job fancy follies" associated with consolidated schools.[8]

When the attendance age was extended to sixteen, some Amish adapted to the change and avoided high school by repeating the eighth grade. There were children who spent as many as three years in the eighth grade, where they functioned as teachers' helpers or studied on their own. An Amish student, Christ, repeated eighth grade twice. The first year his teacher gave him the books and notes he had used as a college freshman and the next year he brought Christ other college texts to study. In later years Christ became a dedicated member of the public school board.

As the Amish population increased, rural schools became crowded but the state refused to build more and so Amish children were forbidden to further crowd the schools by repeating the eighth grade. In many states with an Amish population, problems arose because some parents refused to send their children to high school. Those who did send their children often waited until they were forced to do so by the courts, thereby disrupting classes by adding unwilling children, often several months after school had begun. The Amish were convinced that high school attendance was destructive to the community and harmful to the child. Parents would serve jail terms or migrate rather than permit their children to be removed from their influence at such a critical stage in their education.

Searching for Common Ground

On the local level there have been periodic attempts by the public school system to respect the Amish desire to be separate.[9] In 1854, outside of Lancaster, Pennsylvania, an exclusively Amish school was set apart by the school board for training Amish children. The school had a modified curriculum of reading in the German Bible, spelling, writing, and a little arithmetic. "[G]eography history and grammar, were tabooed, as in noway necessary . . . to make good farmers out of the boys and good housewives out of the girls."[10] The degree of flexibility tolerated is illustrated by the attitude of the non-Amish schoolmaster. When questioned about his opinion as to whether the earth was flat, square, or round, he said he would "teach the subject when required, any way the patrons wanted it taught"! Even today one public school district in Lancaster County operates a one-room school exclusively for Amish children. This anomaly is dwarfed by some one hundred other one-room schools in the county that are operated by the Amish themselves.

In Ohio two exclusively Amish public schools are sometimes referred to as "captured" schools. These small, graded schools were not established for the Amish but the state has kept them open for the Amish. In 1955 one of the township boards in Ohio opened a short-lived school for ninth-grade Amish children so they could meet the attendance requirement while avoiding high school. The school was taught by a public school teacher and the curriculum included English, German, and general mathematics.[11]

The most successful compromise was developed in Pennsylvania in 1955, and later implemented in parts of Ohio and Indiana. The Amish developed a vocational training program for children who had passed the eighth grade but who were still required to attend school. Under the vocational plan the children could work at home, supervised by a member of the community, keeping a diary of "what they worked." One three-hour period per week the children met with an Amish teacher, either in a home or in the parochial school to report on their week's work and to study English, math, German, and whatever else was determined by the local community. Attendance records were kept and forwarded to the state.[12] In those localities where school authorities recognized the vocational program many problems were avoided.[13] But in other areas of the country Amish parents steadfastly refused to send their children to high school.

The response to this Amish "intransigence" eventually pushed the landmark court case *Wisconsin v. Yoder* from the local court to the circuit court, to the Wisconsin Supreme Court, and finally to the United States Supreme Court. Here it was declared in 1972 that the Amish could not be forced to send their children to school beyond the eighth grade.[14] The Supreme Court recognized that education could continue outside the classroom and that "enforcement of the State's requirement of compulsory formal education after the eighth grade would gravely endanger if not destroy the free exercise of . . . [Amish] religious beliefs." The Yoder case legalized the Amish right to be "separate" in the education of their adolescent children.

In order to avoid bussing their children to the consolidated school in the town of Arthur, Illinois, the Amish community built their first parochial school in 1966, their second in 1967, and a third in 1968. Additionally, the Amish "did not feel Sex Education, TV and Physical Education programs were necessary for our way of life. Our hope was to gain better discipline, also we hope to have time to help the so-called slow learners or the one who might need more attention" (Miller 1980:40). Responding to the discontent of Amish families, the Arthur Public School District established two school centers in 1968 exclusively for the Amish. One center has grades one through five, the other grades six through eight. The financing, supervision, curriculum, and hiring of the six teachers is under the administration of the School District. The district officials are advised by an Amish board, elected by the Amish to represent Amish needs and interests. Although the school officials make a conscious effort to respect Amish wishes, the enrollment has remained stable while the number of Amish parochial schools in the county has continued to increase.

The Emergence of Amish Schools

Perhaps if more public school officials had been sympathetic to the Amish desire to remain separate and had retained small local schools with simple physical plants and limited curriculum, the Amish might have remained in the system—but probably not. Specialized public schools for the Amish would likely be challenged by the Civil Liberties Union, would be difficult for states to administer, and the Amish might have been unable to work closely enough with school officials to establish the necessary understanding. In 1946, as prejudice against the Amish was rising, an elderly bishop raised the question of the Amish starting their own schools: "Do you think it is right for us to tell them [school officials] how to run their schools? The world won't stop with their big ideas on education just because of a few Amish. I won't be here to see it, but you might be, when there will be a big change in this public school business" (Byler 1985:221).

Four years later, in a school district in which an Amishman was serving as an elected official on the school board, everything was quiet and peaceful. Public officials were making every effort to please the Amish. Some Amish parents, however, became concerned about one of the books used in the seventh grade. Should the Amish do anything about it? Realizing that in the long run they could not stop the onslaught of change in public education, they decided they should not interfere with the public schools, but rather let the public educate their own children as they saw fit. The Amish would withdraw from the public schools and form their own schools. It was becoming increasingly clear that modern, secular schools were not suitable agents for the socialization of Amish children. The goals of education and the

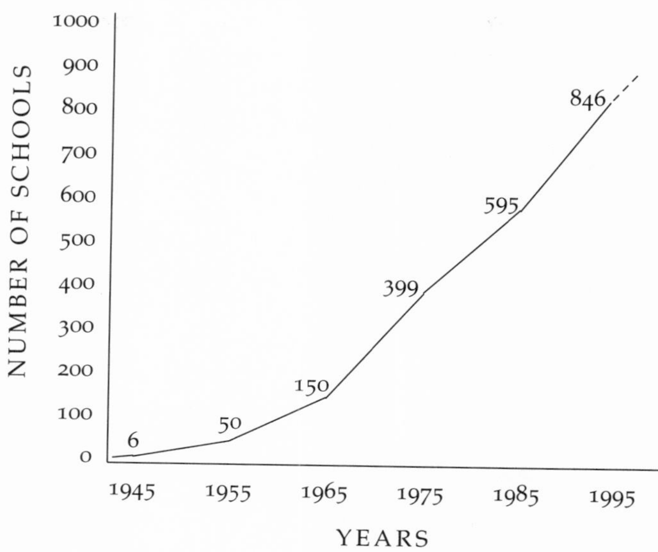

Source: *Blackboard Bulletin*

FIGURE 5.1.
Amish Parochial School Growth in North America: 1945–1995

methods used to obtain these goals for the two cultural systems had become too divergent.

Considering the strong congregational character of the Amish, it is surprising how steady and how fast the school movement grew as shown in figure 5.1. In the early years, and in some communities today, consensus on schooling was difficult to achieve. Specific Amishmen provided leadership to help their coreligionists see the advantages and problems of having their own school system.[15] At the local level judicious visiting, meetings, and informal discussions were important for consensus building and decision making. But local decisions were not enough because the Amish were no longer living in a limited geographical area—they had been spreading to various states and even to Canada. In addition, the Amish school problems were receiving national attention. Many in the general public were incensed when they saw pictures of school officials chasing Amish children into a corn field in Iowa in 1965.[16] Amish schooling had become more than a local issue.

The growth of Amish schools is spectacular when one realizes the small size of the supporting population and the fact that none of their

TABLE 5.1.
The Growth of Amish Schools in North America: 1965–1994

Year	Number of			
	States	*Schools*	*Pupils*[b]	*Teachers*
1965	10	150	5,099	174
1970	14[a]	303	9,789	375
1975	17[a]	399	12,037	491
1980	18	490	14,880	640
1985	18	595	17,373	755
1990	17	722	20,499	976
1994	19	846	23,817	1,155

Source: Compiled by Karen Yoder from the *Blackboard Bulletin*. The 1994 figures are for the 1993–94 school year and are taken from the *Blackboard Bulletin*, November 1993, p. 25.

[a] Includes Honduras.

[b] Schools that did not report their number of pupils were estimated to have *twenty* pupils, and schools that did not report the number of teachers were estimated to have *one* teacher. Figures for 1994 are used unadjusted from the *Blackboard Bulletin*.

leaders had a formal education beyond the eighth grade. Although the first Amish school was started in 1925, by the beginning of World War II there were only 4 Amish operated schools. By 1950 there were about 16 Amish schools, five years later 41, and by 1960 about 82.[17] As shown in table 5.1, by 1990 the number of schools had grown to 722 and by 1992 it topped 800. In 1970 Ohio had the largest number of Amish schools (84) but by 1990 Pennsylvania had the most (248) with Lancaster County alone having over 100 schools.[18] The number of Amish schools in North America is displayed by state in table 5.2.

School building peaked in the late sixties as the parochial school movement continued to spread rapidly among the Amish. Schools founded in 1990 were primarily in new communities and were a response to population growth rather than to a new attitude toward schooling.

In Pennsylvania almost no Amish children attend public schools; in Ohio quite a few go to public schools, including some schools that are primarily attended by Amish pupils. In Indiana about half of the Amish children are in rural public schools. With 140 church districts, Indiana has only 75 schools. In contrast Pennsylvania has 195 church districts and 248 schools.[19] The Amish have lived in Kansas since 1883,

TABLE 5.2.
Amish Operated Schools in North America: 1993–1994

State	Date of oldest school	Number of			
		Schools	*Teachers*	*Pupils*	*Church districts*
Pennsylvania	1938	267	292	7,071	221
Ohio	1944	178	283	5,739	258
Indiana	1948	88	185	3,785	166
Wisconsin	1978	69	80	1,589	53
Missouri	1948	39	46	766	32
Michigan	1958	36	50	824	39
New York	1949	33	37	783	30
Iowa	1962	29	37	592	25
Kentucky	1969	25	35	715	21
Ontario	1953	23	33	568	17
Illinois	1966	15	27	418	21
Minnesota	1974	14	14	260	9
Delaware	1925	10	14	284	8
Tennessee	1945	10	10	202	6
Maryland	1967	5	5	125	6
Oklahoma	1986	2	3	38	4
Montana	1975	1	1	11	2
N. Carolina	1985	1	2	30	1
Virginia	1991	1	1	17	1
Kansas		0	0	0	5
Florida		0	0	0	1
Texas		0	0	0	3
Georgia		0	0	0	1
Totals:		846	1,155	23,817	930

Sources: Figures for number of schools, teachers, and pupils for the 1993–94 school year are adapted from the *Blackboard Bulletin*, November 1993, p. 25. Data in the *Blackboard Bulletin* are based on voluntary reporting. Figures for the number of church districts are for 1992 and taken from David Luthy, "Amish Migration Patterns: 1972–1992," in the appendix of this book.

in Florida since 1927, and in Texas since 1982, yet none of the Amish communities in these states has established Amish schools.

Integrating Schooling and Community Values

The Amish-administered plain schools are called "parochial" schools, but many are, technically speaking, community schools or parent-run private schools because they are administered by community members or clusters of parents rather than directly by the church. In a culture where church and community are coterminous, this distinction is somewhat pedantic. Whether the school is financed by a church district, a cluster of church districts, or by individual church members the purpose of the school remains the same: "to prepare the child for the Amish or Mennonite way of living and the responsibilities of adulthood in an effort to establish the foundations of a society of useful, God-fearing, and law-abiding citizens" (*Guidelines* 1981:8).

The *Guidelines* (1981:1) for Amish schools summarizes their purpose in these words: "The Goal Of The Old Order Amish Parochial Schools Is To Prepare For Usefulness, By Preparing For Eternity." Although theology is not taught, the integration of religion into all aspects of life endows Amish schools with a strong religious orientation. The Amish view is expressed in a booklet of *Guidelines* (1981:72) for their schools:

> With the exception of devotion [*sic*] it is the Amish and Old Order Mennonite theory that the Bible be taught in the home and church, however it is further our aim to teach Religion all day long in our curriculmum [*sic*] (lessons) and on the play ground.
>
> In Arithmetic by accuracy (no cheating).
>
> In English by learning to say what we mean.
>
> In History by humanity (kindness-Mercy).
>
> In Health by teaching cleanliness and thriftiness.
>
> In Geography by learning to make an honest living from the soil.
>
> In Music by singing praises to God.
>
> On the school ground by teaching honesty, respect, sincerity, humbleness and yes, the Golden Rule.
>
> Is Religion then continuously mentioned? Seldom, just enough to bring the whole thing to a point now and then.

The method for teaching religion is further explained in a manual for teachers entitled *Schoolteachers' Signposts* (1985:23): "*Teach religion by action* rather than Bible study. Bible study, we feel, belongs in the church and the home. Remember that 'actions speak louder than words.' . . . Example is the most powerful tool, you see, and by example we are teaching our religion all day long. . . . Be a Christian teacher in *action*. Our precepts must be the Christian virtues such as honesty, respect, love, humility, punctuality, cleanliness, quietness, industriousness, obedience, justice, and the practice of the Golden Rule."

Amish Christianity is highly social. It is best learned in a community setting where it can be constantly practiced in human interaction. Not only is the teaching in the Amish school consistent with that in the home and the church, in many ways the Amish school is a microcosm of the church community. The Amish have never considered home schooling as an alternative to public schools (except for limited periods under unusual circumstances). Home schooling deprives the child of experiences that can be learned only within a social group (Steering Committee 1992:23). The importance of the group is also indicated by the special efforts that the Amish make to provide schooling for their handicapped children. In the larger communities there are special schools for handicapped children and in small communities an extra teacher is hired if there are two or three children who cannot attend the parochial school. The whole school community shares the extra cost.

Over the years profound contrasts have emerged between the plain schools and the public schools. Some of the key differences are contrasted in table 5.3.

One of the interesting contributions of separatist groups is that they give us a glimpse into the society from which they withdrew, because they often preserve specific aspects of the rejected culture (Huntington 1993:21–25). In many ways the Amish parochial schools resemble the one-room schools of rural America in the first half of this century. The curriculum is very similar, as is the pattern of the school day, week, and year.[20] The daily schedule of a one-room public school in 1950 is virtually identical to that followed today in many Amish parochial schools—from the ten-minute recitation periods to scheduling recess. The major curricular change is the introduction of German as a subject in the upper grades. The teacher in the parochial school is responsible for the physical care of the classroom. Consistent with their experience in the home, the children help to carry wood and clean the classroom, enjoying the special chores assigned them and taking

TABLE 5.3.
Contrasts Between Amish Schools and Public Schools

Amish schools	*Public schools*
. . . are run on a human scale.	. . . are run on an organizational scale.
. . . are operated by parents without an administrative bureaucracy.	. . . are operated by professionals with an administrative bureaucracy.
. . . stress drill accuracy and proper sequence.	. . . stress speed, variety and freedom of choice.
. . . train youngsters to stay in their community.	. . . train youngsters to get ahead in life.
. . . stress tradition.	. . . stress progress.
. . . pick teachers because of their Christian example.	. . . pick teachers because of their ability and training.
. . . have teachers who are generalists in subjects.	. . . have teachers who are specialists in subjects.
. . . favor correct knowledge.	. . . favor critical thinking.
. . . value cooperation and humility.	. . . value competition and pride in achievement.
. . . reject technology.	. . . embrace technology.
. . . rank penmanship high as a skill.	. . . rank penmanship low as a skill.
. . . favor group identity.	. . . favor individual expression.
. . . have no kindergarten.	. . . have kindergarten.
. . . use a limited amount of lesson material.	. . . use a great amount of lesson material.
. . . see a child as a future Plain Person with a soul.	. . . see a child as a citizen with an intellect.
. . . hire teachers only from the Plain community.	. . . hire teachers with diverse backgrounds.
. . . stress memorization.	. . . downplay memorization.
. . . see learning as work.	. . . see learning often as fun.
. . . believe truth is revealed in the Bible.	. . . search for truth.
. . . stress believing.	. . . stress questioning.

Source: New Era story by Ed Klimuska (22 May 1989), based on Hostetler and Huntington (1971).

pride in the appearance of their school. Work charts are found on the walls of every parochial school.

When abandoned rural schools were available the Amish often purchased these old public schools and renovated them. New buildings must meet state health and safety requirements and the Amish generally follow the state-approved plans. Physically these schools resemble earlier, rural public schools in size, heating, and sanitation. The Amish schools, however, are often plainer in appearance and simpler in construction. The Amish are careful to choose school sites that provide plenty of outdoor play area for the pupils. Schools usually have some playground equipment and a field large enough to play softball and other running games. There may be a basketball hoop and the parents sometimes construct skating ponds for use during recess and lunchtime. The children may make use of neighboring lanes for sledding.

Teachers

Teachers in Amish schools are expected to teach with their whole life. They are to be of "good Christian character, good educational background and [have] a desire to improve their education" (*Guidelines* 1981:12). They must be obedient to the Ordnung, exemplifying humility, obedience, steadfastness, and love for their fellow man.[21] In order to meet these qualifications the teacher must be a member of the Amish church. This means that qualified Amish schoolteachers have only an eighth-grade formal education and are not certified. This has caused problems in some states, especially in Michigan.

The gender distribution of Amish teachers is shown in table 5.4. The majority of Amish teachers are unmarried women. Early in the parochial school movement there were, especially in the midwest, quite a few male teachers. In 1970 the percentage of male teachers was 18, but by 1990 it had fallen to 14 percent. In 1970 Adams and Allen counties in Indiana had the largest percentage of male teachers with 53 percent; while Lancaster County had virtually none. Among all newly founded schools in 1970, 20 percent of the teachers were men, but by 1990 the percentage of male teachers in newly formed schools had dropped to 5 percent. When the concept of Amish-run schools was new, more men pioneered; as schools have become integrated into Amish culture, more women are teaching, even in newly founded schools.

The majority of Amish schools are still one-room operations with a single teacher, however, the number of one-room schools with two

TABLE 5.4.
The Gender of Amish Teachers (1970 and 1990) in Percentages

	1970	*1990*
Teachers Reporting		
Females	82	86
Males	18	14
Male Teachers in Selected Counties		
Adams and Allen (IN)	53	32
Elkhart and Lagrange (IN)	16	12
Geauga (OH)	41	23
Holmes and Wayne (OH)	22	9
Lancaster (PA)	0	4
Male Teachers in Newly Opened Schools	20	5

Source: The *Blackboard Bulletin*, compiled by Karen Yoder.

teachers or a teacher and a full-time assistant is increasing. Thus the average number of pupils per teacher has fallen from 26 in 1970 to 21 in 1990. The drop in teacher/student ratios may also be related to the founding of new communities, for schools in new areas tend to be smaller than in well-established, older communities.

Training for teachers varies from settlement to settlement but typically continues throughout their career. New teachers can count on help from other Amish teachers and may begin their career assisting an experienced teacher. In areas where there is more than one school, the teachers may gather for supper several times a month. The first national teachers meeting in 1954 was attended by nine teachers (Beiler 1964:58). Twelve years later the attendance had grown to over one hundred school teachers, former school teachers, board members, and ministers. As the number of parochial schools increased and as the Amish migrated to new states, regional meetings were substituted for the annual national meetings. More than four hundred people may participate in the lectures and workshops in some of the regional meetings. Training for beginning teachers is emphasized in special sessions for them. These regional training meetings, often supplemented by local meetings, function as in-service training and encourage teachers to constantly improve. In addition to the formal and informal gatherings of teachers, the monthly *Blackboard Bulletin* provides an important source of information and inspiration for Amish teachers.

Textbooks and Teacher Training

When the Amish parochial schools first were established, they used books that parents and teachers had studied in their childhood: the *Dick and Jane* books, the *McGuffy Readers*, and the *Scott-Foresman New Basic Readers*. Even today the *Strayer Upton Practical Arithmetic* books remain popular, partially because these texts from the 1930s include many farm problems. Prices, however, are far out of line. These and other older texts and activity books are reprinted in the Amish-owned Gordonville Print Shop for use in parochial schools. The vitality of the Amish school system is attested to by the many books written for use in their own schools.

A statewide Old Order Book Society was organized in Pennsylvania in 1957 to discuss what books were appropriate for Amish administered schools. The committee's function broadened to include other educational concerns and in 1976 the Old Order Amish School Committee, which supervised the vocational schools, merged with the Book Society. The Book Society determined what books would be used in Pennsylvania Amish schools and the books printed by the Society were available to Amish schools in other states. However, the Book Society had limited influence on the choice of books used in Amish schools outside of Pennsylvania (Lapp 1991:521–26).

Pathway Publishers, an Amish Publishing house in Ontario, has produced a reading series of thirteen textbooks accompanied by workbooks for grades 1–8. In 1990 Pathway offered fifty-four Old Order titles for use in parochial schools as well as six more books written specifically for Amish schoolteachers. Individual teachers and teachers committees in different communities also produce teachers' aids and textbooks.[22] A group of Old Order Mennonite schoolteachers formed Schoolaid, which publishes educational materials in East Earl, Pennsylvania. They are producing teachers' aids, texts, and workbooks, some of which are used by the Old Order Amish. School materials written by the Amish in various communities are gradually displacing "worldly" books. In 1991 the Steering Committee (1992:24) explained that it "does not feel it should make decisions or commands in using certain books. . . ." The committee recognized state and community differences in schooling requirements and regulations.

About 1951, the few Amish parochial school teachers, consistent with the patterns of their culture, started a circle letter in which they discussed their teaching. The letter came around about every six weeks and provided appreciated support for the men and women who were forging new roles within the community. As the number of teachers grew, the circle letter became inadequate, and someone suggested that there should be a school paper. In 1957 Joseph Stoll began the *Blackboard Bulletin*, a hand-duplicated magazine with eight issues a year, selling for $1.00 for a two-year subscription.[23] Amish authors contributed practical articles on school management and essays describing specific situations they had encountered. Joseph Stoll's (1965) influential *Who Shall Educate our Children?*[24] first appeared as a series of articles in the *Blackboard Bulletin*, as did the essays later reprinted in *The Challenge of the Child* (Stoll 1967), *Tips for Teachers* (1970, 1991), *Teacher Talk* (1974), and *Chalkdust* (1991).

The *Blackboard Bulletin* was the first Amish magazine produced for the national Amish community. It became a new institution, a vehicle that promoted the Amish school system. In 1964 there were about 600 subscribers to the *Bulletin*. By 1990 the number had soared to nearly 16,000. The *Blackboard Bulletin* preceded the chartering of Pathway Publishing Corporation by seven years. The *Blackboard Bulletin* continues to play a significant role in the development and effectiveness of both Old Order Amish and Old Order Mennonite parochial schools and in the education of Amish teachers.

The creation and maintenance of their own formal school system, subject to the regulations of a secular state, created a new institution within the Amish community. A series of new roles for community members emerged and a new attitude toward schooling developed. No longer was the elementary school outside the culture and somewhat isolated from Amish life. It could no longer be criticized as "worldly" when disagreements arose. The elementary school was now within the culture. Consensus beyond the local community was needed to ensure financial and social support and to work with state officials. As the Amish population grows, as government regulation increases, and as medical expenses soar, the Amish are being forced to become more bureaucratic. A single church district can no longer deal with many of these issues in local isolation.

Changing to Persist

How have the Amish balanced change and persistence in education? During three centuries Amish educational beliefs have changed little. The educational goal remains the same: "to prepare for usefulness, by preparing for eternity" (*Guidelines* 1981:72). Though the goal has persisted, the means for achieving the goal have changed somewhat. The family retains primary responsibility for the education of their children, but there have been profound changes in the way the culture schools its children. Schooling has moved from external control to being an integral part of most Amish communities.

Thus Amish culture offers a vivid example of adaptability. They are adapting to changing situations by modifying their institutions in ways that enable them to maintain their basic values. In essence, they are running in order to stand still. In the area of schooling they have been remarkably effective in creating new institutions to reinforce traditional values and historic configurations of their culture. Parochial schools are enabling the Amish to maintain a strong, local, church community—a community that is ideologically, symbolically, and behaviorally separated from the world. This highly functional community protects the Amish family and reinforces the family as a strong and self-reliant unit, enabling Amish parents to educate and thereby socialize their children in order to perpetuate their unique culture. By changing, the Amish are able to persist.

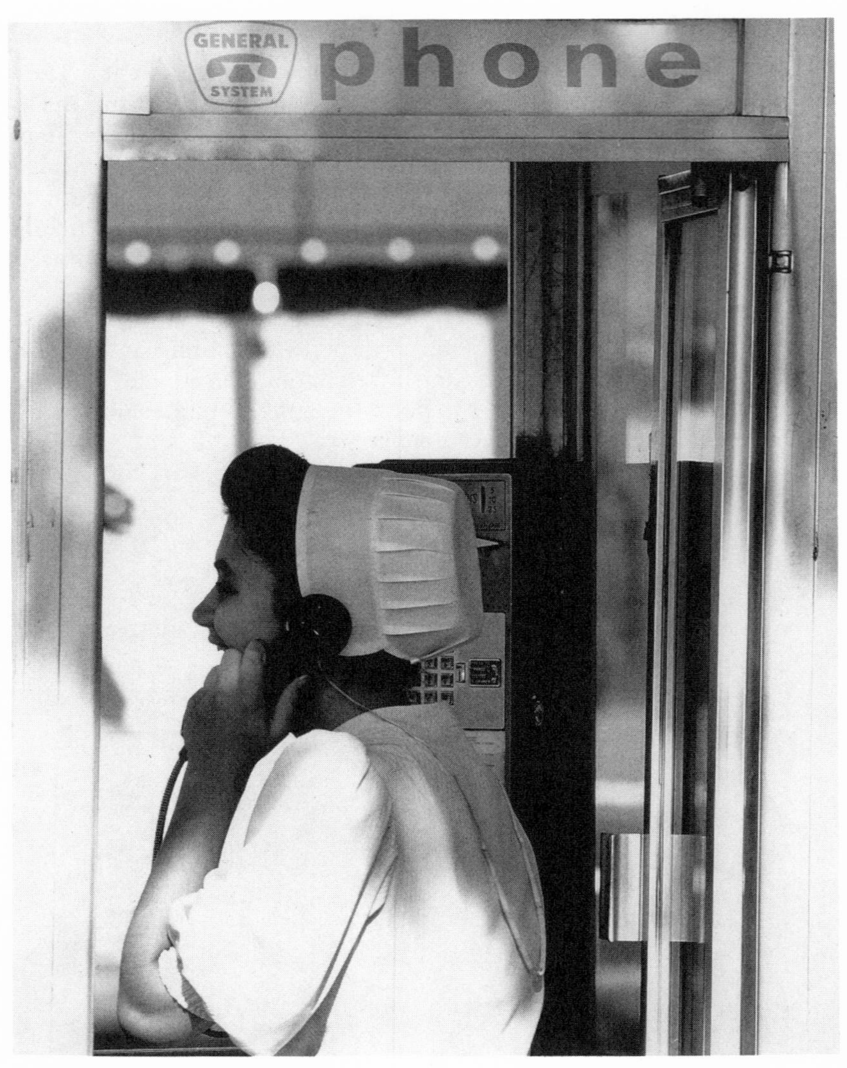

A New Order Amish woman uses a public telephone in Holmes County, Ohio. Some New Order church districts permit the installation of telephones in homes while others prohibit it. (Photograph by Doyle Yoder).

6

Amish on the Line: The Telephone Debates

DIANE ZIMMERMAN UMBLE

The Amish have struggled with a vast assortment of technological changes that have bombarded their communities in the twentieth century. Participation in public education and the use of tractors and automobiles would understandably transform the cultural patterns of a traditional society. But telephones—why would such innocent devices endanger traditional ways? Diane Zimmerman Umble contends that the telephone threatened traditional patterns of communication in Old Order communities. After charting historic debates over the use of the telephone, Umble describes contemporary struggles among the Amish over the role of the telephone.

The Telephone Debates

The Old Order Amish in North America have engaged in ongoing debates about how and where to draw the line on telephone use. At the turn of the century, the debates focused on whether or not to allow telephones in the home. Within the first decade of the new century, the Old Order Amish *Ordnung*, or code of conduct, banned telephones in the home but stopped short of prohibiting telephone use. The decision was a painful one and became entangled in a church split in the Lancaster settlement in 1910.[1] The debates today center on appropriate use of telephones and telephone technologies in Amish businesses as well as the use of loud call bells, flashing lights, toll free numbers, fax machines, answering machines, voice mail, and cellular telephones.

The telephone negotiations represent Amish struggles to manage social change and ensure economic survival while at the same time maintaining traditional values of humility, simplicity, and separation from the world. Rules about appropriate telephone use attempt to preserve the boundary between the Amish community and the outside world. In addition, telephone rules also serve to mark the boundaries distinguishing traditional from more liberal Amish groups. Groups that permit telephones in the home serve as negative reference groups for the Old Order Amish, thereby strengthening their resolve to hold to traditional standards (Kraybill 1989:150).

The ongoing negotiations about appropriate uses of the telephone have led to an interesting array of telephone practices. In recent years, the pressure for access to telephones has increased with the growth of Amish-owned businesses. The rules vary from church district to church district and from settlement to settlement across North America. Some districts permit telephones in or adjacent to a shop. Others maintain that telephones must be outside and separate from the shop. Some bishops encourage their members to use public telephones at mills, stores, and other public places. In Ontario, a telephone is located in an Amish schoolhouse. In the Big Valley settlement in Mifflin County, Pennsylvania, the Amish often use telephones owned by their non-Amish neighbors. In Lancaster County, Pennsylvania, telephone shanties, scattered throughout the countryside, are shared by several families in a particular neighborhood. These "community" telephones have unlisted numbers, and calls are recorded and paid for on an honor system.

In Ohio, shared telephones are often pay phones. Many Ohio Amish use telephone credit cards to pay for long-distance calls, a practice that is less common in the Lancaster settlement. One district may prohibit loud call bells on the telephone, while another may permit such bells. The bishop in one district may object to telephone answering machines, but permit the use of an answering service. The most conservative group of Old Order Amish, the Swartzentrubers, avoid using the telephone except in cases of emergency. While these practices reflect various compromises, they maintain the ban on telephones in homes that was grafted into the Ordnung in the early years of the new century. That historic prohibition provides the context for the contemporary debates over the telephone.

In order to understand the contemporary compromises on telephone access, it is important to understand how and why the telephone came to be banned from the Amish home. The decision against home telephones is best understood by situating the telephone debates within the larger context of communication practices. Amish social rituals structure communication to serve ethnic boundary maintenance.

Rituals of Communication and Boundary Maintenance

At the turn of the century, communication in Old Order communities was organized in and through the rituals of community life and anchored in the home. Worship, work, and socializing all revolved around the home. Births, funerals, and weddings occurred at home. The home was the hub of faith and life. It was the scene of face-to-face, often nonverbal, highly contextualized communication. The home was also a refuge from the complexities and the temptations of the outside world. Old Order rituals of worship, silence, work, and visiting knitted individuals into the fabric of community life and also articulated and nurtured community boundaries. Changes in communication patterns, like the introduction of the telephone, challenged traditional definitions and reordered the taken-for-granted notions about who had access to whom, when and where.[2] In the Amish experience, the introduction of the telephone threatened to fracture the harmony of the community. The telephone threatened to disrupt key social rituals of worship, silence, work, and visiting.

Amish worship services are held biweekly in the home. The three-and-a-half-hour service in the Pennsylvania German dialect includes slow singing, silent prayers, scripture readings, and two sermons. The services ritually express the spirit of *Gelassenheit*, the collective expression of submission and yieldedness. The individual is integrated into and finds expression in the collective activities of waiting, silence, listening, and unison singing.[3]

Communion services in particular mark who is in or out of fellowship and clarify behaviors that are deemed appropriate and inappropriate. Each fall and spring, church leaders meet to discuss issues facing the church. If problems develop (as happened with the introduction of the telephone), communion is postponed until the social harmony can be assured. If individuals resist discipline, they can be expelled. In the preparation for communion as well as in the service itself, individuals renew their commitment to the church, to its rules of behavior, and to each other twice a year. Membership in the community is affirmed, social relationships are repaired, and deviants are expelled. In the process, a common understanding of expected behavior is clarified and community boundaries are reinforced.

Woven throughout the restoration and maintenance of community is a discourse of silence (Hostetler 1984). Amish worship services begin in silence, and periods of silence are interspersed throughout the service. Silence is also a means of negotiating social relationships. It can communicate submission or disapproval. Shunning is the active application of enforced silence for reproof, in the hope that sustained ostracism will restore communication. The Amish also use silence to confront conflicts with the wider culture (Hostetler 1993). Since their beginning, the Amish have upheld prohibitions against taking loyalty oaths, filing lawsuits, and participating in military service. Even faith requires little verbal articulation. From the Amish point of view, the maintenance of a redemptive community is their witness. The common "life" speaks for itself. Silent discourse binds its participants together in a stream of taken-for-granted understandings about what needs to be said and what can remain unspoken. The Amish use of silence, like worship, actively reaffirms and restores community identity and marks off community boundaries.

Work rituals also express community identification. Sandra Cronk (1981:1) says that Old Order people view work as a redemptive ritual, a calling from God. It is pursued for the sake of building and maintaining the community, not for profit or prestige. A family working together on the farm celebrates togetherness and affirms the usefulness of every member of the family. They work together in the house, in the garden, in the barn, and in the fields. Every member, young and old, contributes according to his or her ability. Farm work integrates the family and keeps workers near home in the context of family and community influence. Work patterns at the turn of the twentieth century were governed by the pace and rhythm of the seasons. Recent shifts in occupational patterns have changed work rituals within the Amish community as described in chapters 8, 9, and 10. Work is no longer anchored in the home for many Amish persons.

Old Order Amish visiting rituals allow for regular and extensive communication as a part of worship, work, and, on many other occasions, visiting for its own sake. Worship services are followed by a shared meal that provides the occasion for sharing community news. Shared work also facilitates opportunities for socializing. Work "frolics" bring together extended family and friends to share tasks ranging from house cleaning and quilting to butchering and barn raisings. The "off" Sundays, when worship services are not scheduled, are also devoted to visiting. Informal visiting is routine and extensive among friends and family, both far and near. Frequent visiting strengthens community ties by maintaining a high level of interpersonal awareness and understanding among members. Visiting nurtures belonging, enhances social relations within the community, and funnels communication within ethnic boundaries.

Through communication patterns, Amish communities provide their members with common values, beliefs, rituals, and histories that mark who belongs and who does not, thus providing stability and identity. Rules and rituals about how to communicate, who can communicate with whom, under what circumstances, and about what—all function to construct, reproduce, and repair social boundaries and identities. The rituals of worship, of silence, of work, and of visiting articulate and maintain Old Order orientations within the boundaries of community. The efficacy of these rituals rests on face-to-face, often nonverbal communication; communication that most often occurs at home.

The Coming of the Telephone

With the coming of the telephone, rituals that served to strengthen the identity of an integrated and separated community were challenged. Telephones demanded verbal expression. The telephone mediated face-to-face communication, disrupted social harmony, threatened to change visiting patterns, and intruded into the home.

In the mind of Lancaster's Old Order Amish, the telephone was a principal issue behind the 1910 division of the Lancaster settlement that resulted in the loss of nearly one-fifth of the members (Kraybill 1989:143). Prior to 1910, Amish leaders had taken no firm position on the telephone. Certain Amish families had telephones in their homes. They were connected by homemade lines that linked farm families in the immediate neighborhood on party lines.

Farmers' lines were commonplace in rural areas across the country. Local newspapers often carried accounts describing how such lines could be built with wire, fence posts, and a simple battery operated telephone box. Farmers used these makeshift party lines to communicate with their neighbors long before telephone companies provided service to rural areas. Oral sources in both Pennsylvania and Ohio suggest that while some Amish families had these telephones, most were not connected to organized telephone companies at the time.

One Amishman described the decision-making process in Pennsylvania: "our ministers have conference every year, and what they think should be or what they think shouldn't be, they counsel over it. And then the church people are supposed to listen. . . ." When a few families installed telephones, the telephone question came before the church leaders. Conflicting views over telephones created disunity in the Lancaster community prior to communion. The Amishman went on to explain what happened when the telephone issue came to a head in 1910:

> and these people that had the phone, one said to the other, "What are you going to do? Are you going to put yours away?" One said, "I'm going to wait to see what the ministers come up with." And the other one said, "I'm not going to put mine away." So it caused a division in the church. . . .

Most Amish accounts of the events of 1909 and 1910 are oral. One of the few published accounts, written by an Old Order Amishman born in 1897, reflects common themes in the story:

> About 1909 the phone lines were put up thru [*sic*] the country and our Amish people at least some got them in and it did not seem to make any trouble, then a couple women got to talking about another woman over the phone and this woman also had the phone in and had the receiver down and heard what they said, this made quite a stink and at last came into the *gma* [congregation] to get it straightened out, then the Bishops and ministers made out if that is the way they are going to be used we would better not have them. Some were willing to put them away and others were not so that is when the King *gma* [the splinter group] started, the telephone was one of the issues but I suppose there were some more. (Lapp 1986:7)

Whether the catalyst was the stubbornness of the men, or the gossip of the women, there was dissension within the community over the telephone. An Old Order Amish historian writes that the 1910 split was caused by "indifferent views in church discipline, most concerning newly invented contraptions that our conservative church leaders could not tolerate" (Beiler 1986:14).

In the fall of 1909, when the ministers met to discuss issues facing the community in preparation for fall communion, telephone ownership and the sanction of shunning were on the agenda. After joint consultations with ministers from another county, the Lancaster leaders announced their intentions to hold to the "old order" of their forebears. Their position was explained in preparatory services across the district. They reiterated support for shunning unfaithful members, even those who left the Amish church to join nearby Mennonite churches. And they stated that the telephone had no place in the

Amish home. Thus in the fall of 1909 a ban on home telephones was grafted into the Ordnung in the Lancaster settlement. Other settlements also instituted prohibitions against home telephones, usually without incident. In 1914, one Iowa congregation divided over the telephone. Many Old Order Mennonite groups across North America also had telephone troubles within their congregations (Umble 1991a).[4]

While Old Order Amish accounts are primarily oral, some accounts have been written by descendants of those who left the Amish church in the 1910 division (Glick 1987). Known today as the Beachy Amish, they attribute the Lancaster split to disagreements over strict applications of shunning. In their written histories, the Beachys hold that the division was precipitated by the refusal of progressive-minded members to shun those who left the Amish church for a Mennonite church (Yoder 1987). The Old Order Amish upheld the ban on members who had joined a Mennonite church.[5]

Despite the contentions of Beachy Amish historians, the Old Order Amish continue to view the telephone as a prominent issue in the 1910 division. The Beachy group later built meeting houses and allowed telephones, cars, and electricity (choices all rejected by the Old Order Amish). To the Old Order Amish, the more progressive Beachy Amish represent what happens when "worldliness" is allowed to creep into the church.

At the time of this controversy telephone companies were growing rapidly across the country. Nearly one-quarter of all American homes had telephones by 1909. By 1912, more farm than nonfarm households had telephones (Fischer 1992:93). Telephone advertising aggressively promoted telephones as a "highway" to the world; the "modern way to save one's time and temper."

The Intercourse Telephone Company was founded in the heart of Lancaster's Amish settlement in the summer of 1909. It was connected to the Bell Telephone's trunk lines several months later and by the fall of 1909 it was possible for local persons to talk with "the outside world." The Intercourse Company, consisting of a feisty group of progressive businessmen, carried on a public feud, in the local newspaper, with neighboring New Holland over the granting of franchises to connect lines between the two towns. The Amish virtues of humility and submission were not noticeable characteristics of their aggressive business posture.

To its proponents, the telephone was the hallmark of the progressive farmer, or the efficient businessman, doctor, or lawyer. It was hailed for providing efficient access to current information: market reports, weather reports, transportation schedules. The telephone facilitated business by preventing unnecessary trips to town. Emergencies could be handled quickly by telephone. Some advocates even saw telephones as instruments of "divine service."[6]

The Amish were not blind to the benefits of the telephone. But for them it symbolized a desire to be connected to the larger world. Telephone communication could not be easily monitored or mediated by the rhythms and rituals of community life. The Amish explain that telephone communication was understood to be individualistic, making possible private links with outside sources of information. Telephone service created new business affiliations through the formation of farmers' mutual lines and later telephone companies. Telephone conversations often forced Amish persons to converse in English instead of the Pennsylvania German dialect. People were tempted to use the telephone in ways that could not be monitored by the ethnic community.

The telephone also provided temptations to gossip, "spooning," and other mischief. Visiting over the telephone was not an effective substitute for the monitoring of behavior that traditionally took place in the face-to-face context of community. The telephone required verbal expression, which undermined the practice of silence. And when the telephone caused problems in relationships among church members, it disrupted the harmony of the community. Finally, the telephone had the potential to disturb the pace and style of work routines. The Amish today suggest that telephones get in the way of work. Telephones have the potential to extract the worker from the context of shared work. They are not only a means of communication but a source of interruption and distraction as well.

The negative perceptions of the telephone and the debates swirling about its use reveal concerns about the blurring of boundaries between the community and the outside world. The telephone was not a benign gadget. The Amish doubted its divine qualities. Its use intruded into established patterns of communication and potentially could reorganize a larger set of communication practices. The telephone made community boundaries permeable to new information and new ways of behaving. For better or for worse, the telephone was a direct link to the outside world. Old Order rituals of worship, silence, work, and visiting effectively articulated ethnic boundaries and clarified who was in and who was out of the Amish fold. These rituals contextualized primary communication within the boundaries of the Old Order community. The coming of the telephone threatened to disrupt these historic rituals and extract communication from the control of the religious community.

Contemporary Struggles

Since banning the telephone from homes in 1910, Amish leaders have tried to maintain the primacy of communication within the context of community. For the next twenty years, the Amish upheld the telephone ban. If access to a telephone was necessary, they traveled to a public telephone or used a neighbor's telephone.

In the midthirties, several Amish families made an appeal to church leaders for a shared telephone. They argued that access to a telephone was important in times of emergency—calling a doctor or the fire company. "It was tolerated," according to an Amish leader, "and that was the beginning of the 'community phone.' They had a phone in someone's building but it had to be taken out and put into a phone shanty like the ones we have today" (Kraybill 1989:146).

In the intervening years, community phone shanties have gradually appeared throughout the Lancaster County settlement. Some Amish explain that community phones became necessary because non-Amish neighbors did not appreciate the "barn and tobacco smells" that trailed Amish persons who came to "borrow" a telephone. Others cite economic reasons. Amish dairy farmers in some settlements began using artificial breeding. To maintain their herds, they needed faster access to the inseminator and the veterinarian than the postal service provided. The Amish also explain that medical doctors no longer held open office hours and appointments were necessary. Community telephones thus provided relatively quick access to these outside services.

Community telephones are carefully managed by church leaders. Some Amish families report that they ask permission before installing a telephone shanty. Others simply install one without asking. In the beginning, the telephones were shared, usually by five to seven families. Today often two or three families in some districts share a phone, depending on population density. Telephone shanties or telephones in outbuildings have become increasingly common in the Lancaster settlement. Several Amish persons report that "almost everyone" has access to a telephone these days.

Numbers are usually unlisted and the telephone is primarily used for outgoing calls. Loud call bells to announce incoming calls are discouraged or prohibited. Moreover the telephones are separate from the house. Kraybill reports one grandfather's description of the expectations: "If you have a place of business and need a phone it must be *separate* from the building, and if it's on the farm it must be *separate* from the house. It should be *shared* with the public so that others can use it. It's just not allowed in the house, where would it stop? We stress keeping things small and keeping the family *together*."[7]

Economic pressures today have fostered a new round of debates about telephones. In response to dwindling supplies of farmland, Amish families have developed small businesses in carpentry, light manufacturing, foods, and the like—businesses that often serve both the needs of the Amish community and the general public. About 50 percent of the men eighteen and older in the Lancaster settlement work in nonfarming jobs. Similar trends have been documented in other settlements. In Holmes County, Ohio, a 1981 study found that only 42 percent of the heads of households were involved in full-time farming. Twenty-eight percent were involved in carpentry, construction, and the trades, while the remaining 21 percent held factory jobs (Troyer and Willoughby 1984:52–80). In Indiana 43 percent held factory jobs and only 37 percent were engaged in farming in 1988 (Meyers 1991b:315).

The growth of small businesses is accompanied by demands for a variety of new technologies. Amish entrepreneurs argue that access to the telephone is now a necessity for running a business. Permission to have telephones in the shop varies from district to district, depending on the thinking of the local bishop. In one case, an Amish businessman argued that he needed a telephone exclusively for business purposes. The bishop's reply: "It's either a community telephone or no phone at all."

The emphasis on shared telephones sometimes costs both time and money. An Amishman from Indiana describes a "community telephone house" recently built by an Amish neighbor. It was a "major investment." He estimates that his neighbor spent about sixteen hundred dollars on the building and then had to pay another seven hundred and fifty dollars to the telephone company to install a pay phone. His neighbor runs a small business and uses the telephone for business purposes. Other Amish neighbors can use the telephone as well. They pay a quarter for local calls and use telephone credit cards for long-distance calls. Proceeds from the telephone go to the man who installed it.

Sometimes solutions to logistical problems associated with community telephones can be solved with the creative use of new technology. In Ohio, a roadside telephone serves a small Amish business and an estimated twenty to twenty-four Amish families. So many people were using the phone that business calls could not be made or received. Now two lines are connected to this roadside phone. One line is connected to an answering machine that receives messages for the Amish business. The other is for the use of members of the Amish community who need to make calls.

In Pennsylvania, an Amishwoman describes the "voice box" service they have at the telephone behind their house. By paying three dollars a month to the telephone company, the three families who share this telephone (and manage two family businesses) have programmed their phone to receive recorded messages after fourteen rings. On a regular basis, they retrieve messages by dialing a special identification number. "Having a recording machine attached to the phone would probably be discouraged," she says, "but since this service is offered through the telephone company, it's alright."

Virtually all Amish businesses in the Lancaster County settlement have some type of access to a telephone, either in a shanty or adjacent to the shop. A few have toll-free numbers. While fax machines are prohibited, Amish entrepreneurs do not hesitate to use one accessible in a nearby non-Amish office. Some Amish businessmen have entered into partnerships with non-Amish partners in order to circumvent prohibitions on new technologies.

Cellular telephones are also prohibited in the Lancaster settlement. However, one occasionally hears about someone who discretely keeps a cellular phone in a desk drawer. Some businesses use vehicles equipped with mobile telephones or radios that are leased by non-Amish employees or partners. While church leaders have tolerated increased use of telecommunications for the sake of economic viability, the compromises are not without their ambiguities. Sometimes it is difficult to know where to draw the lines on specific telephone practices.

One line is that telephones are to be used only when "necessary." Businesses are permitted to install telephones with the understanding that they are available to members of the community as necessary. But the distinction between necessity and socializing is often blurred. Most Amish persons repeat the directive that the telephone is not to be used for visiting. Nevertheless, Amish women report that they regularly use the telephone to keep in touch with family members who live at a distance. One Amishwoman granted that she probably uses the phone more since they installed one "out back." She calls both family members and non-Amish friends on a regular basis.

Another rule that is often violated is the expectation that community telephones will be used strictly for outgoing calls. Many people admit to prearranging a time to receive telephone calls. One woman regularly arranges a time to receive calls from her siblings in a midwestern settlement. Day laborers often receive calls at their places of employment.

In the past, it was expected that telephone numbers would be unlisted. Recently, however, Amish business directories are beginning to include telephone numbers in their advertising. Business cards often include the number of a telephone answering service or suggest the best hours to place calls to a phone shanty. One Amishwoman confided that she and her husband had recently decided to list their number in the public telephone directory, because it was "just too expensive" to pay the additional twelve dollars a month to keep the number unlisted.

In recent years, telephone access has increased across most of the Amish settlements in North America. The Lancaster settlement leads in the proliferation of shop telephones and telephone shanties. Kraybill has described the continuum of telephone use in the Holmes County settlement in Ohio in chapter 4. The most conservative groups use public telephones or borrow a neighbor's telephone. The Old Order affiliation uses private telephones at the property line as well as public telephones. About a third of the New Order districts have begun permitting telephones in the home. In general, the smaller, rural, farm-oriented settlements have experienced less pressure for business telephones.

The trend toward increased and easier access to the telephone is not without its critics. Articles in the Amish magazine *Family Life* speak to the ambivalence about the telephone. In an article entitled "Choice of Two Evils" ("Choice" 1976:13) a husband and wife discuss which is worse, having their own telephone or continually pestering their neighbors to use their phone. After a visit to friends who have a home telephone, Fred and Saloma are disgruntled by the interruptions, teens talking on the phone, and the reliance on the telephone for every little thing. The writer attempts to delineate what is "necessary" and "appropriate" telephone use: calls strictly for business that can not be handled by mail, or for emergencies. The writer discourages "gossiping" and "unnecessary" calling. Near the end of the story, Fred wonders about their friends: "will their children be able to see the dangers in having these things which are so handy if the parents make use of them so much as they do?"

Concern about the impact on the next generation is reiterated in another *Family Life* story, "Only One Step" ("Only One" 1985:12–18). Paul comes home frustrated over the inconvenience of going to the service station to use the pay phone. Lydia, his wife, senses that his frustration is symptomatic of his deeper dissatisfaction with the church. In the course of the story, the young couple visits with an older couple who left the church years earlier to join a more liberal group. The older couple laments that they have lost their four children "into the world." The older man confesses: "What else could be expected, since we had already taken a step in that direction? . . . To us it seems the plainer churches still afford the best shelter from all the evils of the world. . . ." Some time later, Lydia finds her husband in the barn loft in tormented prayer. In tears, he admits that he was wrong in his criticism of church rules. In the end, Paul says, "Giving up was the hardest part. But now I see that it was only one small step, too—but this time a step in the right direction." Instead of moving away from the traditions of the church, he was ready to embrace them in humility.

These two stories illustrate how struggles over access to the telephone are seen as struggles of faith. The anonymous writers equate dissatisfaction over telephone prohibitions with willfulness and pride. Readers are challenged to weigh the consequences of handy access to the telephone for the faithfulness of the next generation.

A forty-seven-year-old Amishman echoes the concern about the long-term impact. He says that it may not be the phone in and of itself that causes young people to leave the church. "But one thing leads to another, and so you have this drift. . . . If you get that spirit in a group in a generation or two, pretty soon it becomes uncontrollable." He calls the trend "uncontrollable drift," and it worries him. Handy access to the telephone is viewed as one small step down a road that leads to a loss of faith in the next generation.

Implications for Boundary Maintenance

Amish reconfiguration of telephone access since 1910 represents a negotiated solution—the acceptance of community and business telephones and the maintenance of the traditional ban on telephones in the home. The compromise maintains a degree of separation from the world, while making an accommodation to economic pressures. That accommodation values community over individual needs. It allows access but at a distance. The contemporary compromise upholds tradition, while at the same time preserving community in the face of change. The mechanisms for articulating social boundaries—worship, silence, work, and visiting—continue to regulate Amish social life. But occupational shifts have moved much Amish work away from the home. The shift of focus from home to shop has the potential to blur the once clear rules about interaction with the world.

I have argued that the Amish home was the center of Amish faith and life when the telephone was first introduced. The Amish had good reasons for keeping the phone at bay. In a sense, it violated their sacred space. But while they have protected the home, the telephone and related technologies have invaded the Amish shop. Furthermore, the Amish shop now competes with the home as the center of Amish social interaction.

Many Amish business workers spend most of their time in the shop. Many work primarily with family members or other Amish persons. Others, however, rub shoulders with outsiders for most of their work day. Communication in and around the shop is not monitored or protected by the rituals of community life in the same ways the home is. Business communication is not mediated by the style, rhythms, and rituals that can be practiced at home. The shop is open to the public, as Olshan shows in chapter 8. Silent discourse is untenable for customer interactions. Some Amish leaders fear that the profit motive will undermine the spirit of submission and humility that is cultivated by working the soil. Business owners may come to see fewer connections between their profits and the long-term building of a community of faith.

Shop work also has the potential to dissolve the extended family as a working group. Manufacturing, for example, provides fewer opportunities for the young and the elderly to have meaningful roles in the economic life of the family. The wisdom and experience of an elderly farmer may not be applicable to the struggles his children face in the carpentry business. Young people may work in jobs that force them to interact daily in the world on its own terms. Access to telephones, electricity, and motorized transportation at work could lead to desires for the same technology at home. Furthermore, the demands of running a business and holding regular hours often preclude taking the day off to help with the harvest or butchering. The shop owner may have less flexibility to respond to members of the community in time of need.

Church leaders' repeated prohibitions against visiting by telephone are aimed at protecting visiting rituals. Regular visiting is still a significant part of Amish social life. In fact, the telephone is used to facilitate the logistics of planning visits, both far and near. The telephone serves as a substitute at times, however limited, when distance prevents face-to-face encounters. The Amish appreciate the telephone for its ability to maintain connections with family members who are hospitalized or who live in another settlement.

In the face of economic changes, Amish worship rituals remain unchanged. Meeting in homes brings the congregation into personal domestic space on a regular basis. Hosting worship means that the members of the congregation can observe each other's domestic lifestyle. A shared telephone in or near the shop permits neighbors to observe how one does business as well. Members of the community can informally monitor each other's behavior. Internal codes of behavior can be maintained through regular interaction. Interaction with outsiders, however, has increased significantly as Amish families leave the farm. Articulating and maintaining these boundaries is becoming more difficult.

Contemporary debates about the impact of the telephone focus on how to maintain and repair community boundaries in the face of new links to outsiders beyond the once clear borders of ethnicity. Attempts by church leaders to monitor new technologies and control persons using new-found sources of information illustrate the ongoing battle. The debates express the competing values that are at stake in the continuous renegotiation of appropriate boundaries. Rules about the use of new communications media reveal the dynamics of authority, control, and role expectations of a particular community. Such norms serve to articulate what is expected of those who wish to remain members of the community.

At the turn of the century, the telephone threatened to bring the world into the community through the home. Today, the telephone symbolizes the invasion of the world into the Amish shop. Over the last decade, the physical distance between the telephone and both the home and the shop has been shrinking. Access to the phone has become handier in many settlements. The world is coming closer. It remains to be seen whether the trend is manageable or is growing evidence of uncontrollable drift.

In some communities Amish roadside stands and retail shops cater to the tourist trade. (Photograph by Frank Vane).

7

The Origin and Growth of Amish Tourism

DAVID LUTHY

In their struggle to remain separate the Amish grew increasingly peculiar as the cultural gap between them and the larger society widened in the twentieth century. The growing peculiarity of Amish culture, as well as the expansion of travel, leisure, and mass media, provided the ingredients for the growth of public curiosity. After midcentury the Amish no longer had to merely resist the technological changes that intruded into rural areas, they now faced tourists by the millions, who came to inspect Amish ways and buy their handcrafted products. Amishman David Luthy traces the phenomenal rise of the Amish image in public media—books, drama, tourist paraphernalia—as well as the growth of tourism itself.

Modest Beginnings

In a growing number of settlements the Old Order Amish are being commercially exploited by tourism in various stages of its development. This chapter explores the origin and growth of tourism in the three largest settlements: Lancaster County, Pennsylvania; Holmes County, Ohio; and Lagrange County, Indiana.

Amish tourism is oldest and most highly developed in Lancaster County. Founded in 1760, it is the oldest and second largest Amish community. Since it has become the mecca of Amish tourism and has influenced the direction tourism has taken in other states, it will be studied here in greater detail.[1]

On a sunny Saturday in November 1975, I stood in a sprawling asphalt parking lot in the village of Intercourse (population 600) and stared at rows of chartered busses. They had brought tourists from New York City, Baltimore, Washington, D.C., and various cities in New Jersey to view the Amish of Lancaster County. There were thirty-eight busses parked and, as likely as not, at least that many somewhere on the surrounding roads touring "Amish Country."

I thought thirty-eight busses were quite a lot until I learned that November is one of the quieter months in the flood of tourists who visit the county. August, the busiest month, brings eight times as many. Statistics show that in 1963 there were 1.5 million tourists. The number has risen, especially after *Witness*, the 1985 movie focusing on the Amish, was filmed in Lancaster County. Today between 3.5 and 5 million tourists visit Lancaster annually.

The tourist industry as it exists today in Lancaster County is huge and managed like any large corporation. But it was not always so. For many years I have been interested in tracing it to its beginning. However, the more I studied it, the clearer it became that there is no single identifiable moment or event that created tourism in Lancaster County. Some of the contributing components that have formed it are presented here.

Attention was drawn to the Amish of Lancaster County in 1905 with the publication of *Sabina: A Story of the Amish*, a novel by Helen R. Martin. On its cover in an oval frame is a painting of a lovely Amish maiden wearing a lavender bonnet. It was the second of Mrs. Martin's thirty novels, most of which contain Pennsylvania-German characters of various religious denominations (Thompson 1935).

At about this same time, Isaac Steinfeldt opened a newspaper and tobacco store at 161 North Queen Street in Lancaster. He issued a series of Amish-theme, tinted post cards in repeated printings. Unfortunately none of them are dated, but one that was actually sent through the mail bears a 1915 postmark. Some twenty-five years later he was selling undated matchboxes bearing a colored picture of two Amishmen under the caption "The Amish of Lancaster County, Pennsylvania" on the front side. The left side of the matchbox bears the words: "Complete, Accurate Literature On The Amish Of Lancaster County, Penna." while the opposite side states: "True To Life Amish Dolls and Complete, Accurate Literature On The Amish Of Pennsylvania." Inside the matchbox are matchbooks with colored Amish pictures on the covers and Steinfeldt's imprint along the top edge.

In 1934, Kay Jewelry Company of Lancaster published *Kay's Pennsylvania Dutch Cook Book of Fine Old Recipes*. While its first edition contained nothing pertaining to the Amish, its 1936 edition has a drawing of an Amish couple with two children on the first page. This picture appeared in advertisements for the cookbook into the 1940s. The cookbook is an early example of what might be termed "Amish appeal"—associating the Amish with an item to produce better sales. After all, the cookbook has no Amish content but features recipes from the general Pennsylvania-German culture. This practice would later become very common in the tourist industry with "Amish" being affixed to anything from candy to dried corn—items that are not Amish any more than Quaker Oats are Quaker.

Tourist Booklets First Appear

The first known magazine article actively promoting the Amish appeared in the November 1935 issue of *Travel* (Fuller 1935). "Domain of Abundance: Exploring a Unique Section of America" contains photos of the Amish and tells of the interesting time the author had touring Lancaster County. He even mentions that he cannot imagine anyone who "would not thrill to the sights of Lancaster County and its neighbors."

As tourists were attracted to "Amish Country," entrepreneurs began publishing booklets. In 1937, Berenice Steinfeldt (the aforementioned Isaac's daughter) brought out her thirty-one page booklet, *The Amish of Lancaster County*, which went through at least twenty printings. A subtitle appearing at the bottom of the page states: "A Brief, But Truthful Account of the Actual Life and Customs of the Most Unique Class of People in the United States." The booklet's cream-colored cover shows two Amishmen standing and talking with each other. This drawing is based on an actual photograph that had appeared two years earlier in Fuller's *Travel* article. But instead of a brick wall behind the conversing men as the photograph has, Miss Steinfeldt substituted a rural scene with a picket fence whose gate is painted blue. The "blue gate myth" (that an Amishman who has a marriageable daughter paints the front gate blue) did not originate with Miss Steinfeldt, but her frequently reprinted booklet perpetuated it (Luthy 1981).

The following year, 1938, another tourist booklet appeared, *Little Known Facts About the Amish and Mennonites*, by A. Monroe Aurand, Jr., a Harrisburg publisher and bookseller. This booklet also mentions the blue gate myth. It was sold in souvenir shops along with Aurand's nearly twenty other thirty-two-page booklets dealing with various phases of Pennsylvania-German life. It went through at least fourteen printings during his lifetime and was still in print in 1989. The booklet was published by Gerald Lestz, who publishes a variety of Aurand's booklets under the imprint of "The Aurand Press, Lancaster, PA."

In 1937 the Lancaster County Amish were hurled for the first time into the national news. Overnight, people across the United States were reading about a group of bearded men and bonneted women who refused to accept a $45,000 grant from the federal government's Public Works Administration (PWA) for the erection of a modern consolidated school. The worst financial depression in American history was just ending, and the public found it impossible to believe that anyone would turn down "free" government money. The Lancaster County Amish, however, wanted to retain one-room rural schools and were not interested in the grant.[2]

The *New York Times* gave the Amish situation repeated coverage during 1937. Popular magazines such as *Time* and *Newsweek* also covered the story. *America*, a leading Catholic magazine, printed an article, "Rebecca of Honeybrook Farm" (Blakely 1937), which was quoted for many years to come. A photograph of two Amishmen with the U.S. Capitol in the background appeared on the front cover of the 10 April 1937 issue of *Pathfinder*, now defunct but then a popular Washington, D.C., weekly political commentary. A caption under the picture states: "They Made It Plain That Amishmen Want No Government Gifts."

This publicity, plus the frequent news coverage that followed the Pennsylvania school controversies during the 1940s and 1950s, helped generate an interest in the Amish and a desire to go and see them.

Children's Books and Other Entertainment

The quantity of Amish-theme fictional accounts published for a juvenile audience in the 1930s and 1940s indicates the great interest the public had in the Amish. Children who read the storybooks wished to visit Lancaster County. Many tourists were first introduced to the Amish through children's books.

The first of the children's books to feature the Lancaster County Amish was *Henner's Lydia* by Marguerite De Angeli. It was published in 1936 and reprinted many times. In 1939 Ella Maie Seyfert's *Little Amish Schoolhouse* seized upon the publicity of the PWA school controversy.

In 1940 the bestseller *Rosanna of the Amish*, by Joseph W. Yoder, appeared. Telling the true story of an Irish Catholic baby raised by an

Amish family in Juniata County, Pennsylvania, in the previous century, it was an instant success. The book has been repeatedly reprinted with 360,000 copies in print in 1994.[3] It is the leading Amish children's book sold to Lancaster County tourists.

More children's books featuring the Lancaster County Amish followed quickly. *Lovina* by Katherine Milhouse appeared in 1940. Ella Maie Seyfert's second Amish storybook, *Amish Moving Day*, was published in 1942, followed by Ann Hark's *The Story of the Pennsylvania Dutch* in 1943. While this latter book treats not just the Amish but the larger Pennsylvania-German culture of southeastern Pennsylvania, the numerous full-page color illustrations are mostly scenes of Amish life.

Marguerite De Angeli's second Amish storybook, *Yonie Wondernose*, appeared in 1944, winning a Caldecott Medal, which assured its placement in most public and elementary school libraries across the United States. In 1989 it was one of four best-loved books by Marguerite De Angeli reissued during the centenary of her birth.

An eleven-year lull in the publishing of children's books featuring the Lancaster County Amish followed. Then in 1955 Virginia Sorensen's *Plain Girl* was published. It was the first to be released in a paperback edition as well as a clothbound. That same year saw the publication of *The Witch Tree Symbol* in the very popular Nancy Drew Mystery Series. Set in Lancaster County, its plot and front cover feature Amish characters. In 1956, Ruth Helm's *Wonderful Good Neighbors* was published with Amish illustrations by Kiehl and Christian Newswanger of Lancaster County, whose volume of primitive-style etchings, *Amishland*, had already been published in 1954. In 1963, Lois Lenski's Amish storybook, *Shoo-Fly Girl*, was published and became quite popular, going through at least seven printings.

About 1940 a short motion picture was released with the Lancaster County Amish as its subject. It was described in an article that most likely appeared in the *Lancaster Intelligencer Journal*:

AMISH PICTURES NOW

SHOWING AT GRAND

Short Motion Picture In Technicolor

Was Filmed In The Vicinity

Of Paradise

> A short motion picture featuring the Amish of Lancaster County is being shown in theaters throughout the nation. The picture is in technicolor and was taken here early last summer.
>
> Members of the Amish are shown in the fields, at a country sale, at their meeting houses, and in the market. Most of the pictures were taken in the vicinity of Paradise and along the New Holland pike.
>
> Although very brief, running less than five minutes, the picture is probably the first commercial film ever made to show Lancaster County in its natural summer colors. The film is being shown at the Grand theater here.

Vincent R. Tortora, author of the thirty-page tourist booklet *The Amish Folk of Pennsylvania Dutch Country* (1958), also produced a thirty-two minute, 16mm color-sound motion picture entitled "The Old Order Amish," advertised in 1959. An undated brochure from Tortora's "Photo Arts Press, Lancaster, Penna." in the 1960s also offered "Amish Life Color Slides," "Amish Life View-Masters," and an "Amish Life Filmstrip" for sale or rent.

The first Hollywood-produced movie to contain Amish characters in its plot was *Violent Saturday*, released in May 1955 by Twentieth Century Fox and shown in movie theaters across the United States. Ernest Borgnine portrayed an Amish farmer in whose barn some bank robbers took cover.

Some films have been made strictly for the tourist trade. For example, "The Lancaster Experience," a thirty-seven minute color film, was produced exclusively for the Pennsylvania Dutch Convention and Visitors Bureau of Lancaster County.[4] It was shown to tourists at the bureau's official Visitors Center. A newspaper article describing the film states: "The film can only be shown at the Center, since 4-track sound and special effects are tailored specifically for one location."[5] In 1989 the movie was replaced at the Visitors Center by a multi-image slide presentation, "There Is A Season."

The film *Witness*, starring Harrison Ford and produced by Paramount Pictures, was filmed in Lancaster County. Released in February 1985 and immediately popular, it grossed more than $100 million and drew worldwide attention to the Amish. Soon the cover of a brochure published by the Pennsylvania Dutch Convention and Visitors Bureau invited tourists to come to Lancaster County "as seen in the critically acclaimed movie, *Witness*." The tremendous impact of this movie on tourism in Lancaster County is difficult to fully measure.

Tours and More Books

During the early 1940s the Pennsylvania Turnpike was opened. With an exit near Lancaster, it presented easy access for travelers to visit the Amish section of the county. The prosperity that World War II had brought permitted more Americans to own automobiles and travel more extensively. A large advertisement sponsored by the Pennsylvania Department of Commerce invited tourists to visit the state for a "post-war vacation." The official advertisement bore the caption "Pennsylvania's Plain People" and showed an Amish horse and buggy above the text.

At first tourists merely drove their own cars through the Amish area. Soon, however, interest in Lancaster County Amish reached a point where guided tours began. In 1946 the Hotel Brunswick, located in the city of Lancaster, offered tours of the Amish area and other points of interest in the county. A chartered bus was used with a guide sitting up front talking over a microphone. For $9.75, a person could travel "100 Miles" and see "100 Sights," including a "feast at an Amish farm."

Originally this Amish tour was available only on Saturdays. Quite likely most Amish were not even aware that it passed by their farms. However, in 1950 when Parker Tours of New York City became affiliated with the Hotel Brunswick, its busses were more numerous and more obvious. Then came Caesar Tours, Bingler Tours, and you-name-it tours. In 1954 the Pennsylvania Dutch Folklore Center of Franklin and Marshall College in Lancaster began issuing an attractive annual seventy-two page *Tourist Guide Through the Dutch Country*. More busses and tourists' cars appeared on the county's back roads. And more, and more, and more.

In 1947 the first pictorial account of the Lancaster County Amish, *Meet the Amish*, was published by Rutgers University Press. It was a hardbound volume with the text by John B. Shenk and photographs by Charles S. Rice, both residents of Lancaster County. Inviting the public to come and look at the Amish, the first sentence on the flyleaf of the book's paper jacket states: "Within one day's driving distance of the great northeastern cities and of one-third of the hurrying, worrying population of the United States lies another world, the tiny wedge of land in Lancaster County, Pennsylvania, that belongs to the God-fearing, agrarian Amish."

As the tourists increased, so did the number of booklets and books about the Amish. From 1950 to 1955 the Pennsylvania Dutch Folklore Center of Franklin and Marshall College published a number of booklets for tourists. Among them were *3 Myths About the Pennsylvania Dutch County* (1951), *My Off Is All* (1953a), *Hex, No!* (1953b), and *A Peek At The Amish* (1954), all written by Alfred L. Shoemaker, cofounder of the Folklore Center.

In 1952 *Amish Life*, the most accurate and comprehensive of the tourist booklets, was published by Herald Press of Scottdale, Pennsylvania. Written by John A. Hostetler, later a professor at Temple University, it went through more than thirty printings before being totally revised in 1981. Demand was so great for the original edition that it was reissued in 1982 as *The Amish*. By 1988 more than 727,000 copies were in print.

The year 1952 also saw the publication of Ann Hark's *Blue Hills and Shoofly Pie*, a 284-page volume containing more Amish content than her *Hex Marks the Spot*, published in 1938. In 1953 the Lancaster newspaper, *The Intelligencer Journal*, ran a series of articles by Joseph T. Kingston, a staff writer, and reprinted them that year in a booklet entitled *The Amish Story*. The year 1955 saw the publication of *Such Friendly People* by Joseph S. Hildreth with photographs of the Amish by Charles S. Rice.

Restaurants, Greeting Cards, and other "Dutch Stuff"

Tourists who visited Lancaster County needed to eat. It was only natural that restaurants featuring Pennsylvania Dutch cooking would develop. As early as 1931 Miller's Dutch Restaurant at Ronks had opened its doors. By the early 1950s it could seat 175 people and was using photos of Amish to advertise its "daily specials prepared from famous Penna. Dutch recipes."

A 1940 menu from "The Village," a Lancaster restaurant, contains charcoal sketches of Amish scenes and the statement: "It is due a great deal to the Amish people that Lancaster County is today known as The Garden Spot of the World." This was, perhaps, the same restaurant referred to by A. Monroe Aurand, Jr. (1942:15), in his 1942 booklet *Where to Dine In The Penna. "Dutch" Region*, with these words, "Howard Johnson's 'The Amish Village' just about 3½ miles east of Lancaster. You cannot miss the place. Built in 1941, it is already well-known. . . ."

In 1947, Roy M. Weaver opened Dutch Haven, a luncheonette east of Lancaster on U.S. 30 at Soudersburg. An early photo indicates it sold "Root Beer, Candy, and Sandwiches." Later the building was completely rebuilt and became a full-fledged restaurant famous for its shoofly pie served warm and topped with whipped cream or ice cream. By 1984 more than 2,000 pies from its bakery were being shipped each year by United Parcel Service to people across the United States, generally as gifts from customers. In neighboring York County, some 20,000 shoofly pies were sold each year by high school students going from door to door.[6] Dutch Haven developed into a complex of nine buildings including a gift shop and a model railroad museum.

In 1949 the Hotel Brunswick in Lancaster was advertising Pennsylvania Dutch cooking in all five of its restaurants and using "Yonnie," the caricature of an Amish boy, on advertising brochures and menus. Zinn's Diner opened near the Reading-Lancaster exit on the Pennsylvania Turnpike in 1950. Specializing in Pennsylvania Dutch cooking, the diner used a large caricature of an Amishman on its front sign, which in 1960 was replaced by a much larger-than-life statue of "Amos," an Amishman holding a pitchfork. Immediately popular with the public, the diner was still popular in 1990, with "Amos" towering over customers milling about outside waiting for a vacant table.

The Willows Restaurant five miles east of Lancaster on U.S. 30 was doing a brisk business in the 1950s, especially after the "Amish Farm and House" was opened in 1955 adjacent to it. There tourists could view what formerly had been an Amish farm. Built of stone in 1805, the handsome house soon became a regular stop for tour busses. Not only could tourists get a glimpse of the interior of an Amish house, they could pump a drink of water at the well, undoubtedly a novel experience for urbanites. The farm remained a working farm with animals in the barn for tourists to view. The "Amish Farm and House" was the first staged Amish attraction in the county.

The year 1955 also marked the tenth anniversary of Yorkcraft, Inc., the largest commercial venture using the Amish theme on paper products. It began in 1945 as a family project in the Howard Imhoff home in York, Pennsylvania, but soon occupied a two-story factory. Imhoff, who was a talented artist, drew Amish scenes that were reproduced on greeting cards, note paper, recipe cards, post cards, napkins, coasters, and various other items. His art was so well liked that in 1955 alone the factory used fifty tons of paper (Zehner 1955:7–9).

As early as 1941 Amish figurines were being manufactured. In the June issue that year of *House and Garden*, figurines were shown and described as "An Amish family in miniature for your mantel or hanging shelf. Farmer, wife, and children are iron, painted in natural colors, 5" high. They are from Keith's in Kansas City." In 1949 salt and pepper shakers in the form of an Amishman and Amishwoman were advertised by G. B. Fenstermacher, Route 5, Lancaster, in the November issue of *The Pennsylvania Dutchman*. Other "Amish stuff" followed swiftly. By 1980 the largest distributors were Conestoga Crafts (L. E. Smith, Inc.) of Gettysburg and Garden Spot Gifts, Inc., of Lancaster. Their catalogs included anything from Amish pennants to egg timers.

Plain and Fancy, a musical comedy, opened on 27 January 1955 at the Mark Hellinger Theater in New York City. The play depicted the Amish near Bird-in-Hand in Lancaster County. While it was an inaccurate portrayal of Amish society, it was colorful and well-staged. It attracted thousands of playgoers and was widely reviewed. Even the national weekly Amish newspaper, *The Budget*—published at Sugarcreek, Ohio, and subscribed to by nearly every Amish home—gave the play front-page coverage, stating: "The Amish are rapidly becoming one of the most widely known sects in the nation, principally because of a new musical comedy, *Plain and Fancy*, which has become one of the big theatrical hits of the day."[7]

Many years after *Plain and Fancy*'s successful run on Broadway, some people have credited it with having created Amish tourism in Lancaster County. While the play certainly contributed to the growth of tourism, the tourist industry was already deeply rooted in Lancaster County when the play hit Broadway. *Plain and Fancy* was not "the goose that laid the golden eggs of tourism" as a *U.S. News and World Report* article stated in 1979. The eggs had already been laid by 1955, but *Plain and Fancy* helped to hatch them. Since then Lancaster County has grown into one of the top ten tourist attractions in the United States.

Holmes County, Ohio

The largest Old Order Amish settlement in the world is situated among the rolling hills of Ohio's northeast quarter. Centered in Holmes County, it has spread into the adjoining counties of Wayne and Tuscarawas. Amish pioneers began settling there in 1808, just five years after Ohio had entered the Union. By 1992 the settlement had grown to include 143 congregations compared to 103 in Lancaster, the second largest settlement.

Tourism is a fairly recent phenomenon in Holmes County. In the April 1968 issue of *Travel*, writer Bill Thomas focused on "Ohio's Amish County" and stated that tourism was nonexistent there:

> The northeastern section of Ohio boasts the largest Amish population of any state in the U.S. The country of the Plain people of Ohio re-

> mains one of America's most offbeat travel attractions, mainly because it has been unheralded and unpublicized. . . . There are no organized tours such as in the Amish lands around Lancaster, Pa., although you may wander on your own and find plenty of unforgettable sights and experiences.

Thomas, however, was not correct in his observation. Tourism, although not readily apparent to the casual observer, had begun in Holmes County before 1968. Eleven years earlier in the 23 June 1957 issue of Cleveland's daily newspaper, *The Plain Dealer*, staff writer Grace Goulder in her column "Ohio Scenes and Citizens" featured a drive-it-yourself Amish tour of Holmes County as "Goulder Tour No. 3." She described her own travels through the area, suggesting routes for tourists to follow and places to stop. She remarked, "This is delightful hinterland anywhere you go. Life is placid, paced to horse-and-buggy speed. Even if you get lost, you will enjoy yourself." A road map accompanied the article showing Dundee, Barrs Mills, Sugarcreek, Farmerstown, Charm, Berlin, Walnut Creek, and Trail—small towns that form the heart of the Amish settlement.

Three years later in 1960 organized tours were being brought to Holmes County with a noon meal served at the home of an Amish mother and daughter, Elva and Betty Miller of rural Millersburg, a service discontinued in 1978. In 1973 they published *Mrs. Miller's Amish Cookbook*, which sheds some light on their venture in its foreword:

> We started serving dinners in our home nearly 14 years ago (1960) to groups of tourists brought to us by a tour agency. We first served in our living room which seated 40 people, but as the groups got larger, we added a dining room which seated 50. Seven years later (1967) we added another dining room and can now seat 120 at one time. We serve an average of 1,300 people each month. Dinners are by reservation only.

According to a 1961 brochure entitled "Meet Your Amish Neighbors," Alma Kaufman (a reporter for *The Daily Record* in Wooster, Ohio), was arranging six-hour bus tours through Holmes County for Flair Travel Consultants of Wooster. In 1971, Betty Goodman of Cleveland began organizing tours to Holmes County. Having gotten to know some Amish personally, she received permission for each tour group of some forty people to stop briefly at a one-room Amish school. Her groups generally consisted of school children from grades 2 to 12. However, she also developed some adult tours on which tourists purchased "a lot of crafts, baked goods, vegetables, etc. from the

Amish."[8] She attempted to dispel misconceptions about the Amish by portraying them accurately and sympathetically. Her brochure entitled "There's No Place Like Holmes" (n.d.) contains the classic statement concerning the Amish: "Their lives may be simple, but the people are not."

By 1974 the American Automobile Association included a self-conducted tour "of interesting Amish regions of the state" in its annual Ohio booklet. Ohio newspapers frequently reprinted the tour's map and text as an assistance to the state's promotion of tourism.

In 1975 photographer Fred J. Wilson of Massillon in neighboring Stark County published a brochure, "Welcome to Ohio's Amishland," with the subheading: "A Map To Guide You On Main Roads Through The Amish Area." Wilson had been taking candid photos of the Amish since the 1950s to illustrate his wife's lectures on "Amish Customs and Religion."[9] Wilson's Amish photographs grace the cover and interior pages of *Wonderful Good Cooking*, a cookbook that was first printed in 1974 and has been repeatedly reprinted. In 1976 his photographs appeared in the forty-page, large format *A Visitor's Guide To Ohio's Amish Country*. And in 1982 his six different "Amish Country Note Cards" were selling for $5.95 postpaid per set.

By 1975 tourists were traveling to hilly Holmes County in such numbers that Elaine Sommers Rich in her column "Thinking With" in the 25 March issue of the *Mennonite Weekly Review* quoted a friend's letter, which stated: "You should see Holmes County these years—such tourists! Charter busloads as high as eight in one day during the summer. We local folk hardly find room to park in town when we need a loaf of bread." That same year saw "Amish Hayride Tours" advertised as available daily from 11 A.M. to 8 P.M. at the junction of U.S. 62 and State Route 39 in the village of Berlin ("Amish Hayride" 1975:11).

By 1976 the Ohio Department of Transportation was including a detailed description in its promotional literature of "Ohio's Amish Country," focusing on touring Holmes County. In 1979 the Ohio Department of Economic and Community Development published a separate brochure, "Ohio's Amish Country," in its "Travel Ohio" series. And in 1987 *Farm & Ranch Living*, a magazine with a large national readership, began including an annual "Amish Community Tour" of Holmes County in its offering of "World Wide Country Tours."

The hub of tourism in Holmes County is the village of Berlin (pronounced with the accent on the first syllable), which had a population of only four hundred in the 1980 census. The village has but one main road passing through it, a two-lane merger of U.S. 62 and State Route

39, which during the height of the tourist season has traffic moving more slowly than people strolling on the sidewalks.

One mile east of Berlin is a major attraction that began in 1976 as "The Amish Farm" but ten years later was expanded and renamed "Amish Heritage Village." Situated on forty-three acres, it consists of nearly twenty buildings. Besides touring what once was an Amish farmstead, visitors can browse in various shops or take a fifteen-minute horse and buggy ride through the surrounding fields. The "Der Dutch Peddlar" arts and crafts festival, which began in 1987, is held on this property twice a year: three days in July and two days in October. The 1989 festival attracted more than 125 artisans and craftspeople, some of them Amish. It is sponsored by the publishers of *Down Home Country*, the cover of which declares that it is "Ohio's Complete Amish Country Tour Guide." Published sporadically between 1983 and 1991, it contained advertisements for restaurants, cheese houses, gift shops, and tourist attractions. Its center foldout map shows many winding township roads throughout the eastern section of Holmes County. Also included are pages listing "Home Based Cottage Industries" many of which have Amish owners.

Another major attraction near Berlin is the Mennonite Information Center, founded in 1981. Besides providing tourists with basic information and a twenty-minute slide presentation, "The Amish and Mennonite Story," it offers them the opportunity of viewing a unique 10′ × 265′ mural whose scenes trace the Amish and Mennonites back to their Anabaptist martyr forebears in sixteenth-century Europe.

In 1989 it was estimated that one million tourists were visiting Holmes County each year and spending $45 million.[10] The April issue of *Ohio Magazine* in 1988 included the Amish as one of the "Seven Wonders of Ohio" and referred to them as "Ohio's biggest 'non-commercial' tourist attraction."

There is very little about tourism in Holmes County that could be validly called noncommercial. This was superbly pointed out by Joe Ionne in "The Selling of the Amish," which appeared as the cover story in the 10 June 1979 issue of *The Columbus Dispatch Sunday Magazine*. He states that: "Commercialism and accompanying sightseeing has stuck in its ugly head, invading the privacy of these tillers of the soil."[11] His opinions on tourism were echoed ten years later by Paul Locher, associate news editor of Wooster's *The Daily Record*:

> For more than a decade now I've watched as tour buses—at first just a trickle of them, and now a virtual torrent—have come rolling into southern Wayne and eastern Holmes counties, their passengers anx-

> ious to explore the countryside and see the "plain people" who live and work on the picturesque farmsteads. . . .
>
> Tiny hamlets like Berlin, which once reposed lazily on summer afternoons, recalling the charm, atmosphere, and pace of bygone days, have been overrun with throngs of tourists. . . .
>
> "You're all exploiting the Amish and the area's cultural heritage," say I.
>
> OOPS! Did I say the forbidden phrase, exploit the Amish? I did, didn't I. And why not. Let's call a spade a spade here. . . .
>
> If you want to see the future of Holmes County as it is presently heading, you don't need a crystal ball. Just head east about 400 miles on U.S. 30 to Lancaster, Pa., and you'll see clearly what could well happen here.[12]

Tourism in Holmes County, which definitely has been influenced by tourism in Lancaster County, will undoubtedly continue to grow. Perhaps, though, because the area's very hilly terrain produces traffic congestion, it may never reach the proportions of tourism in Lancaster County. Only time will tell.

Lagrange County, Indiana

The third largest Old Order settlement is situated in northern Indiana. Amish farmers from Somerset County, Pennsylvania, began settling there in 1841, some locating in Newbury Township, Lagrange County, and others in neighboring Clinton Township, Elkhart County. By 1992 the settlement had grown to contain seventy-eight congregations or "church districts," of which three-fourths are in Lagrange County. A few straddle the county line with households in both counties (Miller 1988:48).

The promotion of Amish tourism in Lagrange and Elkhart Counties began about a decade later than in Holmes County, Ohio. The earliest discovered printed item relating to tourism in those counties is a four-page brochure, "Amish," published in 1966 by the Chamber of Commerce of Goshen, the county seat of Elkhart County. It contains a brief history of the Amish and recommends further reading in four authoritative books. Apparently enough tourists by that date were asking about the area's Amish residents to warrant the publication of a special brochure. A year later in the June 1967 issue of *Travel*, an article entitled "Overlooked Indiana" (Steinmeier 1967:30) told tourists the location of the Amish settlement and cautioned them to "drive slowly on the roads, especially at dusk, for it's often then you'll meet people as they travel along in their black buggies."

The area's first major Amish-theme restaurant, "Das Dutchman Essenhaus," was constructed in 1970 northeast of Goshen and a little southwest of Middlebury at the corner of C.R. 16 and U.S. 20 in Elkhart County. Built in the style of a large Amish barn, it opened for business on 1 January 1971. Three major additions made to it by 1985 developed it into much more than a restaurant. The complex contained a furniture store, a retail bakery, a gallery of country art, and assorted gift shops.

The adjoining farm was purchased and its old chicken barn renovated into a two-story gift shop, "Dutch Country Gifts." South of it another building, "Country Cupboard," has been built where the restaurant's salad dressings, other specialty foods, and gifts are sold. Nearly all the shops on the property sell Amish quilts. In 1985 construction began on the thirty-two-unit "Essenhaus Country Inn." A local historical volume, *Middlebury The Town Beautiful 1836–1986* (1986), states, "This restaurant is one of the best known in northern Indiana and neighboring states, and has become a major tourist attraction . . . serving 5,000 to 6,000 meals on a busy summer day."

While Amish tourism was starting at Middlebury in Elkhart County, it also was beginning at Shipshewana in Lagrange County. With a population of less than five hundred, Shipshewana has become the center of the two-county tourism just as the village of Berlin is in Holmes County and Intercourse in Lancaster County.

The development of tourism in Shipshewana is closely intertwined with the growth of the Shipshewana Auction and Flea Market. In 1922 a livestock auction was begun at Shipshewana, and by 1947 it was common to see "five or six people selling baked goods or old tools" in the parking lot on sale days (*Shipshewana* 1984:9). Each Wednesday there was a livestock auction plus a consignment auction of miscellaneous items. Gradually more vendors set up stands beside the auction barn, and more customers came. The flea market grew remarkably during 1972–1977, mainly by word-of-mouth advertising. By 1977 some two hundred vendors were setting up stands attracting 10,000 to 15,000 shoppers on a single day.[13] In 1977 the management allowed the vendors for the first time to set up stands on Tuesday morning, thus turning the flea market into a two-day affair. By 1986 there were 1,050 booths, 14 acres of free parking, and as many as 30,000 shoppers/tourists a day. The relationship between the flea market and tourism has been succinctly expressed by one observer, "The Shipshewana Auction and Flea Market first drew the crowds, but the Amish keep the tourists coming back" (Kurowski 1990:66).

In 1977 *Welcome to Shipshewana* (1977) was published for the first time. It is an annual, free, tabloid-format newspaper for tourists. Besides containing a large detailed map of places to visit and numerous advertisements, it has brief descriptions of "Where To Shop," "Places To Eat," etc. Also in 1977, the American Automobile Association published an article, "Indiana's Amish Country," in the July issue of its *Michigan Living Motor News* (August 1977).

In 1979 a number of local businessmen financed the construction of a new cheese factory named "Deutsch Kase Haus" three miles west of Shipshewana along the Middlebury-Shipshewana Road. Besides providing a much needed market for Amish farmers' Grade B milk, it has become a popular stopping place for tourists. The retail store has Amish employees and two large windows where customers can watch the Amish cheesemakers at work in the adjoining room.

A thirty-two-page magazine, *Amish Country*, began publication at Middlebury in 1980, focusing on tourism in both Elkhart and Lagrange Counties. The following year it was increased to thirty-six pages. In 1982 it was renamed *Amish Heritage* and published in two thirty-six-page issues. In 1983 the title changed to *Heritage Country* with a subtitle "Guide To Indiana Amish Country." Two forty-eight-page issues were published that year. In 1990 it had reached two ninety-two-page issues. In 1993 it was renamed *Country Ways Guide & Journal*. It now covers tourism in Ohio and Illinois as well as in Indiana. Besides containing many advertisements, it has feature articles and regular columnists. Printed on quality coated paper and with beautiful colored photography, it is a very attractive magazine.

A visitors center called "Menno-Hof" was opened in May 1988 on land across the road from the Shipshewana Auction and Flea Market. Built in the style of an Amish farmstead, it consists of a large, white frame house with an attached red barn. The center is nonprofit, operated by the Mennonites and Amish-Mennonites of northern Indiana. It offers tourists a highly educational tour of Amish and Mennonite faith, history, and life via a slide presentation and a self-guided tour of exhibits with audio and visual messages placed throughout the various rooms. No admission fee is charged, but donations are suggested and accepted. Seven months after it opened to the public, the center had already hosted more than 32,000 visitors from all 50 U.S. states and 54 countries ("Menno-Hof" 1989).

While the promoters of tourism are enjoying the influx of visitors to

Shipshewana, many of the village's residents and their Amish neighbors are not. Writing in the 1 February 1989 issue of *The Budget* (a weekly newspaper containing reports from most Amish communities), O. Vernon Miller, an Amish correspondent from Shipshewana, commented:

> A big basement is being dug for another new building to promote and accommodate tourism. Many residents are getting quite perturbed at the continuous rush to develop more projects to lure tourists and yearn for the good old days when the town was nice and quiet. . . . During the summer, town officials have problems with traffic and parking, and the sewer system is so overloaded that they just have to open the gates and let her run. Likewise in summer the town is so overrun with tourists, it seems like a herd of animals trampling all over, disrespectful of people's properties. Others call this progress![14]

But there is no stopping the growth of tourism in Shipshewana. Writing in the 11 April 1990 issue of the same newspaper, O. Vernon Miller reported that another house had been purchased by "a merchant of the tourist trade" and would succumb to the work of a wrecking crew with the land paved for a parking lot for tourists. Miller stated that it was "the 24th house in town to be converted for the use of the tourist trade, mostly craft shops, bed and breakfast homes, etc."[15] The Amish in northern Indiana have not yet seen tourism reach its zenith.

While this study has focused on the tourist industry in the three largest Amish settlements, tourism exists in many other communities as well. One of the most highly promoted tourist attractions is "Amish Acres" at Nappanee, Indiana, where the Amish have lived since 1839. Another is "Amishville" at Berne, Indiana, where the Amish first settled in 1850. Then there is "Rockome" at Arthur, Illinois, where the Amish migrated in 1864. A smaller settlement that attracts many tourists is the Kalona, Iowa, community where the Amish located in 1846. It is safe to say that any sizeable Amish settlement within several hours driving time of large cities is being affected by tourism.

Part III

Occupational Changes

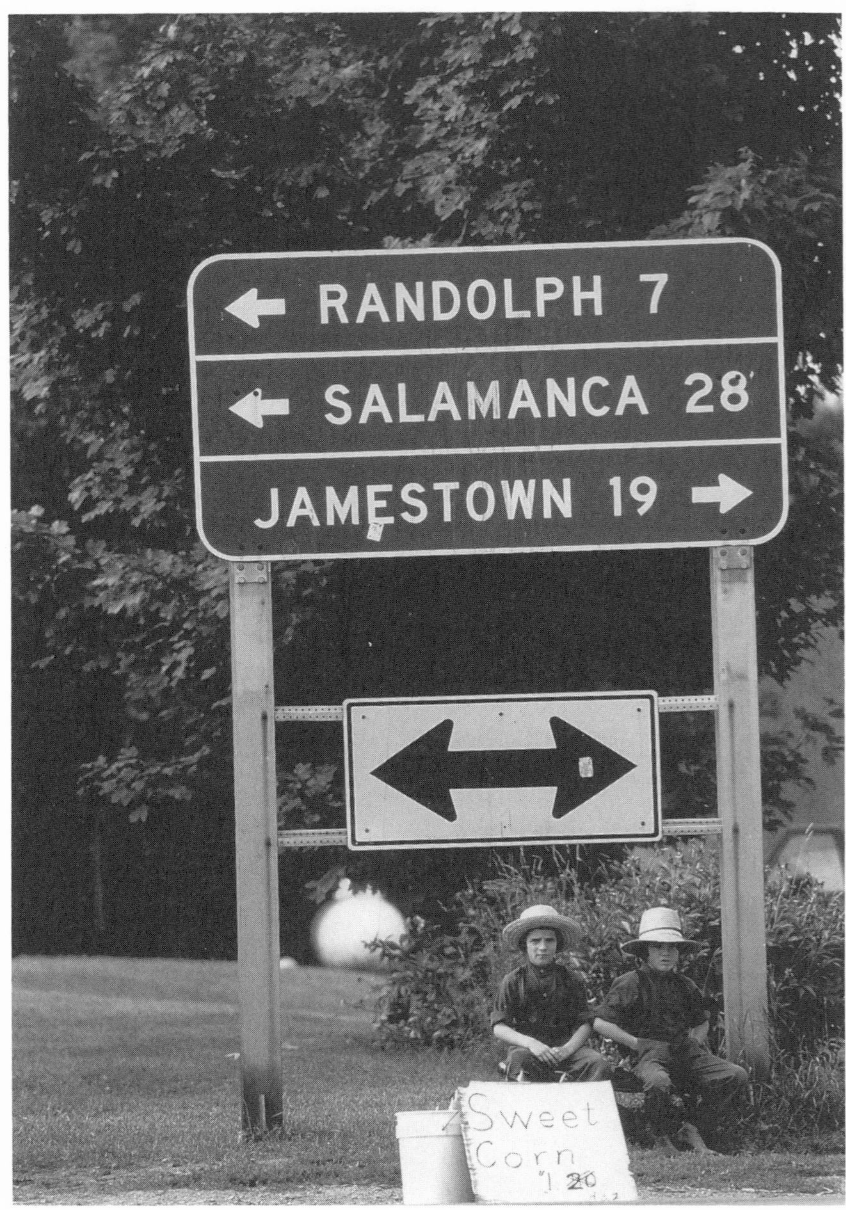

Two Amish children sell sweet corn at a roadside stand in Conewango, New York. Innocent roadside stands may be a first step in the "opening" of Amish society to the larger world. (Photograph by Doyle Yoder).

8

Amish Cottage Industries as Trojan Horse

MARC A. OLSHAN

Traditional Amish culture has been shaped by its longtime association with farming. Rural isolation helped to perpetuate the seclusion and separation of Amish life. In recent years, however, many Amish persons have developed small businesses and cottage industries on their farms and in other cases have given up farming entirely. In this chapter, based on field observations in New York State, Marc A. Olshan argues that the proliferation of cottage industries symbolizes a rather dramatic "opening" of Amish society to the larger world—an opening that will surely bring substantial consequences in their struggle with modernity.[1]

The Economic Context

The image of the Old Order Amish as a people apart is a well-established icon of American culture.[2] Literary examples of the aloof, solemn Amishman are common (Bourjaily 1980). The stereotype is familiar enough to be parodied in popular magazines (McConnachie and Heath 1976). Journalists confidently refer to the Amish ability to maintain their distance from the outside world ("Christdag" 1985). In those few cases where they engage in self-description, the Amish also choose to emphasize "separation from the world" as central to their identity.[3]

Social scientists have, for the most part, been far more circumspect in their characterizations. Recent analyses of Amish society have made clear the importance of separation as a normative stance while fully acknowledging the extent of Amish entanglement with the larger society.[4] Inevitably the ideal of separation has been tempered by economic exigencies.

The need to generate cash, driven primarily by the rising cost of land, has forced a steadily rising proportion of Amishmen to turn to nonagricultural occupations. The trend is well documented across a variety of major Amish settlements. For example, rising land prices and large family size explain why only slightly over one-third of Amish in one large Indiana settlement are full-time farmers, while almost half work in trailer factories (Rechlin in Lewis 1976a:5).

Likewise, "a trend away from farming" in the Lancaster County, Pennsylvania, settlement is attributed to the high cost of land (Ericksen et al. 1980:59). In the Arthur, Illinois, settlement, expensive land and credit have meant that "Amish young people are almost shut off from buying new land for the purpose of farming" (Miller 1978:13). In Holmes County, Ohio, center of the most populous Amish settlement, less than half of the heads of households reported themselves as full-time farmers in 1981 (Troyer and Willoughby 1984:61). In Geauga County, site of another large Ohio settlement, less than one-third farm (Foster 1984a).

Even when the agricultural base has been maintained, there is increasing pressure to abandon traditional diversified farming for specialization in cash crops (Stoltzfus 1973). This in turn "has meant greater market involvement and led to a sensitivity and vulnerability to national trends of supply and demand that was uncommon in the past" (Martineau and MacQueen 1977:384). As early as 1942, one observer noted that "the Amish farmer's production and consumption are closely tied up with the market economy. . . . Self-sufficiency is in retreat" (Kollmorgan 1942:47).

The increased need for cash is also explained by an unrelenting growth in two other areas: taxes and medical care. Although the Amish generally send their children to private schools, they pay taxes to support the local public school system as well. Nor are they exempt from other varieties of taxation, including state and federal income tax. The Amish have also been affected by the rising cost of medical care. The use of modern medical technology is not proscribed. In the absence of commercial health insurance, a single large bill may threaten a family's solvency.

Medical expenses create a degree of community vulnerability as well. The Amish are not a communal group in the sense of collective ownership of property, but they are in some limited respects financially tied together. A moral obligation to help one's neighbor serves as an informal vehicle for spreading the burden of medical expenses. In some settlements a more institutionalized response has been implemented. Programs variously known as Amish Church Aid, Hospital Aid, and Health Aid are the functional equivalents of hospitalization insurance. After paying an initial fee, members are typically assessed for additional payments as the need arises for funds to pay submitted hospital bills. Examples include the Hospitalization Plan for Lagrange and Adams Counties (Indiana), the Amish Health Aid Plan for Geauga County (Ohio), and the Church Fund of Holmes County (Ohio). While such programs mitigate the impact of a large hospital bill for a specific family, they also mean that all other member families must be prepared to make intermittent cash payments.

The need for cash to purchase property, pay taxes and medical bills, and buy myriad items not made within the Amish community, such as kerosene, glass, roofing material, etc., has pushed a growing number of Amish to "work away" or "work out." Jobs outside the Amish community that once would have meant excommunication are now routinely accepted. But the negative consequences of working with or for non-Amish remain. The potential subversion of values through exposure to worldly culture, the equation of time with money and the consequent threat to participation in community events, the provision of fringe benefits by employers, and the father's absence from the home all undermine Amish culture (Kraybill 1989:193–94).

Given the incompatibility of "working away" with the values of separation, self-sufficiency, and family, it is not surprising that many Amish have turned to the alternative of cottage industry. Running a business from one's own home would seem to eliminate the subversive consequences of wage labor noted above. Leaders in one Canadian settlement described their decision to open a mail order business, based in part on locally made products:

> We felt we could provide a service to those outside our way of life by making available some of the self-help tools we use every day. As well, the high price of farmland is forcing our community to develop cottage industries producing hand-made furniture, harnesses, etc. . . . Our community puts great emphasis on home-centered, family-oriented occupations. We do not feel it is good for a family to have the father, let alone the mother, working away from home, leaving children unattended and untrained. (Stoll and Stoll 1980:13)

Another Amishman argued that cottage industry grew naturally from Anabaptist roots. In the preface to the *Old Order Shop and Service*

Directory, a compilation of hundreds of traditional and nontraditional Amish-run businesses, he writes: "This diversified trade stems from a Swiss-German pattern of farming. . . ." And later: "Moreover our forefathers were denied the right to hold land in prime farming valleys and were driven back to remote areas in the mountains, causing them to resort to side line trades. . . . The evidence is clear that these despised groups soon became skilled tradesmen as well as practical farmers. . . ." (Beiler 1977).

Nonetheless, the compatibility of cottage industry with Amish values is not self-evident. As a means to an end, namely economic survival, cottage industry has been welcomed by many Amish. But a greater reliance on cottage industry also requires redefining normative behavior, especially in regard to relations with non-Amish. In particular, that complex of norms that make up the role of "seller" may be associated with values that are inconsistent with traditional Amish values. The utility of cottage industry as a vehicle for perpetuating Amish culture is problematic. An examination of its impact may offer some insight into how changes at the macroeconomic level may translate into altered definitions of what is appropriate behavior, and finally into a corresponding shift in values.

The New York Settlements

Most studies of the Amish have concentrated on a handful of the largest settlements, chief among them Lancaster County, Pennsylvania. But Lancaster is in many respects atypical of the over nine hundred church districts scattered from Montana to North Carolina, and from Texas to upstate New York.[5] Lancaster's urban character, its highly developed tourist industry, and the fact that its Old Order Amish population are all members of the same church affiliation, make the Amish there unique.

Given the frequent schisms that have marked Old Order history, it would be imprudent to identify any Amish group as "typical." But New York's fifteen Amish settlements are arguably as representative a cross-section of Amish society as might be imagined. Its settlers come from over two dozen Amish communities (including Lancaster) in ten states and Ontario. They cover almost the entire gamut of Old Order ideological positions—from the more progressive who use diesel powered milking machines to the ultraconservative Swartzentruber faction. With thirty church districts, New York ranks seventh in size of the twenty-two states and one Canadian province with an Amish population.[6]

The findings presented here are based on visits to all of the New York settlements, which included interviews with Amish leaders (in almost all cases bishops or ministers). Quotations not otherwise credited derive from those interviews. Another important source of information is *Die Botschaft*, an Amish-edited weekly newspaper. It is composed for the most part of letters from community "scribes," individuals who volunteer to pass on the news from their area, making it available to all subscribers. Publicly recorded tax maps, deeds, and indentures were also examined for many of the newer settlements.

The general pattern of economic pressures depicted in the previously noted studies exists in New York as well. Agriculture alone cannot sustain most Amish families. In New York the trend toward occupational diversity has been accelerated by problems with dairying, a sector that had been the cornerstone of Amish farm income.[7] State laws regulating the marketing of milk have been tightened since the first few settlements were established. The maximum allowable bacteria count has been lowered as has the maximum allowable temperature below which milk must be cooled. Amish across the state uniformly expressed the belief that dairying had become a more uncertain proposition.

One Amishman who was still shipping milk commented: "The rules have gotten stricter. It used to be 200,000 bacteria count. Now it's 100,000. That's just about impossible. Anything goes wrong and you're in trouble." The wife of a man who no longer farms, and who now operates a woodworking shop, explained: "We couldn't cope with the milk inspectors. We'd get one thing right and they'd want something else."[8]

The changes in regulations have had a direct impact on dairy farmers, especially those who want to participate in the Grade A market (i.e., for liquid milk, as opposed to manufacturing grade milk used for making cheese). To receive the higher price for Grade A milk means either installing a diesel powered bulk cooling tank or finding a non-Amish partner who will set up a tank to be used as a milk dumping station. Amish dairymen in the area then bring their milk, in cans, to this location, where it is picked up by a tank truck. Various settlements have opted for both arrangements, but in many cases farmers simply have left dairying for other occupations. Sometimes they went into another type of specialized agriculture such as raising heifers to be sold to large, commercial dairy operations or raising calves for veal.

Old Order settlements are scattered over ten New York counties, in all but the southeast quadrant of the state. In every settlement cottage industries constitute a significant component of economic activity. The previous generation's concerns with finding a farm have given way to the much more open-ended question of finding a way to make a living. The economic squeeze out of agriculture is reflected in one bishop's comment that "Most of our people can't afford a farm." In another settlement, where only two families out of eleven were shipping milk, an Amishman reported that most men were working at carpentry and "They have more work than they can handle."

Another measurable indicator of economic pressure is the extent to which real estate is financed. Of the properties purchased in four New York settlements established in the mid-1970s, a little over one-third were mortgaged. About two-fifths of the mortgaged properties were financed through the previous owner; the remaining properties were financed through commercial sources. For three settlements founded since 1983, over half of the properties purchased were financed, with the ratio between private and commercial sources remaining almost exactly what it was for the older settlements. Many families are renting property and, as in the past under unfavorable economic conditions, some are sharing houses with relatives.

Given this financial reality, wage labor and cottage industry have become increasingly attractive options for many Amish. The expanded range of possibilities from which Amishmen can now choose is suggested by one *Die Botschaft* scribe recently arrived in New York: "Seems like the craft business is more interesting to the young fellows. Here I have to figure out what I could make that would sell."

A minister in another settlement, describing the situation there, observed: "Farming should be self-sufficient. It used to be but it isn't anymore. Seems a man has to have a sideline to make it." Some of those who more enthusiastically embrace the small business strategy have created multiple "sidelines." A case in point was reported by another *Die Botschaft* correspondent reporting from New York: "There at D.'s it is getting to be quite a business place with a hardware and tin shop combination and saw mill and lumber yard . . . and now horse shoeing and also a well drilling outfit so I don't know what they would need next unless it would be a bank or a post office."

Goods and services offered by New York Amish include those in more traditional areas such as baked goods, cheese, rocking chairs, firewood, quilts, maple syrup, as well as sawmills, pallet shops, harness making, blacksmithing, and woodworking. Amish businesses now also include greenhouses, gas and diesel engine sales and repair, horsetraining, hide tanning, leather shops, upholstery shops, furniture refinishing, shoe stores, and the sale of a variety of other items from lawn furniture to rugs. The Amish sometimes sell products through intermediaries but most commonly they are sold from the home or at a roadside stand or other outbuilding on the property. This latter approach is typical of New York cottage industry and is the arrangement that will be addressed here.

Sometimes two or three rough, hand-lettered placards advertising various products will be nailed to fences and trees in the same yard. For example, a single homestead displayed signs reading "Fresh Baked Goods," "Woodworking," and "Quilt Shop." But the most commonly seen sign, and the one that conveys the impact of cottage industry most powerfully, offers no particular good or service. Usually store-bought, most often in a standard format of red letters against black background, it reads "OPEN," or in the slightly more emphatic version, "COME IN—WE'RE OPEN." It would be difficult to imagine a more graphic denial of the claim to separation. Placed in the window of an Amish home or tacked to its door, this otherwise innocuous notice is transformed into an unequivocal sign of social change.

The Consequences Of Cottage Industry

As a farmer, the Amishman was free to be aloof, contemptuous, or indifferent to unwanted visitors. He and his family could meet intruders with a wall of silence, literally or figuratively turning their backs. The "open" sign denies the Amishman this strategy. The acknowledgment that one is open exemplifies the kind of significant gesture that Goffman (1967:34) contends is used "to initiate a spate of communication and as a means for the persons concerned to accredit each other as legitimate participants." The Amish family accredits, in this sense, any passerby who is inclined to stop. The "open" sign represents an implicit invitation, allaying the feelings of uneasiness, embarrassment, or guilt that before kept all but the most insensitive from intruding.

The passing stranger and the Amishman are then in "a state of talk—that is, they have declared themselves officially open to one another for purposes of spoken communication and guarantee together to maintain a flow of words" (Goffman 1967:34). Of course a troublemaker or overly inquisitive individual can be cut off or asked to leave. But this is less of a solution than it is an ongoing consequence of offering goods and services to the public. It is one more situation that the Amishman must be prepared to handle, different in degree but not in kind from another consequence of "being open": a necessarily growing concern with what Goffman refers to as face-work.

The Amishman's concern with threats to the face of others as well as to his own face, even in very ephemeral interactions, arises from two sources. First, by accrediting the customer as a legitimate participant, by allowing the birth of the interaction in the first place, the Amishman takes on a degree of responsibility. As Goffman (1967:113) notes, "a conversation has a life of its own and makes demands on its own behalf. It is a little social system with its own boundary-maintaining tendencies; it is a little patch of commitment and loyalty. . . ."

Goffman's evocative language perfectly fits the type of interaction under discussion. The "little patch" of commitment is indeed far outweighed by the enormous cultural differences between Amish seller and non-Amish buyer. Its existence, however, represents a significant shift from the relationship, or its absence, that existed before between Amish isolate and non-Amish interloper. The institutionalized avoidance that before obviated the need for daily interactions with strangers has been lost as an option to those who engage in the kind of cottage industry under discussion here.

A second source of the need to be more concerned with face-work can be found in the role of seller. The norms associated with that role are foreign to Amish culture and in some ways antithetical to it. For example, a seller ought to be polite, friendly, outgoing, and ready to please. The Amish have little use for what passes for politeness in the larger society. The "please," "thank you," and "have a nice day" of contemporary social intercourse tend to be seen as gratuitous hypocrisies by Amish. Conveying a demeanor of being eager to satisfy is likewise incompatible with the role of being Amish. To identify this role conflict is not to predict that Amishmen will perforce compromise their Amishness or engage in ingratiating behavior. After all, the public's expectations are mixed as well. Up to a point they may tolerate a degree of reservedness that would otherwise drive them to take their business elsewhere. There remains, however, a fundamental tension between the role of Amishman and the role of seller that precludes the simultaneously earnest performance of both. The Amishman is confronted with working out a strategy that will allow for commercial success as well as cultural survival. That strategy will necessarily mirror a greater concern with how to manage a more or less constant interfacing with the public.

Management of interaction with the public has been crucial in allowing the Amish to successfully maintain a degree of separation from the larger society. One reason why the Amish were willing to take the issue of mandatory education to the U.S. Supreme Court was that they would not have been in a position to control the high school environment in which their children otherwise would have spent several years.[9] They fully recognized the threat implicit in that lack of control.

On a smaller and less institutionalized scale, some degree of control is lost with a public declaration of openness. The timing, content, and circumstances of interactions are left largely to the discretion of the non-Amish buyer. Even when the shop or sales area is located in an outbuilding rather than in the house itself, the visitor may choose to wander around the premises and, as a potential customer, do so with relative impunity. When the shop area is unattended, as is often the case owing to the demands of family or chores, the visitor has a virtual carte blanche to approach the house or engage children in conversation, in search of someone to wait on him or her.

In the case of the Canadian settlement cited earlier, what was intended as a mail order business drew a constant stream of visitors: "There were up to 15 cars in the laneway and on the road at one time. . . . We couldn't even get a meal without being interrupted and some people came late at night."[10]

Most Amish businesses post a "No Sunday Sales" sign, maintaining, on at least one day, the degree of avoidance that existed before the surge in cottage industry. During the rest of the week, they are fair game. The customer's language, mannerisms, dress, and paraphernalia, including vehicles, radios, jewelry, and other worldly accoutrements, are beyond the Amishman's control, intruding sporadically and, if the business is successful, frequently.[11]

What makes these intrusions problematic is only in part the discrepancy between Amish and American culture that they highlight. Most Amish are quite familiar with American culture and don't expect the rest of the world to live as they do. In fact, what the Amish perceive as the excesses and blasphemies, even the coerciveness, of the larger society can serve to reinforce Amish values. The concept of relative advantage, as developed by Wolf (1990), may be useful in explaining this apparent anomaly.

Wolf (1990:41) defines relative advantage as "a collective process by which a group of people come to define their situation, values, or character in reference to that of another group's . . . in a manner which gives them a sense of satisfaction." The other group, the comparative reference group, may be more powerful or superior along some dimension judged important by them. But measured by the criteria judged important by the group in question, such as character, values, or godliness, the comparative reference group is at a disadvantage. The result is a reinforced sense of group identification, group solidarity, and self-esteem. Members of such a group not only feel a sense of relative advantage "but often a sense of group smugness or contentment with their lot. . . ." (Wolf 1990:52).

The attitude of the Old Order Amish toward the larger society has often been consistent with this particular social construction of reality. The idea of smugness may be innately subjective but in interactions with the Amish it comes through so clearly and frequently that it would be disingenuous to deny it.[12] An example is contained in this letter from a New York scribe to *Die Botschaft*. The scribe, who had gone along on an outing of Amish students to a local public school, comments on the extensive resources available to the public school children, and concludes: "I don't believe I'd want to go to a school like that, a room for every different subject. How thankful we should be for our schools, the way they were back when we went to school. The schools (worldly) have almost whatever they wish for, but all the money they spent, and I wonder if their pupils know that much more than ours? Maybe worldly wisdom."

An Amishman living in a New York community that had been in conflict with local authorities over the Amish failure to use slow-moving vehicle symbols on their buggies argued: "It's probably not a bad thing that we get crowded once in a while by the law. It helps us draw the line." Encountered as an abstraction or a short stay in the county jail, or examined at arm's length on an occasional field trip, the "world" serves to confirm the superiority of Amish values and the relative advantage of their way of life. But as a frequent visitor, arriving in a late model car, knocking on the door, asking questions, and coming and going at will, the "world" threatens to upset the rhythm of Amish life and undermine its values. It is this erosion of control over interactions with the public that makes them so problematic.

The Amish Reaction

Despite the fact that in some settlements cottage industry has played a significant economic role for a dozen years or more, discussion of its consequences is only recently beginning to appear in Amish publications. In response to a question concerning the appropriateness of "making things for the tourist trade" that appeared in *Family Life*, an Amish monthly, several readers expressed concern. The combination of uneasiness and resignation that characterized the discussion is reflected in the following excerpt from one reader's letter: "Perhaps the best answer might be to move to a place where the land is cheaper and try to farm. But alas, if you checked it out, many of the people in these new settlements are having a hard time unless there is a side line such as a saw mill or produce growing or some shops. Some people end up in a shop or factory again."

In another *Family Life* issue featuring "a special section on the production of questionable items and its adverse effects on ourselves and our communities," an Amish author addressed the question of "What is happening to us?" In answering he observed that "many of our people are beginning to wonder if it is fitting for them to sell so much directly to the customer" (Wagler 1990:18).

The same tentative concern is shown in a recent Amish-edited directory. Regarding the situation in Lancaster County, Pennsylvania, the author comments:

> These conditions have lured our people to employment unthought of twenty years ago. We are reluctant to release today's statistics, but without pointing our finger or to accuse anyone we must face the facts. Perhaps some of these things come from material necessity: There are over 100 Amish construction crews in Lancaster County, some travel as far as Delaware and perhaps further instate to work in developments that destroy farmland. There are about the same amount of woodwork shops of which many cater to the tourist trade. We have many shops that restore carriages and related items that are pleasing to the world fashion today.

In assessing the consequences of engaging in these kinds of enterprises the author concludes: "Only time can tell—or is time running out?" (*Amish Directory* 1989).

Another Amish commentator, addressing the impact of a greater involvement with the cash economy that "came to us in the name of progress and efficiency" concluded:

> But I am afraid it is not progress. Because in a subtle way, in a sneaky, below-the-surface, behind-the-scenes sort of way, it changes our entire way of living. Worse yet, it changes our way of thinking. When that line of reasoning is followed to its logical end, it will put our lives out of balance, alter our lifestyles and our communities. . . . [I]t is a kind of reasoning, if we pursue it in the future as we have in the past, that will eventually destroy our Christian values in our homes, communities and churches, even as it has already done so in the larger society around us. (Stoll 1990:8)

In the New York settlements concern was far more muted. When asked directly about the impact of the various cottage industries in his community, one bishop replied: "I don't like to see too much of it. But we haven't had any real problems with it. In the Spring, people [i.e. customers] are coming and going in immodest dress. Sometimes people will use indecent language that the children might pick up. It might make some Amish more forward. We might lose some individuals but the church won't lose its basic values."

The bishop went on to identify, as a more serious problem, Amish working for non-Amish at construction sites where electric power tools are used. Another bishop in a different settlement made the same point. He acknowledged the problem of customers in "indecent dress" and others wanting to be served on Sundays because, "They just don't know our ways." He cited, however, working for wages as "the real problem," since it often meant working only eight hours a day, thus leading to idleness.

Cottage industry may be less problematic than "working away." And it may be a logical and even necessary response to an economic environment in which agriculture is not a viable alternative for most families. But its consequences will not necessarily be trivial. The nature of those consequences is only now beginning to manifest itself. A recently reported scene in Lancaster County is suggestive of how the relationship between Amish seller and non-Amish buyer might influence Amish behavior. The reporter described Amish children selling craft items to tourists, a common enough event in Lancaster, but "What made the happening unusual was that tourists were taking turns having their picture taken with the Amish kids. At an early age, they obviously had learned an important business lesson: the customer is always right."[13]

Even if such incidents remain anomalous, and thus newsworthy, a significant shift is taking place. Non-Amish behavior and points of view can no longer be so easily dismissed as irrelevant. The customer may not always be right, but he is now very much part of the Amish world.

Discussion and Conclusions

Cottage industry now plays an important role in Amish economic survival. The pages of a recent *Old Order Shop & Service Directory* confirm this conclusion "in the number of ads and the varieties of merchandise and services offered. They reflect what is happening in the Amish communities as members find new methods to earn income to meet today's rising costs, and to supplement farming or even substitute for it" (Beiler 1988:3). The growing importance of cottage industry is also demonstrated by the almost one hundred shops and businesses maintained by fewer than four hundred families in the Arthur, Illinois, settlement, which one observer referred to as "the emerging shop-culture" (Miller 1978:19).

A report on Amish-run restaurants, bake shops, and other home businesses in Ohio settlements recognized their growing economic importance as well as "the threat of worldliness that comes with such commerce."[14] In an aside that tellingly illustrates the new openness and vulnerability associated with cottage industry, the author notes: "Doing business with an Amish family offers a rare opportunity for a glimpse into their simple and, by their own choice, often difficult way of life."[15] The opportunity for that glimpse is now no longer especially rare. In Lancaster County many home-based Amish shops actually cater to tourists or serve both Amish and non-Amish customers (Kraybill 1989:201–202). And the trend is toward an even further shift away from farming to cottage industries.[16]

The economic pressures responsible for the development of this sector are unambiguous. At the level of the baked goods shop or dry goods store, these macro-level economic forces manifest themselves by shaping the context and, indirectly, the scripts of endlessly iterated Goffmanesque interactions between non-Amish customer and Amish seller. These more or less routinized contacts, and the roles that are associated with them, represent a new type of threat to the perpetuation of Amish culture.

For almost a hundred years following their birth in the midnineteenth century, the Old Order Amish have consciously rejected the criterion of efficiency (as defined by the larger society) as a master value. Economic pressures toward specialization and expansion that transformed the rest of American agriculture were muted in Amish society by the ideological mandates of the church. For the most part, the Old Order continued to cultivate small, diversified farms by horsepower.

Whatever competitive disadvantage might have resulted from this partial resistance to the dictates of efficiency was mitigated by accepting, even idealizing, a standard of living that was grossly incompatible with the rising expectations of the rest of the population. The widening gap during this period between Amish and American society can only be explained by the primacy of religious ideology in Amish decision making.

Beginning in the early 1970s, however, already growing economic pressures intensified to the point that, for an increasing proportion of Amish, the old patterns were no longer viable. Their move away from agriculture recapitulates the earlier move that took place in the larger society, but with a difference: The industrialization and commercialization of agriculture in American society as a whole may have been lamented in some quarters but were not systematically resisted. Now, despite their resistance, the Amish are being forced to consider new ways of earning a living. The shift to wage labor and cottage industry effectively illustrates the limits of ideological influence in the contest between doing what is correct and what is economically necessary. Granted, church rules have changed as have more informal norms dealing with lifestyle and contacts with outsiders. But these changes only confirm the potency of the economic forces arrayed against traditional Amish life.

The Amish farmer arguably represents the last and best expression of Thomas Jefferson's virtuous "cultivator of the earth." Jefferson attributed the virtue of the yeoman farmer to his economic autonomy. He argued that commerce led to moral corruption in those who practiced it, because they depended for their subsistence on the "casualties and caprice of customers" (Jefferson 1894:269).[17] One might take issue with Jefferson's stance toward what he called the "vixen of commerce." But his insight concerning the nature of the relationship between buyer and seller, in contrast to the relationship between self-sufficient husbandman and the rest of society, is germane to understanding the potential impact of cottage industry on Amish culture.

Cottage industry has been welcomed by many Amish as an alternative to the problems of wage labor. But cottage industry carries with it a potential for forcing the realignment of Amish life to accord with the dictates of commerce. The consequent increased contact between Amish and non-Amish, and the new roles associated with that contact, represent an opening of Amish society. This opening, however, is not a process that began only with the rise of cottage industry. Even a cursory examination of Amish history shows that Amish relations with the larger society have been no more static than Amish society itself. Nor is this further evolution in relations a prelude to inevitable assimilation. That commercial contacts are not necessarily antithetical to successful boundary maintenance is demonstrated by the case of Hasidic communities in the United States.[18] The literal, physical opening of Amish homes and places of business to the public does not inexorably lead to the dissolution of Amish culture. What remains to be seen is how successful the Amish will be in perpetuating the values of an agrarian society once agriculture is no longer the foundation of economic life.

This retail hardware store is typical of the many Amish-owned retail outlets that have flourished in Lancaster County, Pennsylvania, in recent years. (Photograph by Dennis Hughes).

9

The Rise of Microenterprises

DONALD B. KRAYBILL AND STEVEN M. NOLT

The Amish settlement in Lancaster County, Pennsylvania, has been dramatically squeezed by the pressures of suburbanization in recent decades. Declining farmland, rising land prices, and a burgeoning Amish population have made it difficult for young couples to enter farming. Rather than migrate or enter factory work many entrepreneurs have developed microenterprises. Donald B. Kraybill and Steven M. Nolt tell the story of the mushrooming microenterprises that now dot the landscape of Lancaster's Amish settlement. Kraybill and Nolt identify some of the moral boundaries of nonfarm work and also speculate on its long-term consequences for Amish life.

The Legacy of the Land

The Amish of Lancaster County, Pennsylvania, have always been linked to the land. Until the 1970s nearly all of them were engaged in farming. Those who were not tilling the soil were involved in small crafts and enterprises that were linked with agriculture. Indeed at midcentury, employment in an outside factory was cause for excommunication (Kollmorgen 1942:23). Church leaders feared that factory work, the "lunch pail threat" as they sometimes called it, would undermine their way of life by pulling families apart and placing adults in "foreign" cultural settings where they might face many temptations that would compromise their Amish convictions. The many perks provided by the factory—paid vacations, insurance, and pensions—would surely undercut the dependency of members on the church community. Given their stubborn resistance to the factory and their love of the soil, why in recent years have the Amish so quickly deserted their cows and plows for carpentry shops?

The Lancaster settlement began about 1790 and now ranks second to Holmes County, Ohio, in size.[1] Lancaster County enjoys an enviable reputation for fertile limestone soil and vigorous agricultural productivity. The Amish settlement is distinguished for its longevity and density but in recent years it has achieved the dubious distinction of being one of the most progressive Amish communities in North America. Amish use of advanced technology is widespread. Modern agricultural techniques are widely used in farming—bulk milk tanks, machine milkers, artificial insemination, nutrition management for dairy herds, professional crop management, and extensive automation of farm implements within, however, some limits. Newer homes are quite modern in appearance, with state-of-the-art gas appliances, indoor bathrooms, lovely cabinetry, and a growing use of professional landscaping.

Lancaster County sits on the edge of the ever-expanding eastern megalopolis. Rapid suburban growth and a proliferation of service industries, not to mention the annual influx of some four million tourists, have accelerated Amish interaction with the outside world and provided the incentives for assimilation and social change. These conditions have not only prodded the Amish toward greater use of technology but have also spawned hundreds of Amish microenterprises. This development, more than any other, promises to dramatically alter the cultural landscape of Amish society over the generations.

Adjacent to several metropolitan areas (Philadelphia, Harrisburg, and Baltimore) Lancaster County has experienced dramatic population growth in the last four decades. Between 1960 and 1970 its population was growing faster than any other metropolitan area in the state. The population soared from some 235,000 in 1950 to 423,000 by 1990. The flow of tourists into Lancaster County jumped from about 1.5 million in 1963 to nearly 4 million by 1974. The swelling population and steady stream of tourists spawned sprawling suburbs and shopping malls, setting up dozens of confrontations in the eighties between commercial developers and the often vocal advocates of land preservation.

The new demographics of Lancaster County disturbed the traditional ways of Amish life and forced a crisis upon them in the seventies and eighties. Two of the culprits—shrinking farmland and skyrocketing land prices—resulted from the growing urbanization that was creeping across Lancaster County. A third factor that also triggered the crisis was the booming Amish population itself—a problem, of course, of their own making.

In the 1940s choice farmland in the heart of the Amish settlement could be purchased for $300 to $400 per acre. By 1981 Lancaster County farmland was selling for an average of $4,550 per acre and in the early nineties it was not unusual to pay $7,000 or $8,000 per acre for prime land. Developers naturally were willing to pay far more for strategic locations. At $7,000 per acre a typical farm might cost $700,000, a price that was virtually impossible to pay with only farm income. While prices were skyrocketing the available crop land was steadily shrinking—covered over by developments, malls, industrial parks, asphalt lots, lawns, and golf courses.

On top of the land-squeeze the Amish community was enjoying prolific vitality. With an average of 6 to 7 children per family, most of whom remained with the church, the Amish community was doubling nearly every twenty years. The community of some 5,700 persons in 1960 had jumped to nearly 11,000 by 1980. Even if urbanization and development were suddenly frozen, Amish growth itself would have eventually created the occupational crisis. In any event, all of these factors made it very difficult, often impossible, for young Amish families to enter farming in the seventies and eighties.

The Lancaster Amish responded to the crisis in four ways. They began buying farms in the southern end of the county and soon inched across its borders into Lebanon, Chester, and York counties. Second, they planted new settlements in other rural counties of Pennsylvania, sometimes at a considerable distance from Lancaster. Indeed, nearly a dozen new settlements were spawned by the Lancaster mother settlement between 1940 and 1978. In the early nineties families were moving to Kentucky and Indiana in search of farmland at a reasonable price. A third response to the demographic crunch involved the subdivision of farms. Homesteads were split in half and more intensive farming operations provided income for two Amish families. Fourth, in the late sixties and early seventies the Amish began creating small businesses and cottage industries.[2] Since 1970 these have flourished and provide many of the jobs in the Amish community today.[3]

A Profile of Microenterprises

The data reported in this chapter were gathered through face-to-face interviews with 114 Amish business owners living in the 13 church districts that constituted the sample for the study.[4] Included were enterprises that met three criteria: (1) an annual sales volume exceeding $1,000, (2) the owner's intention to establish a formal business, and (3) public evidence of entrepreneurial activity—letterheads, road signs, and business cards. Informal enterprises with annual sales under $1,000 were excluded—neighborly sales of milk and eggs, small produce stands, and the sale of garden vegetables to friends.

Interviewers identified 118 enterprises in 419 households in the 13 church districts that comprised the sample. Each church district had an average of 9.1 enterprises. The number of households with a business owner ranged from 48 percent in one district to a mere 13 percent in the most rural district. Based on the results of the sample, the entire settlement has about 950 Amish-owned enterprises. These small ventures have created about 2,000 full-time jobs, or 3,400 total jobs if part-time positions are counted. The enterprises range from one-person operations to a few sizeable establishments that employ upwards of a dozen persons. About one-third of the enterprises are "sideline" operations, often attached to a farm. They provide seasonal or part-time work in tandem with other work or part-time employment for someone in retirement.

One astonishing mark of the microenterprises in the Lancaster settlement is their relative youth. A mere 6 percent were founded before 1960 and fully 60 percent sprang up in the twelve-year period between 1980 and 1992. In other words about six hundred enterprises have flowered to full bloom in slightly over a decade. On top of the burgeoning entrepreneurial activity interviewers found no bankruptcy and virtually no evidence of business failures.[5] The rapidity of new starts coupled with few failures has contributed to this dramatic shift in Amish occupational patterns in the last two decades.

The type of entrepreneurial activity in the Lancaster settlement is displayed in table 9.1. Although some of the activity is farm-related, many of the enterprises are not directly tied to the agricultural economy. Fully one-quarter of the businesses are involved in some type of woodworking—furniture of one sort or another, cabinetmaking, storage barns, or general carpentry. A variety of small wood products is manufactured by Amish shops—dog houses, bird houses, cupolas, gazebos, picnic tables, and lawn furniture. Nearly 10 percent of the entrepreneurs are contractors who do both residential and commercial construction. Another sizeable group of shops fabricates metal and manufactures a variety of equipment.

Amish enterprises vary in size, location, and function. The three major types are small cottage industries, larger manufacturing establishments, and mobile work crews. Home-based operations, often

TABLE 9.1.
Type of Microenterprises in the Lancaster Settlement*

	Percent	*N*
Contractors	8.5	10
Retail (local interest)	7.6	9
Furniture manufacture/sales	6.8	8
Harness shops	6.8	8
Lawn furniture/ornaments	6.8	8
Retail (quilts/crafts)	6.8	8
Agricultural equipment	5.1	6
General woodworking	5.1	6
Greenhouses	5.1	6
Roadside produce	4.2	5
Bakeries	3.4	4
Cabinet shops	3.4	4
Storage barns/gazebos	3.4	4
Welding	3.4	4
Animal sales	2.5	3
Blacksmith shops	2.5	3
Farmers market stand	2.5	3
Metal fabrication	2.5	3
Carriage shops/wheelwright	1.7	2
Machine shops	1.7	2
Silo construction	1.7	2
Tax accountants	1.7	2
Toy manufacture/sales	1.7	2
Other	5.0	6
Total	100%	118

*Based on a sample of thirteen church districts.

located on farms, are housed in tobacco sheds or other farm buildings retrofitted for the new task. Bakeshops, craft shops, machine shops, hardware stores, health food stores, and greenhouses are a few of the hundreds that are often annexed to a barn or house. In some cases, new buildings are constructed for the enterprise. Many home-based shops cater to tourists, the Amish, and non-Amish neighbors. These shops, like the old mom-and-pop grocery stores of bygone America, are family operations. Several adults, an uncle, cousin, or sister, may assist the nuclear family as part- or full-time employees. Children help or hinder the operation, as the case may be. These cottage industries, lodged at home, range from one-person operations to those employing half a dozen people. One thing is certain: work in these settings is securely under the family's control. "What we're trying to do really," said one proprietor, "is keep the family together."

Larger shops or manufacturing concerns are established in newly erected buildings on the edge of a farm, on a plot with a house, or on rare occasions in an industrial park. These formal shops, with as many as fifteen employees, articulate with the outside business community. Blacksmith shops and welding shops that manufacture horse-drawn equipment cater primarily to the Amish. Other businesses, such as cabinet shops and hydraulic shops, serve both Amish and non-Amish customers. Many retail outlets—harness, hardware, paint, household appliance, and food stores—also sell to both groups. Some metal fabrication shops thrive on subcontracts with larger non-Amish businesses, as well as with other Amish manufacturers.

Mobile work crews are a third type of Amish enterprise. Amish construction crews travel to building sites in Lancaster County and to other counties as well. Trucks and vans provided by non-Amish employees or hired drivers transport the work crews. Carpentry and construction work have always been acceptable alternatives to farm work, and today carpentry rates second to farming as a preferred occupation. Amish construction crews, using the latest power tools operated by portable electric generators or on-site electricity, engage in subcontract and general construction on both residential and commercial buildings. Amish cabinet shops produce high-quality cabinetry, which is sometimes installed out of state.

As the Amish have struggled to keep their work at home and their families together, they have encountered encroaching zoning regulations. Ironically, the zoning laws that had protected their farms from developers and large industry now prevent some of them from building commercial establishments on their own farms. The proliferation of cottage industries and small manufacturing operations, often built in agricultural zones, has caused tension with public officials. In some townships, zoning officials have overlooked violations, but others have closed down Amish businesses. Many townships have worked with the Amish to design zoning codes that would control in sensible ways the size of small businesses in rural areas. Under pressure from the Amish, one township amended its agricultural zoning ordinance to permit home industries if they did not exceed 2,500 square feet or employ more than four workers, including the owner. Another township has a limit of two nonfamily employees—an interesting twist of secular law to enforce Amish values of smallness and family involvement.

The Entrepreneurs

The rise of Amish enterprises violates many of the assumptions about the prerequisites for starting a small business. The owners have virtually no training beyond the eighth-grade education they received in one-room Amish schools—let alone any college, business, or technical training. Indeed, 93 percent of the owners reported no training beyond the eighth grade. Those who had taken additional schooling may have taken a special course or seminar in hydraulics, plastics, or plumbing. An Amish tax accountant might enroll in an H&R Block class or a Penn State extension seminar. A few others have taken Dale Carnegie courses on "Human Relations" or a seminar on "How to Run a Small Business." Because the church does not permit the use of computers, entrepreneurs are not computer literate. Thus most business owners have virtually no formal education.

For the most part the training of Amish entrepreneurs and employees is rooted in old-fashioned apprenticeship—learning by trial and error under the supervision of a mentor. Book learning for the most part is ridiculed. One Amish shop owner expressed his opinion that the larger society's work force is overeducated and underexperienced. "American business would be more productive if business people would actually work in shops and try to weld something or make something with wood and see how it's done instead of just reading about it in books," he suggested. There are some exceptions however. A craftsman planning to build rolltop desks gathered all the literature he could find on desk making before opening his shop. After reading extensively he developed a new type of desk tambour that is now selling well.

These enterprises typically start with very little capital—surely without government subsidized loans. Furthermore, many are experiments. They begin without elaborate strategic plans and marketing strategies—more likely with a few notes on the back of an envelope or in a conversation with a neighbor. For the most part these entrepreneurs have not inherited or purchased their business but are primarily first generation entrepreneurs. When asked how they got started, fully 83 percent reported, "I had the idea and started it myself." Only 5 percent inherited the enterprise from their parents.

Without a long history of entrepreneurship within their families, owners are learning managerial skills on the job. Fifty percent were under 35 years of age when they started their enterprise. A quarter of the entrepreneurs were over 45 when they began their operation. This reflects the traditional practice where fathers move into early retirement to make room for sons to take over the family farm. Thus the recent burst of entrepreneurial activity is prodded by young persons embarking on a career as well as by adults moving into early retirement. Fully 93 percent of the owners had grown up on a farm and 60 percent had operated a farm themselves before starting their enterprise. Many indicated that management skills related to farming were transferable and helpful in managing their businesses. Although many of the shops are still located on the edge of a farm or near the family homestead, over two-thirds of the owners no longer spend any time farming. In other words, the bulk of these shops are not part-time "sidelines" but are pursuits that demand a full-time commitment.

About 20 percent of the owners are women. Their business activities conform to traditional gender expectations—bakeries, greenhouses, quilts, handicrafts, and vegetable markets. The women, however, are managers, which introduces a new twist into this patriarchal society. If the sample of 13 districts is representative of the larger community, there are likely more than 175 enterprises in the Lancaster settlement that are operated by women. Some women entrepreneurs are single, others are married. Despite the church's patriarchal structure of leadership, church officials have freely permitted women to become involved in business activities. "If a woman wants to start up a business, getting her husband's okay may be the hardest thing in getting started," said one Amishman.

Married women are strongly discouraged from working in formal jobs away from home. But because much of their entrepreneurial activity can be done within the context of home and family, it is viewed as less threatening to the community than full-time employment outside. Many female entrepreneurs operate their businesses alongside their household and family duties. Other family members often help in its operation. Still, many married businesswomen feel pulled between traditional roles and their business activities. One female entrepreneur mused, "Some times I feel guilty and wonder, 'Did I put too much into the business and not enough into the family?' "

The Moral Boundaries of Work

The phenomenal growth of these microenterprises has been funneled in specific directions by several constraints in the moral order of Amish society. First, the eighth-grade lid on education hinders Amish youth from entering the endless smorgasbord of occupations in the larger society. Without higher education Amish teens cannot aspire to becoming surgeons, professors, pilots, lawyers, or play hundreds of other occupational roles that demand professional training. This means that the brightest and best, the cream of the crop as the Amish would say, will likely enter business because it is the only viable alternative to farming. There are of course talented farmers in Amish circles, but with opportunities for farming shrinking, many of those looking for a challenge often find it in business. To put it another way, those in mainstream society who end up in professions will, in Amish society, likely try their hand at business. Business involvements provide a window of opportunity for those who are otherwise blocked from mainstream occupations by the constraints of Amish culture.

The *Ordnung* of the church also exercises moral constraints over Amish business activity. Religious taboos on certain kinds of work channel entrepreneurial activity in prescribed directions. The ban on electricity makes it difficult to operate certain types of retail activities, especially those that require refrigeration. Projects requiring computerization are also off limits because the church prohibits the ownership of computers. The sale of automobiles, video, television, jewelry, and fashion clothing would of course violate the moral sensibilities of Amish life. Restrictions on the ownership of automobiles also limit the type and nature of business activity. Many businesses hire vehicles on a regular basis, but sales work and other jobs that require automatic mobility would be impossible for an Amish person. These cultural restrictions focus entrepreneurial activities on traditional work—construction, carpentry, crafts, food, and light manufacturing.

A third norm that has encouraged the proliferation of shops is the Amish preference for small-scale structures. "Bigness," said one Amish carpenter, "ruins everything." Church leaders fear that too much power, concentrated in the hands of one person, will lead to arrogance and undue influence. It will, in short, disturb the egalitarian nature of the Amish community. Successful entrepreneurs might snub the church and begin "making their own rules," one retired farmer and shop owner fears. Consequently the church frowns when business operations become too large. It is rare to find an Amish business with more than a dozen employees. Indeed, only 6 percent of the enterprises had more than six employees. Amish commitment to small-scale values and the cultural taboo against large-scale operations have prodded the proliferation of small shops. Rather than concentrating entrepreneurial energy in several large operations the cultural commitment to small-scale values defuses it throughout the settlement. This keeps entrepreneurial activity, enthusiasm, and satisfaction widely dispersed.

The fourth constraint that energizes Amish enterprises is their selective use of technology. The Amish community has traditionally forbidden the installation of private telephones, the ownership of vehicles, and the use of 110 volt electricity from public utility lines. As noted above, these limitations block Amish access to certain types of work. But these restrictions have also fostered a spirit of ingenuity as shop owners have tried to create competitive enterprises that nevertheless are harnessed by the cultural constraints of Amish society. A wide array of modern equipment in Amish shops in the Lancaster settlement is powered by air and hydraulic motors. The air and hydraulic pumps are operated by large diesel engines. The technological restrictions in Amish life have encouraged an inventive spirit that, rather than stifling creativity, has actually spurred Amish mechanics to experiment. In a variety of ingenious ways they have circumvented cultural taboos in search of efficient sources of power and productive modes of mechanization.

The cultural constraints on education, diversity, size, and technology—although restrictive in nature—have nevertheless in subtle ways funneled Amish energies into creative entrepreneurial activity. The taboo on higher education imposed a vertical lid that has lured the best and brightest into the world of business and marketing. The horizontal limits that forbid certain types of work reinforce traditional occupations and provide a strong infrastructure of skills, knowledge, and ethnic connections. The limits on size impose a human scale on things and spread entrepreneurial activity across the settlement, preventing the alienation that sometimes accompanies employment in large-scale enterprises. Finally the technological restrictions have stirred creative imagination to find new ways to rig and power the machines in Amish shops. All of these cultural constraints in ironic ways have energized Amish entrepreneurial activity and focused business behavior in culturally prescribed directions.

The Sources of Amish Success

When asked why their businesses are flourishing, most entrepreneurs cloak their answers in the traditional raiment of Amish humility. Nevertheless all the evidence points to almost stunning success—despite the lack of formal training and the first generation nature of many of the ventures. As noted earlier very few Amish businesses have failed. Most of them are not merely surviving but are doing well financially. Profitability data are not available, but annual sales figures show that most shops are not merely selling handmade brooms! Fully 45 percent report annual sales between $50,000 and $500,000. Moreover, 14 percent enjoy annual sales above $500,000. About sixty of the enterprises in the Lancaster area have annual sales exceeding a million dollars. What are the sources for such success—to use a word that's feared in Amish vocabulary?

Many factors feed this robust entrepreneurial activity. First of all the work ethic is alive and thriving in Amish culture. Shop owners and their employees work long hours, take few breaks, and rarely take holidays or go on vacations. Said one Amish furniture maker, "If I worked from 9 to 4 and then watched TV the rest of the evening, I wouldn't make it on what I get an hour." Hard work is applauded and slothfulness is despised. Idleness is still considered the door to the devil's workshop. The basic values of agrarian culture—independence, thrift, ingenuity, self-sufficiency, and brute labor, now transferred to the shop—have served Amish entrepreneurs well.

Secondly, the austerity of Amish life also undergirds the shops. Laced with traditional simplicity and humility, many of the operations are modest in appearance. In recent years business cards and advertising specialties—mugs, calendars, and the like—are being used more and more, as are roadside signs. Nevertheless, advertising efforts and expenditures are relatively low. Overhead costs are remarkably low without air conditioning, carpeted offices, computerized equipment, utility bills, and the accoutrements of executive suites. Most retail and wholesale businesses have modest and simple showrooms and display areas. In virtually all the shops, owner/managers work alongside their employees throughout the day—another benefit of small-scale size. It is also rare to find a full-time bookkeeper. Typically a spouse or part-time employee serves in this role. The more sizeable operations do have makeshift offices, but these are often empty except for doing paperwork in the early morning or evening or for private discussions with an occasional visitor.

Compensation factors also contribute to the success of these small ventures. About 90 percent of all employees come from within the ethnic community. Federal legislation exempts the Amish from paying Social Security because the church views it as a form of insurance.[6] In the state of Pennsylvania Amish employers are also exempt from paying Workers' Compensation. Virtually none of the Amish businesses provide a pension plan for their employees because retirees, traditionally at least, have lived in an apartment on the homestead and were cared for by their children. In addition, few shops provide paid holidays or health insurance, not to mention other fringe benefits. The Amish church has traditionally provided assistance for excessive health costs through various informal mutual aid programs. All of these factors lower payroll costs for Amish employers. The labor rates in Amish shops are commensurate with those paid by similar non-Amish enterprises but are substantially lower than those in unionized companies. All things considered, these favorable compensation factors substantially reduce labor costs and give Amish entrepreneurs a competitive edge in the marketplace.

A fourth factor contributing to the success of Amish enterprises is favorable product perception. Amish products carry a mystique that enhances their marketability. They are viewed as handcrafted, high quality, and unique. Public perception of Amish craftsmanship is very positive. In one study of attitudes toward Amish products, 97 percent of the respondents rated the quality of Amish products as "higher or much higher" than non-Amish products.[7]

Likewise 97 percent rated the overall value (what you get for what you pay) of Amish products as "higher or much higher" than nonethnic products. In any event, the positive public perception of Amish products is a powerful market force that boosts the viability of Amish enterprises.

The Consequences of Occupational Change

The emergence of microenterprises is a most significant and profound change that is reshaping the character of the Lancaster settlement in the last quarter of the twentieth century. As Olshan has argued in chapter 8, it is indeed the opening of Amish society. Although the ramifications of this shift will surely be pervasive it is difficult to fully anticipate their long-term consequence. The Amish detour around factory work is an attempt to control the terms and conditions of their work—a negotiated attempt to protect and preserve their identity as a people. Cottage industries and microenterprises embody many traditional Amish values and certainly are more congruent with Amish virtues than the culture of the modern factory. Moreover these enterprises are relatively friendly to family values and the ritual calendar of the church. Nevertheless, this occupational shift poses undeniable challenges to the persistence of Amish life.

The development of microenterprises is fostering the emergence of a three-tier society. The historic agrarian base bestowed at least the appearance of a homogeneous society, void of the typical class distinctions produced by variations in education, income, and occupation. With the advent of the shops, three social class groupings are taking shape. Farmers of course continue to represent a sizeable cluster of wealth and lifestyle patterns, but their wealth is largely frozen in land and assets. The entrepreneurial class by contrast has ready access to financial resources, and the profitability of many enterprises produces considerable means. Access to wealth brings larger and more stylish housing, greater travel, and a more affluent lifestyle than that found among farmers. The third social class consists of day laborers working in shops for modest hourly wages and with few fringe benefits. They enjoy the social and financial support of the larger Amish community and certainly are not destitute, but their financial status is quite limited.[8] Compared with the sharp inequalities of modern life these differences in Amish society are rather mild, but their long-term consequences will certainly change the homogeneity of Amish life.

The growth of microenterprises will surely have an impact on the Amish family. It minimizes the lunch pail threat somewhat, by keeping fathers nearby home, but many fathers are not as nearby as they were on the farm. Consequently for some families the burden of child rearing falls heavily on the mothers. Children are also more insulated and separated from their father's work. Said one Amish father sadly, "I worked away. My wife did very good raising the children on her own. But it's not like farming with them, not like working with them yourself." Although some children are able to work in certain cottage industries, they are less of an economic asset than they were on the farm. If children become a liability, will Amish families also shrink in size like many others around the globe who have moved off the farm?

The farm provided ample, indeed unending work, seven days a week. In contrast, shop employees may only work forty to fifty hours a week. "The young people have too much free time," one father warned. "They go out there and work their eight or nine hours and then they come home and they're free." Shop employment gives teenagers more leisure time as well as more money in their pockets. This not only leads to new temptations but over the generations will likely foster new attitudes toward work and leisure itself.

In many ways, the involvement of women as owners and employees offers new opportunities for creative work not available on the farm or in traditional domestic work. The occupational shift also promises to erase some gender inequities by giving at least some women more access to finances and management—in short, to more power.

And although the microenterprises provide an ethnic context for work that is more friendly than the large factory, they nevertheless do increase interaction with the outside world. This is especially true for business owners, who are constantly interacting with salespersons, suppliers, distributors, and other competitors. The entrepreneurs learn the ways, the values, and the language of the world. They become more fluent in English, conversant in the jargon of marketing, wise in the ways of the market place—in short, immersed in the rationality and logic of the larger culture. This exposure threatens many traditional Amish values: *Gelassenheit*, separation from the world, humility, and the rejection of force. Entrepreneurs, in other words, are tempted with individualism, arrogance, greed, and the use of the law to protect their economic interests.

Will the entrepreneurs who absorb the rational values of the larger society continue to be content to drive a horse and carriage to Sunday services and have the patience to sing the laboriously long hymns and listen to untrained ministers preach lengthy sermons? Will the managers of million-dollar enterprises quietly fall in line with the traditional values of patriarchal authority? Or will they want to apply the problem-solving logic and strategic analysis of their business life to the practices of the church? Will the wealthy in the long run be able to resist the many pleasures of modern life now becoming ever so easily available to them?

Moreover, the transformation from plows to business will erase forever the peasant innocence of Amish life—a shift that may have profound implications for their relationship with the outside world. No longer barefoot farmers, whose peculiar ways can be attributed to rural naivete, Amish entrepreneurs will likely be subject to the same legal and regulatory restrictions as their non-Amish competitors without the public indulgence they have sometimes enjoyed in the past. The power brokers of modern life and all their functionaries will no doubt insist that the Amish play on a level playing field despite the implications of their religious convictions.

Many of the legal and political concessions that have been forged for the Amish over the years have been based on the assumption that they were innocent farmers seeking to preserve a sharp separation from the world. That assumption will surely erode as they enter the fray of business. What, for example, might have been the outcome of the Supreme Court's 1972 decision in *Wisconsin v. Yoder* if less than half of the Amish had been farming at the time?

The creation of hundreds of microenterprises represents a negotiated settlement with modernity. In essence Lancaster's Amish have said, "yes, we will leave our plows behind" but "no, we won't work in factories." Microenterprises symbolize a midway point—halfway between farm and factory. The Amish in the Lancaster settlement were willing to be pushed off the land—willing to give up their three-hundred-year love affair with the soil, but not willing to send their sons and daughters off to work in an alien context. Like professionals of a sort, they sought to control the terms and conditions of their own work.

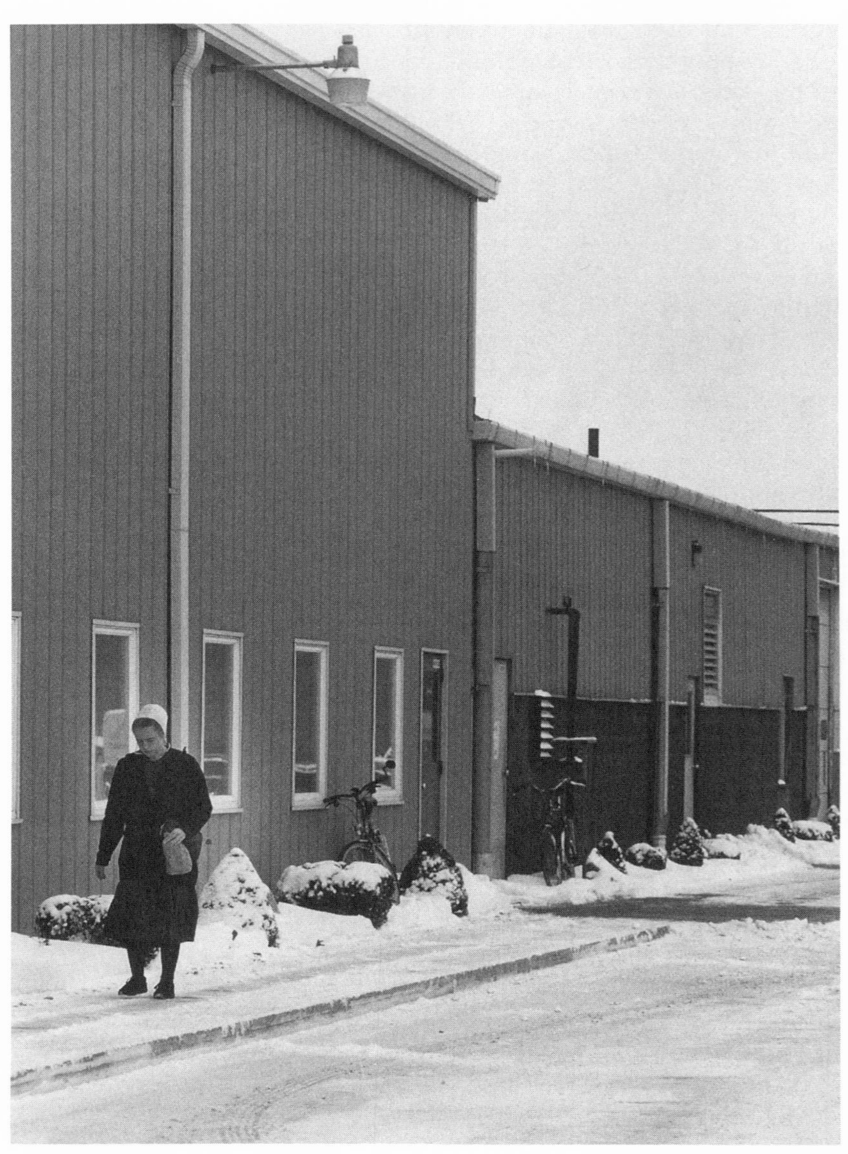

An Amish woman leaves work at Jayco, Inc., a manufacturer of recreational vehicles in Middlebury, Indiana, that employs many Amish. (Photograph by Lynne Echtenkamp).

10

Lunch Pails and Factories

THOMAS J. MEYERS

Many observers have argued that the survival of Amish society rests on an agrarian way of life. Unlike their Lancaster cousins, many of the Amish in the Elkhart-Lagrange settlement of Indiana have left their cows and have taken up factory employment. This settlement offers an interesting case study in which to explore the linkage between Amish culture and an agricultural way of life. Thomas Meyers assesses the impact of factory work and concludes that although employment away from home will bring changes it will not lead to the demise of Amish society.

The Beginning of the End?

"On a recent visit to Goshen, Indiana, I was told that the Amish in that area were too prolific for the resources of the land. No more land was for sale. Hence Amish young men are going into factories. 'That,' I remarked to myself, 'spells the beginning of the end' " (Gross 1980:16). This pessimistic conclusion was reached by the eminent church historian Roland Bainton after visiting Goshen, Indiana, in the fall of 1974. He had learned that many Amishmen were seeking employment in the recreational vehicle and mobile home industries of northern Indiana. Bainton's line of reasoning was consistent with that of most scholars—the Amish could not survive without an agrarian base. Rural agricultural communities provided a niche for a people who wanted to be separate from the larger society. But when the boundary lines crumbled these "peculiar" people would surely be seduced by the dominant culture. Daily contact with the "English" world would replace the horse and buggy with the automobile. Telephones and electricity would become the norm in Amish homes as a way of life disappeared in a blaze of rapid acculturation.

Nearly twenty years have elapsed since Professor Bainton made his prediction, yet the Amish community in northern Indiana is thriving despite some rather dramatic changes. The Elkhart-Lagrange Old Order Amish settlement has made the transition from an agricultural community to one in which farmers are in the minority. This chapter explores both the causes and the consequences of this significant transition.

The Elkhart-Lagrange settlement hosts the third largest concentration of Old Order Amish in the world. Situated in northern Indiana, it borders the state of Michigan and covers the eastern half of Elkhart County and most of Lagrange County.[1] The qualitative data presented in this chapter have been gathered in interviews with Amish and non-Amish people in this community over the past thirteen years. The quantitative data were taken from settlement directories produced by the Amish.

Forces Promoting Change

Why have the Amish in northern Indiana abandoned agriculture? The answer is relatively simple: a rapid increase in the Amish population, coupled with limited and expensive farmland, made it difficult for young persons to start farming. As table 10.1 demonstrates, in less than twenty-five years the population of the settlement has more than doubled. This increase is largely attributed to natural population growth. Families in this settlement continue to be quite large, with an average of 7.4 children.

This increase is consistent with growth rates in other communities.

TABLE 10.1.
Settlement Size and Composition by Year[2]

Year	*Church districts*	*Households*	*Children*	*Members*	*Total pop.*
1964	30	NA	NA	NA	5,219
1970	37	1,205	NA	NA	6,720
1980	51	1,561	5,398	3,177	8,575
1988	66	2,100	6,262	4,792	11,154

TABLE 10.2.
People Remaining Amish, Leaving the Amish, or Migrating, by Year

	Remaining	*Leaving*	*Migrating*	*Total*	
Year of birth	%	%	%	%	N
1920–1929[a]	75	18	6	100	(772)
1930–1939[a]	70	22	8	100	(1,095)
1940–1949[a]	78	14	8	100	(1,737)
1950–1959[b]	83	10	7	100	(2,349)
1960–1969[b,c]	92	5	3	100	(1,983)

[a] Data taken from 1980 *Indiana Amish Directory* (Gingerich 1980).
[b] Data taken from 1988 *Indiana Amish Directory* (Miller 1988).
[c] This cohort includes young people in their late teens and early twenties (835 out of 2,818) who are not members. Therefore, only those people who have left their parental home are included in the analysis.

Luthy (1992:21) reports that in the decade from 1981 to 1991 the number of Amish church districts in North America increased from 569 to 898. Using Kraybill's (1993b) estimated average of 150 individuals (children and adults) per district, the total Amish population in North America likely increased from 85,350 to 134,700 in ten years time!

The increase in the Elkhart-Lagrange population gradually expanded the geographic size of the settlement. However, there is little farmland available at the edges of the existing community for further expansion. Some farms have been subdivided, but this strategy also has its limits. In some other settlements as population density increased many Amish chose to search for farmland in another part of the country.[3] As table 10.2 demonstrates, migration has not been an attractive alternative for many people in the Elkhart-Lagrange settlement. The data suggest that migration has actually decreased slightly among persons born since 1950.

Table 10.2 was constructed by gleaning information from two community directories (Gingerich 1980; Miller 1988). Those persons identified as leaving the church were children who left their parental home and were identified by their parents as deciding not to join the Amish church. The data in table 10.2 suggest that the retention of Amish youth in the Elkhart-Lagrange settlement is on the rise. An increasing number of young people are choosing to remain within the faith of their parents, which only exacerbates the problems of population pressure and available land.[4]

The rapid Amish population growth has coincided with an increase in the price of farmland and a slump in the farm economy. The average price per acre of farmland and buildings in the state of Indiana increased from $406 in 1970 to $1,498 in 1979 (U.S. Census, 1979:691). Although the price of land decreased slightly in the following decade to $1,244 in 1990 (U.S. Census 1992:648), purchasing a farm continues to be an expensive proposition. Prime agricultural land in northern Indiana generally sells above the state average.

Many Amish have been leery of beginning their married lives with a major debt load. In addition to the price of land there are the concomitant costs of equipment and livestock. In 1981, when farmland in the Shipshewana, Indiana, area sold for between $2,000 and $3,000 per acre and top quality dairy cattle sold for $1,900 a head, an Amish farmer commented on a young person who went deep in debt to get established in farming: "A young fellow bought six of those cows ($1,900 per head) and one of these days he's gonna wake up to the fact that he isn't going to be able to pay for them and put bread on the table at the same time."

Another farmer described his difficulty "making ends meet" this way: "I put oats in [the ground] this year. It used to be that you paid 1 or 2 dollars a bushel for seed, now they're 5 dollars. I bought certified or near certified seed which cost me a little more, next year I'll just use my own seed. I sold my beans—now I'll be honest—for $5,000; and I put in some new tile and bought some other things and I didn't make any money. When I got done, I lost." Another informant described his unsuccessful poultry business: "About six years ago I put up a hen house and for some reason the floor fell out and we lost a lot of chickens. I used to have a dream where I saw those chickens down in there and tried to get them out but I couldn't."

Finding alternatives to a financially difficult and stressful start in farming has become increasingly attractive to young Amishmen. With factory workers typically earning in excess of $30,000 as laborers in the Elkhart-Lagrange area, industrial employment has become a tantalizing option.

Idealized Farming

Both the scholarly community and the Amish have idealized the Amish farming tradition. Scholars such as Martineau and MacQueen (1977) and Ericksen et al. (1980) have argued that farming is the heart of Amish culture and that with the demise of an agrarian way of life the future of Amish society is in jeopardy. Amish publications make frequent references to "working away" (meaning off the farm) and the pitfalls associated with such employment. One anonymous writer, in the Amish publication *Family Life* ("Sam Buys" 1972:13), summarized the dangers of working in industry:

> Probably most of us, if we have really considered the matter would agree working in factories is not good for building up the church. The following points, as a general rule do not work for the good: 1. Working with worldly people who practice smoking, swearing, telling dirty stories, etc. 2. Men and women working together, especially under such conditions. 3. Fathers away from home, many times leaving too early to have devotions with the family. 4. Too much money available. Many people would say they want to work away so they can get started farming but it seems the number of farmers are getting fewer and fewer.

An elderly Amish minister described the stark contrast between farming and "working away" in the following manner. "Farming is working with creation. There is something in the soil that man is attracted to. Man was made from the soil you know and he likes to see things grow. In a factory there are manmade things not things from the Lord. The farm is healthier and you're closer to God."

This is the idealized, frontstage, description of agrarian life. However, if one goes backstage in Amish society there is a reluctant admission that farming is not necessarily the ideal occupation for everyone. One Amishman remarked: "My (oldest) son has no desire to farm because he has seen the hard life that his parents lead, particularly in terms of finances. Our second son isn't interested because he knows our situation. Farming is a lot of work and it's hard to make ends meet."

Amish farmers, especially those who have large debts, often have a difficult time making ends meet. Although there are advantages to their relatively simple technology, the growing season is the same whether a farmer uses a tractor or a horse. The Amish farmer has to compete with non-Amish neighbors in the same market. During planting season, farmers work from the early hours of the morning until long after dark, particularly when the weather has not been cooperative. As one man said, "when your neighbor has a tractor and can plough eight furrows in the time it takes you to do one, it can be discouraging."

Because of the financial risks and hard work involved in farming, Amish informants report that many young Amish persons would not remain Amish if they had to farm. In the words of one minister, "there are a lot of big husky guys who could be farming but aren't." One farmer stated the cultural ideal this way, "farming is the best way of life," and then added, "I don't really like farming. I don't like to work in the dirt and I don't like to be out in the hot sun making hay. Years ago, before I had help [sons] I was so tired at the end of the day that I could barely make it up the hill in front of the house."

The Rise of Industrial Employment

A gradual movement away from farming in northern Indiana began in the late 1930s and early 1940s, when small groups of Amishmen began to work in the mobile home industry. Ironically, these peace-loving people were producing modular homes for military bases. Companies formed to provide housing for thousands of servicemen and their families who were flocking to military installations in the context of World War II. Elkhart County, Indiana, became a major locus of the mobile home industry during this era.

To the outsider it may seem strange that the pacifist Amish would produce a product for the military, particularly during wartime. Likewise most non-Amish find it puzzling to learn that Amish people now work in factories that specialize in van conversions or produce large recreational vehicles. The issue today is the same as it was in the forties—economic survival. Work is a means to an end. The typical Amishman has little concern for the final use of the product he is producing. He willingly provides labor to produce a product that will be used by persons who inhabit the "kingdoms of this world." His primary concern is how he spends his paycheck among his own people, whom he considers to be among the redeemed in the Kingdom of God.[5]

With the end of World War II more and more recreational vehicle factories began to open their doors in Elkhart County. A Mennonite man remembers his summer employment at a "trailer" factory in Goshen, Indiana: "In the summer of 1947, I worked in Solly Kropf and Henry Cripe's 'trailer' factory. This factory employed 45 Amishmen and a few non-Amish, mostly Mennonites. But approximately 90 percent of the craftsmen were Amish. I had my regular 3 or 4 Amish riders that I picked up every morning and took home in the evening. As I recall they paid me 25 cents a day, including those for whom I had to drive out of my direct route to Goshen."[6]

One of the first factories to employ large numbers of Amish was the

TABLE 10.3.
Occupation of Household Heads by Year

	Farm		Factory		Shop		Carpenter		Other		Total	
	%	N	%	N	%	N	%	N	%	N	%	N
1970	61	(557)	26	(236)	4	(36)	4	(37)	5	(45)	100	(911)
1980	54	(646)	28	(339)	6	(75)	6	(66)	6	(70)	100	(1,196)
1988	35	(580)	45	(740)	8	(133)	5	(84)	6	(101)	100	(1,638)

Source: The Indiana Amish Directories (Cross and Gingerich 1970), (Gingerich 1980), and (Miller 1988).
Note: Because of difficulties establishing the employment status of older persons, only men under the age of 65 were included.

Starcraft Corporation which initially specialized in agricultural equipment when it began producing steam thresher tanks in 1903. By 1926 the Star Tank and Boat Co., as it was then called, began to manufacture galvanized steel boats for use in farm ponds (*Goshen* 1981:136). In the 1950s livestock tanks and hog feeders were added to their line of products. Later they produced fiberglass boats and eventually a variety of recreational vehicles. By the 1950s at least fifty Amishmen worked in this plant. Although these men were initially involved in the production of agricultural equipment, they soon moved into all aspects of recreational vehicle production.

During the decade of the 1960s many mobile home and recreational vehicle factories were established in northern Indiana. Some of them explicitly targeted this area because of the large supply of Amish and Mennonite workers. Owners knew that these men were hard workers, would not unionize, and would often work below industry pay standards. A company history of Coachmen Industries in Middlebury, Indiana, explains the owner's reasons for selecting the site for a recreational vehicle factory: "The area is inhabited by many of Amish/Mennonite descent, and when the time came that he [the owner] would need additional help, Claude was aware that their traditional building skills would be invaluable. Their reputation for giving a day's labor for a day's pay also concurred with his philosophy of giving a dollar value for a dollar received" (Coachmen 1964:12).

When I asked an Amish minister how the church made the decision to allow members to seek employment in industry, he said, "the church didn't! It just sort of happened. When farmland became scarce, it just was practical for men to work in factories."

The data in table 10.3 demonstrate the steady increase in the number of Amish persons seeking employment outside of agriculture since 1970. In addition to factory work there have always been a small number of individuals who have worked in construction, handicrafts, or in their own cottage industries.

The Factory Culture

Many factory workers begin their day with early morning chores. They are typically on their way to work by 6 A.M. They travel by bicycle, horse and buggy, or with a "taxi" driver. Most Amishmen work in plants that are nearby their homes. There are some however, who commute more than ten miles to work. In this case a man may spend an hour on his bicycle traveling to work. Typically other men from the same church district will work together in a factory. Small businesses may employ less than fifty Amishmen, while the larger companies may employ several hundred.

Amish workers typically describe the benefits of factory employment in monetary terms—receiving a steady income. In many respects their attitude toward work is typical of other working-class people. Unlike the middle class, their identity is less tied to their work, which they see as simply a means to an end. Work in an alien cultural environment is tolerated for at least eight hours a day, after which they can return to preferred Amish lifestyles. Many Amishmen describe their work in an uncomplimentary fashion. The most frequent complaints reflect the pressures of working in a large organization and away from home.

Most Amish factory workers dislike the strong press of production. A farmer who left factory work said: "When I worked in the factory I was always pushed to work faster and then I would sweat. I didn't like when people came around and just slopped their things down any way. I always found that they didn't care in that rat race. I'd rather work slowly and see that things are done right." Another man with more than twenty years of factory experience complained: "In factory life the more you do, the more they want you to do. If the boss finds out you can do a lot of work, the more you work, the more they want you to do. Bosses are all different but they're all the same. I don't want to brag but everybody seems to want to get more work out of me."

"A farmer can do what he wants, he's his own boss," added another factory worker. The issue is not just simply setting one's own work pace; there is also interpersonal conflict. Working under someone may become a problem, not because of submitting to a superior, but because it creates interpersonal conflicts, which the Amish like to avoid as much as possible.

As one man said, "When pressure builds up I get mad. After that I feel weak all over. I've always had a problem with my temper. I try to keep my cool at all times. But when so many people work together in the same spot, trying to get things done, there are problems. I put paneling on the walls, the electricians come after me and put sockets and wiring in and they try to rush me sometimes or if the guy in front of me doesn't get his work done, then I get mad."

The schedule of factory work is determined by the needs of the organization. The pace of work may slow when business declines, or increase when orders are strong. Many Amish experience some conflict between their work schedule and the rhythm of Amish life. Secular holidays that the Amish do not observe may be observed by the factory. Conversely the Amish prefer to rest and fast on days such as Good Friday and Ascension Day, which the factory may ignore. One factory worker commented: "In the factory you got to be there to punch a clock. Most factory workers can spend a weekend away and they don't have to worry about morning and evening chores, but they do have to be there every day. A farmer can take a day off and go to a wedding or a sale if he wants to." Another man is very grateful because his Mennonite plant manager "knows how the Amish do. He respects our holidays. We can take off for weddings or funerals, but in some factories they give them a hard time for that."

Occasionally Amishmen find themselves in leadership positions in industry that do not conform to the egalitarian patterns of Amish life. Ordained officials are the only individuals with real power in the Amish community. However, this power is rarely utilized unilaterally. The German word for minister is *Diener* or servant. A person in this position is expected to function as a servant. Although ordained officials command respect and certainly influence decision making, they are nevertheless brothers in the faith and are not expected to rule with an iron hand. An Amish bishop usually acts with the counsel of fellow ministers and the congregation. In Amish leadership meetings, specifically the annual *Dienerversammelung* (ministers meeting), leaders try to prohibit hierarchical structures from emerging. In Indiana the chair of these meetings rotates each year, to prevent any individual from becoming too powerful.[7] This flat model of servant-leader does not fit the hierarchical structure of business.

An Amish informant said, "the most difficult thing about my work is getting along with my guys when I have to bawl them out for something. I don't like to do it." Another group leader said, "the factory is a lot of stress . . . to keep things moving, to keep everything so it will fit in place. There is responsibility on any leader but I have to keep the lines supplied and keep people motivated so they will work. If you're in a bad mood, workers will be in a bad mood. There is one fellow who is depressed and doesn't get his work done. I have to help him to get his work done. I could have fired him but I can't do that because the man has a family and responsibilities. With the economy the way it is, it's very difficult to get another job."

The power of a foreman or a manager has no equivalent in Amish society. When a government official went to inspect an Amish school that was under construction, he asked to speak with the foreman and the response was silence. Finally someone spoke up and said, "we don't have one." The formal, rationalized structure of a factory bureaucracy is at variance with the oral, egalitarian patterns in Amish culture.

Another frequent complaint of factory workers is the amount of time they must spend away from home. One Amishman recalled: "When I worked in the factory I used to come home and hold the children on my lap a little. One day I came home and went straight out to the fields. My little girl was sitting there but I just went straight out. The next day I did the same thing and just as I was going out the door she started to cry. I decided right then and there that this was enough, it wasn't worth it." Many other fathers have also lamented that factory workers cannot be home working with their sons.

The Impact of Factory Work

The Amish purchase few of the products manufactured by the industries where they work. The major contribution of these factories to Amish society is the employment that they offer. The one exception is the mobile home. It is not uncommon to find a young Amish couple starting their married life in a mobile home on a plot of land on the edge of an existing farm. Twenty years ago the following advertisement would certainly not have appeared in a local Amish publication. "Custom Amish Modular! No Wiring!" Shipshewana Homes. . . ."[8]

Most Amish factory workers live in the countryside. Although some live on farms and may work the land before and after "working away," many live on small plots with a house and a small horse barn. Country roads in eastern Elkhart and western Lagrange counties are dotted with these "factory homes."

When asked about the changes associated with factory work, Amish

TABLE 10.4.
Defection by Gender and Year

	Women		Men		Total	
Year of birth	%	N	%	N	%	N
1920–1929[a]	49	(67)	51	(70)	100	(137)
1930–1939[a]	38	(88)	62	(146)	100	(234)
1940–1949[a]	40	(97)	60	(148)	100	(245)
1950–1959[b]	30	(75)	70	(171)	100	(246)
1960–1969[b,c]	18	(18)	82	(84)	100	(102)

[a] Data from 1980 *Indiana Amish Directory* (Gingerich 1980).
[b] Data from 1988 *Indiana Amish Directory* (Miller 1988).
[c] This cohort includes many young people in their late teens and early twenties (835 out of 2,818) who are not members. Therefore, only those who had left their parental home were included in the analysis.

persons typically note that factory workers have more available cash. The factory employee's substantial paycheck may be used to purchase better furniture than that found in the typical farm house. Extra money may also enable the family to eat in a restaurant, or take a vacation to another Amish community, or travel across the country. As one Amish farmer who has worked in a factory put it: "When you make more money you spend more. You get more of what you want and not what you need."

The problem of surplus cash is most acute for young men. Prior to the age of twenty-one (when one "comes of age") young persons turn over their paychecks to their parents. They may be given a small portion as spending money but most of the paycheck goes into the family coffer. There is some evidence that this traditional pattern is changing with factory work.

Factory employment is also luring some young Amish males into the non-Amish world. As reported above, the rate of defection is decreasing, however there is some evidence that young men are choosing to leave the faith in larger numbers than young women. As shown in table 10.4, the percentage of males leaving the Amish has steadily increased while the female defection rate has dropped.

Males have always had more opportunities than women to explore the outside world. Young men typically have access to a buggy at the age of sixteen and are permitted more liberties than young women in testing the limits of Amish society.[9] This exploration of the world may include purchasing a car and living for a period of time in an apartment in a town. For many of these young men, employment is off the farm. Factory employment, in particular, provides more cash to make major purchases such as automobiles. An Amish father told the following story about his son's experience experimenting with "the world":

> Henry Glick bought a car and Aaron [the farmer's son] started to run around with him. Aaron later got a job in a factory without my permission. He started keeping $10.00 a week and later kept $20.00 and then still more out of his check. I told him if he wanted to stay at home he must follow the Amish way of giving the parents all of the money that he earns and we would decide how much he is to get back. Well, Aaron decided to leave home and he got an apartment with Henry and three other boys in Middlebury. Aaron bought a car and the rest of the boys shared the two cars. These boys soon discovered that it cost money to keep a car and pay rent. They got into financial trouble and one day Aaron came driving in the lane with a sale sign on his car and asked if he could come home. I said, "yes," if he promised to put the car away. He also wanted to join church. I told him that he would have to talk to the bishop about that.

The transition away from agriculture has triggered a variety of changes related to the shift from a rhythm of life based on the seasons and weather to one that is organized by the clock and the marketplace. The Amish now face some of the challenges that the larger society grappled with as a result of the industrial revolution.

Work has always been an important component of daily life. When asked what he likes to do in his leisure time an Amish farmer may smile and simply respond, "work." The factory worker, on the other hand, has time on his hands in the evening, and weekends as well. He may need to fill this time with a visit to town. As one farmer suggested: "They think they need to be going all the time instead of staying at home. They see all those people (non-Amish) everyday and aren't separate anymore like they were on the farm."

The factory worker with time and money to spare may be tempted to push the limits of his church. He may purchase a power boat equipped with the latest fish-finder radar. He will pull this behind his buggy to a local lake to fish. The church may turn its back on such an anomaly and other members may quickly follow suit. Such experimentation may also spur a series of conversations about how to "hold the line" on appropriate technology.

There is also some evidence that community life is changing as local bonds weaken with men working in factories. In the past, local farmers often joined together to thresh wheat in what was known as a "threshing ring." As the threshing machine moved from farm to farm the "ring" of men worked cooperatively to harvest grain. Industrial employment unravels such bonds of community solidarity. As one Amishwoman laments, "when people earn a lot of money they think that they can take care of themselves and don't really need others. Our community used to have a bond. We helped each other out. [Then] some [began to] work away and didn't think they had to help their farmer neighbor."

Factory work tends to accentuate the individual by isolating his work from community efforts in un-Amish ways. An Amishman who cuts lumber in a large mobile home factory described the conflict that he experiences between his desire to help others in need and his boss' emphasis on production. "People are always coming to me with something they want to cut and it's hard for me to turn them down. My group leader is the type . . . I have a clipboard in front of me with the orders that I have to fill . . . he says you get your work done and don't worry about them. It's hard on me to turn somebody down. I feel I ought to take a minute and help a person out. What's hard on me is to tell a person I ain't got the time. That's the part about the factory I don't like."

Status in Amish society is often linked to three things: family of origin, ordination, and success in farming. It is not coincidental to find all three elements among the most reputable families. These families have kept all of their children in the church, they have a patriarch on the ministerial team, and they operate a successful farming enterprise. Other families may have the reputation of maintaining a tidy home and yard and raising children who behave properly in church. Others manage their family and religious life well, but business failures tarnish their reputation.

Factory work has added a new form of status that is earned because of involvement in "worldly" work. For example, one minister has become very adept at the use of a company computer. Others in the factory and in his home community are quite impressed with his expertise with such a "modern" skill. This new form of prestige adds a new dimension to social stratification in Amish life.

Changes in Amish family life also parallel changes in the dominant industrial culture. Farming is a labor intensive occupation where children are an economic asset. In contrast, factory workers typically live on a plot of land with only a small garden. Other than the routine

TABLE 10.5.
Mean Number of Children by Occupation of Household Head

	Farm	*Factory*	*Shop*	*Carpenter*	*Other*	*Total*
Mean number of children	8.6	6.6	7.2	7.9	6.8	7.4
N =	104	44	27	16	14	205

Source: The 1988 *Indiana Amish Directory* (Miller 1988).
Note: Only households with completed families and with men 45–64 years of age and still employed are included.

chores of caring for a driving horse and a few farm animals there is little work for children. Family size typically shrinks with industrialization and the Amish are no exception. As table 10.5 indicates, the average number of children for factory workers is 6.6 compared to 8.6 for farmers. Foster (1984b:8) reports a similar pattern in Geauga County, Ohio. His data suggest that farm families in that settlement average 9.0 live births per completed family in contrast to 6.4 births for factory employees. The shift to factory employment is apparently weakening the Amish prohibition against family planning.

A significant change for women who are married to factory workers is the responsibility for childcare while their husbands are away from home. Amishwomen are following a pattern that developed much earlier in the larger society—they are becoming housewives rather than partners in the production of the family livelihood. While their husbands are away making a living for the family, they remain at home, often with more than six children. "The farm is where the family is," said one Amishwoman. . . . "I often say that I'm a widow through the day. With only 10 acres it is hard to keep all the boys working."

Social Change and the Survival of Amish Culture

Will these changes ultimately undermine the Amish way of life? The evidence, thus far, is uncertain. The information in table 10.6 shows that children who grow up in the families of factory workers are no more likely to leave the Amish fold than children of farmers or other related occupations. There is no statistically significant difference in the rates of defection between factory versus nonfactory workers.[10]

Although personal observations suggest that factory employment may encourage some young men to leave the Amish, the data in table 10.6 suggest that factory workers are only 5 percent less successful than farmers in keeping their children in the faith.

The primary identity of the factory worker continues to be that of an Amishman. His occupational role is secondary. His work is a means, a very important one, to an end, i.e., a paycheck. For some young factory workers it is possible to remain Amish precisely because they do not have to make the sacrifices required of a farmer. As one informant said, "if they all had to farm with horses there would be far fewer Amishmen today."

Although it is clear that factory work has brought changes in Amish society, such as the decline in family size noted above, the Amish have survived the shift by adapting in ways that have helped to preserve their culture. The key to maintaining Amish culture is the creation of social structures that encourage social interaction with other Amish people. Such networks prevent the Amish person from being stranded in a non-Amish environment for an extended period of time. Despite their involvement in factory employment, Amish friendship networks on the job and in the community consist primarily of other Amish people. These networks of ethnicity reinforce and help to preserve Amish culture.

It is rare for an Amish person to be the only representative of his faith in a factory. In my study of Amish factory workers about forty-seven other Amishmen on the average worked in each respondent's factory (Meyers 1983). When I asked Amish factory workers about their primary language at work, 40 percent indicated that they spoke Pennsylvania German. Factory workers frequently reported that they regularly eat lunch with, ride to work with, or talk at breaks with

TABLE 10.6.
Defection by Father's Occupation for Children under 40 Who Have Left Home

Child's affiliation	*Farm*		*Factory*		*Shop*		*Carpenter*		*Other*	
	%	N	%	N	%	N	%	N	%	N
Amish	86	(633)	81	(96)	82	(133)	80	(84)	86	(48)
Non-Amish	14	(101)	19	(23)	18	(29)	20	(21)	14	(8)
Totals	100	(734)	100	(119)	100	(162)	100	(105)	100	(56)

Source: The 1980 *Indiana Amish Directory* (Gingerich 1980) and a random sample of 33 districts (approximately one-half of the settlement) in the 1988 *Indiana Amish Directory* (Miller 1988).

at least two or three other Amish friends. As one informant said, "a couple of us guys get together to eat lunch. Some of them have been friends of mine for a long time. We often talk about keeping the right attitude."

The evidence so far suggests that the so-called "lunch pail threat" (Kraybill 1989:192) does not mean the demise of the Amish community in this settlement. It does however, certainly mean that changes will continue to occur in this community.

Conclusion

Rapid population growth and a scarcity of agricultural land have pushed many Amish in northern Indiana into nonfarm occupations. Although the movement into industry began in the context of World War II, it was in the late 1960s and early 1970s that large numbers of Amishmen began working in recreational vehicle and mobile home industries in Elkhart and Lagrange counties.

Many scholars and even Amish people themselves have suggested that farming is the only occupation that is suitable to undergird Amish culture. However, beneath the surface of Amish society alternate forms of livelihood are increasingly being accepted. Alternative modes of earning a living may even indirectly benefit the Amish by providing a means to earn a living during the day, which in turn makes it easier to be Amish in evenings and on weekends.

Most Amish factory workers view their work as simply a way of earning a living. For most of them the factory culture is an alien environment that they tolerate but do not enjoy. In the factory they may encounter a pace of life and an organizational culture that clashes with the values of their community. There are conflicts between the holidays of their community and the holidays of the dominant culture. They also must come to terms with the fact that their work separates them from their families for significant amounts of time. The families of factory workers are smaller than those of farmers. Mothers must also find ways to occupy their children when their husbands are working away. Factory workers typically earn more than farmers. With extra cash they are able to purchase more things for their homes, to take longer vacations, and to purchase items that may exceed the limits of the church's *Ordnung*.

Factory employment has brought changes to Amish society in northern Indiana. But although the Amish in the Elkhart-Lagrange settlement are changing, there is little evidence of their demise. Fewer people are leaving the church today than earlier in the century. Furthermore, when children of factory workers are compared with children of farmers there is little difference in rates of defection. The Amish will likely survive this major change in their way of life by successfully adapting and finding new ways to preserve their identity as a people.

Part IV

Theoretical Perspectives

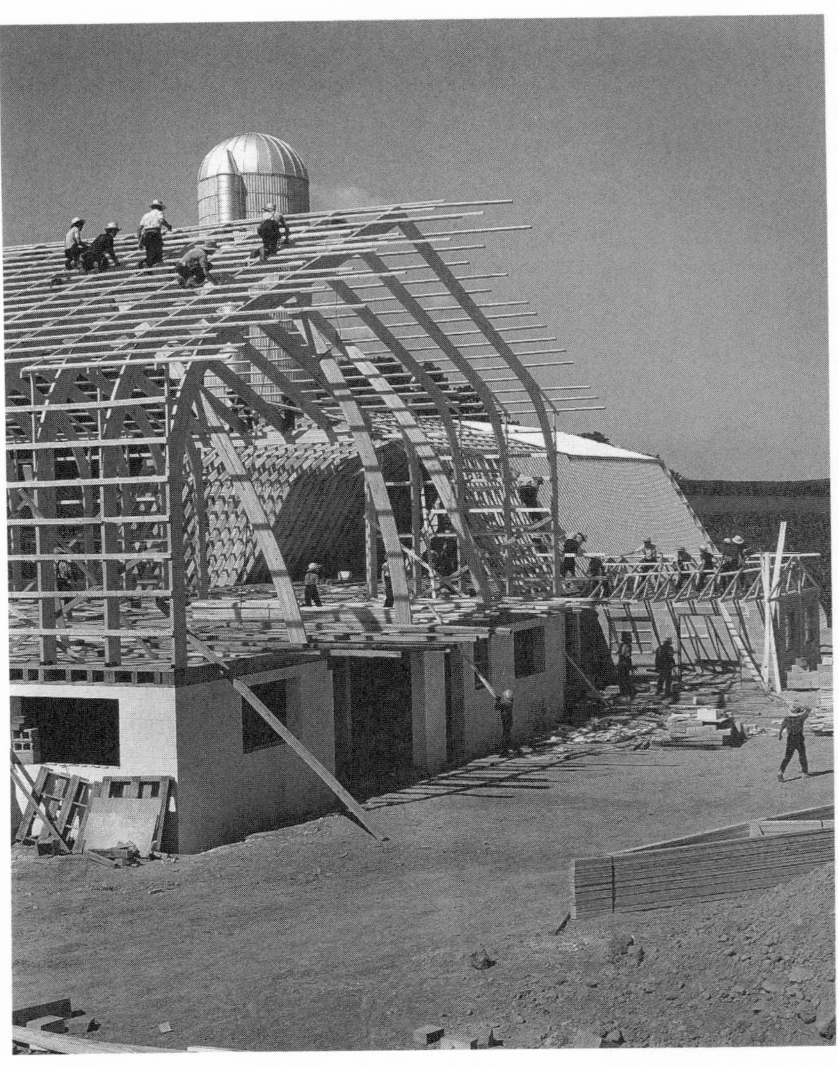

Prefabricated trusses used in a traditional barn raising symbolize the blend of modern and folk societies in Amish life. (Photograph by Dennis Hughes).

11

Modernity, the Folk Society, and the Old Order Amish

MARC A. OLSHAN

For many years the Amish have been portrayed as a small folk society that follows traditional patterns of social life without making deliberate choices about their future. In this seminal chapter, Marc A. Olshan overturns such assumptions and argues that the Amish exhibit modern ways to the extent that they self-consciously make choices and attempt to control their own destiny. Noting a variety of strategic decisions, Olshan contends that the Amish can serve as a model for other groups who want to selectively adapt to the forces of modernity.[1]

Introduction

Offering the Old Order Amish as one example of the unreflective folk society has itself become something of an unthinking ritual—a ritual performed by social scientists. The Amish have been characterized as a "folk society" (Kephart and Zellner 1991:39), a "simple folk society" (Cross 1976:18), and an "economically self-sufficient folk society" (Hoover and Hoover 1979:100). Hostetler (1993:9) feels that the folk society, as conceptualized by Robert Redfield, "lends itself well to understanding the tradition-directed character of Amish society." Such characterizations are ritualistic to the extent that they reflect an uncritical acceptance of a reified conceptual schema that inhibits rather than encourages understanding.

An unreflective, unself-conscious folk character is also implied by those who invoke intuition or instinct as an explanation for Amish behavior. With regard to educational institutions, Albert Keim (1975:2) avers that "the Amish, almost instinctively, sense the potential harm to their way of life in modern American schooling." Likewise, Hostetler (1993:394–95) claims that in making occupational choices the Amish "know intuitively that if they lose their agricultural base, they will lose to a large extent the qualities that go into the making of an Amish community." He further claims that "the Amish are intuitively aware of the danger of large-scale enterprises." The same depiction of a passive or intuitive level of decision making is offered by another observer of the Amish, John Ruth: "They have a little seismograph inside them; they know when innovation will disrupt community" (Nagel 1978). Presumably intuition and instinct are consistent with the putative traditional or folk character of the Amish. As explanations of behavior, however, they are untenable.[2]

I will argue here that the gap between the folk society and "intuitive" behavior on the one hand and contemporary Amish society on the other is far greater than can be legitimately ascribed to the inevitable, and therefore admissible, differences that exist between any ideal type and its closest empirical expression. Hostetler's (1993:23) observation that the model of the folk society (or any of the other models he outlines) should serve as a benchmark reflects an awareness that no abstract concept (such as the ideal type folk society) is found perfectly mirrored in reality. After a point, however, the invocation of an ideal type is misleading even when offered as a heuristic device or as a rough approximation of what we might expect to find empirically. That point is reached when elements that are antithetical to the essential character of the ideal type must be ignored or glossed over.

One can agree with Redfield's (1960:146) statement that "in every isolated little community there is civilization; in every city there is the folk society" without conceding that it is useful to characterize cities as exemplars of the folk society. In short, I am arguing not only that the Amish are less folklike than they have been represented to be. I am suggesting that they have been fundamentally misrepresented. Further, this misrepresentation should not be attributed to putative flaws in Redfield's conception of what constitutes a folk society, but rather to the claim that Redfield's ideal type represents a useful conceptual tool for understanding the Amish.

Redfield's (1947:295–305) ideal type folk society is small, having no more people in it than can come to know each other well. It is isolated, its population having no communication with outsiders and never leaving the small territory they occupy. No books, no historical sense, and no theology exist in the folk society. The folk society is "economically independent of all others." In the folk society, economic behavior characteristic of the market is absent. No money is used and "there is no place for the motive of commercial gain." Most important for the argument to be presented here, behavior in the folk society is "traditional, spontaneous, and uncritical."

The discrepancies that exist between the reality of Amish life and the ideal typical modern society are less salient than those that exist between Amish society and the ideal typical folk society. Nor is this evaluation based only on the truism that the ideal typical folk society is in a null set. It is equally true that the ideal typical modern society, or any ideal type, is in a null set as well. In any case there is no justification for a continued association of Amish society with the concept of the folk society. Generating a more meaningful characterization of the Amish will require going beyond the essentially physical, and to some extent superficial, criteria emphasized by Hostetler and others and acknowledging the dimension of self-consciousness that permeates Amish society.

The Definition of Modernity

Hostetler (1993:364), and by implication most others who have analyzed Amish society, defines modernization as "the acceptance of technology and material culture." Such a narrow, one-dimensional criterion totally ignores the subjective orientation of a group. It fails to take into consideration their motivations, the extent of their familiarity with contemporary technology, or their degree of philosophical or theological sophistication. A definition of modernity tied to the level of technology "accepted" or utilized will not distinguish the Amish from groups utilizing the same level of technology but who (unlike the Amish) are totally unaware of the existence of any technology other than what they already possess. That such disparate groups might be characterized as equally modern clearly reveals the weakness of the definition.

The following alternative definition of modernity, offered by Berger (1974), not only differentiates between the two types of groups noted above but also provides the conceptual leverage for understanding the Amish in a far more realistic manner. For Berger, modernity exists to the extent that fatalism is rejected and any course of events is perceived as the outcome of a series of conscious choices. For modern beings, life is pervaded by alternatives. "Modernity means (in intention if not in fact) that men take control over the world and over themselves. *What previously was experienced as fate now becomes an arena of choices.*"[3]

Modernity, as here defined, thus is not associated with particular technologies, types of social organization, or beliefs and values. The essence of modernity is the perception of choice: "Nothing can be more modern than the idea that man has a choice between different paths of social development. One of the most pervasive characteristics of traditional societies is the notion that there is no choice, that the structures of the given society are inevitable, rooted in human nature, or indeed in the very constitution of the cosmos" (Berger et al. 1973:177).

Even for Redfield (1953:113) the contrast between the folk society and modern civilization rested on the difference between the slow, unpremeditated growth of culture in the former and the attempts of man "to take control of this process and to direct it where he wills" in the latter. Decisions in primitive societies are not the product of much reflective thought. "People do the kind of things they do, not because somebody just thought up that kind of thing, or because anybody ordered them to do so, but because it seems to the people to flow from the very necessity of existence that they do that kind of thing" (Redfield 1953:14).

The folk society is transformed into civilization "through the appearance and development of the idea of reform, of alteration of human existence, including the alteration of man himself, by deliberate intention and design" (Redfield 1953:113). It was precisely the idea of reform that gave birth to the Swiss Brethren in 1525. This group, from which the Amish split in 1693, represented one of the most radical expressions of the Reformation. The attempts of Jacob Ammann, spiritual leader of the group that eventually came to be known as the Amish, to further purify the practices and membership of the Swiss Brethren exemplify yet another manifestation of the reform impulse.

This reformistic, self-conscious, reflective stance, presupposing the existence of alternative realities, is one distinguishing characteristic of the Amish and of modern humanity in general. This conception of modernity does not confuse a physical phenomenon (the creation of particular configurations of material wealth) with what is actually a social-psychological orientation. Modernity is collective self-awareness, not the capability to produce I-beams and isotopes. The fact that technological sophistication is one possible correlate of modernity, or even that it always has been in the past, does not justify equating the two. Technology may be self-consciously eschewed as well as embraced.

The Amish as a Modern People

To the extent that the Amish self-consciously manipulate their path of social development, selectively rejecting some technology and forms of social organization and accepting others, they manifest what Berger et al. (1973) identified as the essence of modernity. An appreciation of this phenomenon is the basis for Huntington's (1957:144) characterization of the Amish as a "contrived" or "consciously maintained folk society." Such a designation reflects, on the one hand, the voluntary nature of the group, the rationalized, self-imposed nature of their isolation, and their self-conscious awareness of their culture, and on the other hand, the traditional social institutions and cultural trappings characteristic of a folk society (Huntington 1957:107, 1040). "The very essence of the two [that is, self-consciousness and the folk society] are different although the final products have many characteristics in common" (Huntington 1957:1044). Likewise, Gutkind (1952:28) questioned the utility of the folk society characterization on the grounds that "The Amish people have accepted the notion of social change, the fact that culture is dynamic rather than static. A folk culture has not."

The comments of Gutkind and Huntington are unusual among observers of the Amish. Huntington's thesis concerning the voluntary, self-conscious nature of Amish society seems especially fertile. Unfortunately, she does not develop this line of reasoning beyond what is noted above. In the following material I will describe several tangible expressions of self-consciousness, including illustrations from two sectors of Amish society, agriculture and education, where intuition has been invoked as an explanatory variable.

The Amish attitude toward innovation is not adequately summarized by the epigram that they themselves sometimes employ: "The old is the best, and the new is of the devil" (Hostetler 1993:11). The selective rejection of certain technologies and the arguments used (within the Amish community) for retention of others reflect a sociological and technological sophistication that goes well beyond a blind and wholesale adherence to traditional practices. The Amish actually exhibit a keen sensitivity to the varying ramifications associated with the acceptance of different types of innovations. Such a high degree of awareness, of sensitivity to the potential impact of technological change on culture, cannot be reconciled with the passive, nonintrospective, unself-conscious character of a folk society.

A prime instance of this selectivity born of awareness is the way in which tractors have been rejected while new generations of agricultural implements have been employed by Amish farmers, sometimes even before their acceptance by non-Amish neighbors. For example, in the Plain City, Ohio, settlement, where tractors had been forbidden (except for belt work) in 1930, the Amish introduced mechanical hay loaders and manure spreaders before their use by non-Amish farmers in the area (Yutzy 1961:14). A similar situation was reported in *The Budget* in 1978 in Lawrence County, Pennsylvania, where, according to an Amishman who had farmed there, the Amish "led the way to modernization with such advanced machinery as grain binders, manure spreaders, and side delivery rakes." Bachman (1961:81) also observed that, "Farm machinery on an Amish farm is modern. That the forefathers used less-complicated implements, and few labor-saving machines does not appear to influence them to any extent in this matter. The most modern cultivators, hay-making equipment, self-binders, spraying equipment, etc., are all in common use among them. . . . The only restriction, in the matter of farm machinery, is in the use of the tractor."

The explanation of why modern farm implements may be used while the use of tractors in the field is forbidden constitutes clear evidence of the self-conscious quality of Amish decision making. The Amish recognized the potentially negative impact of tractors, in several distinct areas, on the culture they wished to maintain. That recognition is reflected in the arguments that were, and are, used within Amish communities. One Amishman, now living in Canada, related that as a boy in Reno County, Kansas, he had listened to the debates that took place in the 1930s over whether or not tractors would be used. The pressure to allow tractors was particularly severe in Kansas because there the plowing for winter wheat had to be done during the hottest part of the summer. It proved to be too much for the horses. Eventually many Amish did purchase tractors and today would not be considered Old Order. Of interest here, however, is the rationale for not allowing tractors that was offered by those who maintained their Old Order affiliation. The former Reno County resident summarized the argument as the realization that "tractors would lead into the world." In other words, the introduction of tractors would make it unlikely that the Amish would be able to successfully comply with the biblical injunction to "be not conformed to this world."

Specifically, one argument against tractors offered by two Reno County bishops was that "they would lead to bigger farms necessitating the use of trucks" (Wagler 1968:15). The causal relationship between using tractors in the fields and automobiles or trucks on the road has been a clear source of opposition to tractors. "With tractors doing the work there would be less need for horses; and the danger would be great, they feel, that the horse would be replaced by the automobile also in traveling on the road: and opposition to the use of the automobile is quite strong" (Bachman 1961:82).

In Kansas it wasn't long before the tractors themselves were used for road transportation. They were hitched to two-wheeled trailers, some of which were constructed especially to transport family members. Gradually the tractor and trailer replaced the horse and buggy as the common means of weekday transportation (Wagler 1968:18). From the perspective of the Old Order, "tractors have a tendency to be the forerunners of cars. If we are persuaded that we do not want the cars, then we should abstain from any thing which has a tendency to break down the barrier against their entrance and acceptance in the church" ("Are All Things" n.d.: 20).

The opposition to motorized transportation, and cars in particular, is in turn based on a well-articulated series of arguments that can only be characterized as extremely rational, given the objective of maintaining Amish society separate from the world. In a pamphlet printed by Pathway Publishers (operated by Old Order Amish), eight reasons are listed that demonstrate the negative influence of automobile ownership on the Amish way of life:

1. It breaks down non-conformity.
2. It is a major contributing factor to the moral decay of the nation.
3. The modern automobile is built for luxury.
4. They are expensive.
5. They are dangerous.
6. It puts the church members further apart (. . . members have a tendency to buy farms or houses many miles out of the community).
7. It has a tendency to bring in radios.
8. It brings in insurance. ("Are All Things" n.d.:8–10)

Each of these reasons is logically explained, and possible counterarguments are answered. One does not have to agree with the line of reasoning offered or with the ultimate objectives sought to acknowledge that there is more to Amish resistance to automobiles (and tractors) than the simple assertion that they are "of the devil."

Concerning the continued use of horses, the Amish are also able to muster a whole series of arguments based on positive advantages they hold over tractors. These include lower operation and depreciation expenses (horses may even appreciate in value if handled and fed right), an absence of soil compaction problems (Getz 1946:76), soil improvement through manure production (Ortmayer 1947:43), the ability of horses to create their own replacements, and the ability of horses to work earlier in the spring, in wet fields, than tractors.[4] There is, in addition, a general independence associated with horse-powered agriculture that is not lost on the Amish; a relative freedom from dependency on oil supplies, spare parts, and mechanics.

A second manifestation of self-consciousness is the selective adaptation of particular forms of social organization. The most salient of these organizational innovations is the parochial school. For a period of over two centuries there were no Amish-run schools. The "traditional" mode of education was the public school system. The first Amish-operated elementary school did not open until 1925. That first school, and the over eight hundred others now in existence ("School Directory" 1993), represent an informed and astute response to changes in the public educational sector.

Specifically, the Amish perceived the process of school consolidation as a threat to their continued existence. The replacement of small neighborhood schools by central school systems meant that parents had significantly less to say about who would do the teaching and what would be taught. The larger student population was much less homogeneous than before, and the buildings boasted electricity, indoor plumbing, and other innovations that were not appreciated by the Amish. Consolidation also meant that children were likely to ride school busses as part of their daily routine, another unwelcome development.

In describing the Amish response, Hostetler and Huntington (1971:35) conclude "the Amish sensed intuitively what scientists know empirically, that when a secular system of education displaces the indigenous method of training, the basis for a traditional way of life is swept away." The Amish response was not based on some undefined intuitive factor, however, but rather on a clear-sighted comprehension of the consequences of consolidation. The well-reasoned arguments against public education offered by Amish author Joseph Stoll

(1965:23), for example, cannot meaningfully be characterized as either instinctive or intuitive:

> How can we parents expect our children to grow up untainted by the world, if we voluntarily send them into a worldly environment, where they associate with worldly companions, and are taught by men and women not of our faith six hours a day, five days a week, for the greater part of the year?
>
> . . . There is something about human nature that wants to be one with the crowd, that hates to be different. To expect our children to wear different clothes, have different haircuts, and different interests than the majority do, and to stand firm in their differences, is expecting much, perhaps too much. (Stoll 1965:23,53)

The articulate fashion in which Stoll argues against a public school education for Amish children may be unusual, but, as Stoll (1965:17) points out, the arguments themselves have been invoked by Amish communities at least since the end of the nineteenth century. With the extension of school consolidation, Amish parents voiced the same concerns in one community after another. One particularly well-documented confrontation took place in 1937 in East Lampeter Township of Lancaster County, where the Amish resisted sending their children to a newly constructed central school on the grounds that such a school would lead the next generation into worldly ways.[5] In East Lampeter and in the many other locations where consolidated schools were rejected, the Amish were guided by something other than a passive adherence to old institutions.[6] The new Amish-run parochial schools were a rational and innovative response to a threat that was perceived clearly and realistically. The one-room schoolhouse is not a manifestation of a primitive level of social organization. Instead, its existence is an indication of the sophistication of a people who understand the need for controlling the socialization of their children and who have been able to successfully implement the mechanism by which the control is achieved.

Other organizational innovations include the Old Order Amish Steering Committee and the various Amish Aid societies. The Steering Committee was formed in 1966 in response to problems with the system of alternative service set up by the federal government for conscientious objectors. Many Amish youth had been assigned to work in hospitals where a standard eight-hour shift left them with more free time than they were accustomed to:

> . . . many boys go with good intentions but by having so much idle time, become involved with amusements, with the nurses or in other ways are led astray to the extent that when they could return home and become church members there are so many that no longer prefer to. . . . It was agreed that it would be good to appoint one district man for each Amish community and to form a committee to work between the Old Order Amish and Washington, D.C., to see what could be done. (Steering Committee 1972:1)

The Amish recognized that the formation of a national committee was necessary to deal effectively with particular federal agencies. The concept of such a centralized, nationwide council working beyond the boundaries of individual communities is totally alien to the Old Order philosophy. Yet in this one area the Amish leadership evaluated the threat as significant enough to justify a departure from standard patterns of interaction with the non-Amish world. The creation of a specialized national steering committee, limited in its scope and authority, to deal with a specific set of problems is not the response of a traditional people. Nor is it the response of a people that is being pushed unaware, headlong down the path of acculturation. Whatever innovations are accepted by the Amish, their justification and intended impact are to enhance the survival of the same values and style of life that have characterized the Amish for over three hundred years.

Organizational innovation to enhance survival (in this case, financial survival) is similarly evidenced in the creation of three types of Amish Aid societies. These mutual aid societies take the place of insurance companies, which are proscribed. The first Amish risk-sharing plans, generally called "Amish Aid," were founded in the 1870s. Coverage was limited to loss from fire and storm. As new financial risks developed, the Amish responded by creating new organizations. For example, the growing possibility of liability suits, resulting primarily from buggy-automobile accidents, led to the founding of the first "Old Order Amish Liability Aid" plan in 1965. Likewise, with the dramatic rise of hospital costs in the 1960s, "Hospital Aid" programs were established.[7]

In the type of technology they utilize and in the organizational innovations they have selectively introduced, the Amish have demonstrated a remarkable sensitivity to and control over the process of change. Attempts to characterize societies as modern or traditional must go beyond an evaluation of the cultural content or external characteristics of those societies. The use of horses, kerosene lamps, and one-room schoolhouses cannot be explained as a repudiation of modernity. Nor does the use of unsophisticated technology indicate an absence of self-consciousness or an uncritical approach to existing social institutions. In fact, in the context of the contemporary United States, its use represents the very essence of self-conscious choice.

Discussion

If the Amish can no longer be dismissed as an anachronism, the living representation of an earlier cultural stage, then they arguably become a potential model for other contemporary groups. It is not necessary to repudiate reason or modernity to advocate a way of life that neither passively clings to tradition nor is antithetical to the essence of modernity as defined here.

Many of those who have suggested that aspects of Amish life might well be emulated in the context of a non-Amish, highly developed society have done so with an apparent sense of irony. During World War II, shortages of consumer goods turned the Amish into "models for the nation's consumers. Their self-denial and avoidance of 'luxury goods' fits in the new national pattern amazingly well."[8] Energy shortages in 1973 and 1979 again generated photographs of Amish buggies plodding past long gas lines as well as articles touting the advantages of a society in which the demand for energy is minimal.[9] During the last energy crisis the Amish were described as "a society that knows no energy crisis because it has so little need for energy, so little desire for what most of us regard as necessities, and because it is a conserving—not a consuming—community. People often speak nowadays of how we will live in the post-industrial age, and we realized that the Amish have been there all along. We wanted to say, 'We have seen the past, and it works' " (Ketchum 1979:19).

In a similar vein, Stoltzfus (1973:205) concluded that "the Amish experience is a living, more-than-hypothetical alternative to the pattern of conventional gratifications. Folk cultures of other traditions may also be helpful to the search for answers in this area." But the continued identification of the Amish as a people of the past and their continued characterization as a folk society actually represent stumbling blocks to taking their example seriously.

One cannot choose to emulate a society in which there is no choice; that is, a society in which all institutions are passively and uncritically accepted as givens. To truly be a member of such a traditional society would preclude the possibility of selecting options, of making choices. For modern individuals to be at home in an uncritical, traditional social context would require nothing less than the equivalent of a cultural lobotomy. Such a radical reorientation is not required in the case of the Amish, once their self-conscious, selective, and, in short, modern nature is understood.

The ultimate value or desirability of the Amish way of life is not at issue here. That evaluation will differ according to one's ethical or ideological predilections. However, the basis for a realistic evaluation of the Amish and of their potential relevance does depend on the recognition that they are guided by a self-conscious awareness of who they are and where they want to go rather than by intuition or an unthinking traditionalism.

Old Order Amish Steering Committee

CHAIRMAN - *Voice of the Old Order Amish* - **NATIONAL**

Gordonville, Penna. 17529

RECOMMENDATION SCHEDULE SHEET

TO WHOM IT MAY CONCERN: – NOTICE––This Schedule Is Used NATIONAL

FOR Old Order Amish or Mennonite SELF PAY Hospital Patients who for religious reasons are opposed to accepting Public Hospital Insurance; Medicare; Medicate or other Public assistance and where it would be a problem for applicant to pay entire statement on his or her own, without charitable assistance. Further in appreciation for accepting enclosed check as settlement in full, applicant will commit himself to the fact that no legal action will be taken against the Hospital or Doctors in this case, now or ever, nor will the itemized statement be send off to be analyst.

APPLICANT: Bill should be paid in full in sixty (60) and in no instance more then ninety (90) days if the following allowance is to be taken. Your check should be clearly marked, "ACCOUNT SETTLED IN FULL".

COMBINED Hospital Statement of $1,000.00 or less should be paid in full unless Hospital voluntarily suggests that a allowance may be taken.

COMBINED Hospital Statement of $1,000.00 to $2,000.00 a 10% allowance would be suggested by your Committee as a charitable contribution by the Hospital or Doctor.

COMBINED Hospital Statement of $2,000.00 to $20,000.00 a 15% allowance would be suggested.

COMBINED Hospital Statement of $20,000.00 to $50,000.00 a 20% allowance would be suggested.

COMBINED Hospital Statement of $50,000.00 or over a 25 or 30% allowance would be suggested, depending on size and nature of the statement and Hospital stay.

ABOVE Schedule is also suggested for Doctors issuing their seperate statements with the exception of starting at $600.00 instead of $1,000.00.

REASON FOR ABOVE SUGGESTIONS

HOSPITAL Statements are extremely high for an individual to pay.(Let us ask ourselves, "Would we be able to meet this statement without charitable assistance"?

IN Many cases the home community, the home church or neighboring churches assist."Under these circumstances, would the Hospital not also wish to assist"?

SHOULD The patient not be able to pay or to receive assistance, would the Hospital receive 100% payment from Insurance, the State or elsewhere?

SHOULD The patient not be able to pay or receive assistance, Would it not be more profitable and respectful for all concerned, to allow a charitable reduction then to stretch out the statement for years on small affordable monthly payments?

WE As a conscientious, religious people, desire to pay our honest statements but with the extremely high Hospital and Doctor bills of which many of the charges we do not understand or fully agree with, we feel it more proper to deduct a reasonable amount and pay the balance, then to make a issue of not being able to pay or not satisfied with the bill.

WE Trust that you as a Hospital staff or Doctor will understand and agree, however if you cannot accept the enclosed check as settlement IN FULL, please return the check so that a satisfactory salution may be found with the people assisting as well as the Hospital. If the check is NOT returned the statement will be considered settled in full.THANK YOU.

Very truly yours, D. S. Kinsinger
Old Order Amish Steering Committee, NATIONAL

______________________ Signature of Bishop   ______________________ Signature of Applicant

P. S. NOTICE TO APPLICANT; Should the check be returned it is suggested by your committee that if further Hospital care is needed, you or your family favor or patronize a Hospital or Dr. that will appreciate and assist above arrangement with a charitable contribution.

Revised October 1, 1986
All Previous Printings Obsolete

A medical discount form prepared by the Old Order Amish Steering Committee asks hospitals to provide discounts ranging from ten to thirty percent for Amish patients who pay their bills promptly. Most Amish object to receiving medicare or medicaid benefits for religious reasons.

12

Homespun Bureaucracy: A Case Study in Organizational Evolution

MARC A. OLSHAN

The conspicuous absence of formal organizations signals one of the remarkable ways in which the Amish have remained a separate people. Missing from their society are the centralized structures, agencies, professional bureaucrats, and policy manuals which typify many religious communities. The Amish struggle with modernity has, however, produced an embryonic form of what Marc A. Olshan calls a homespun bureaucracy. In this chapter he suggests that the Amish paradoxically were forced by the growing encroachment of the state to develop their own bureaucratic forms—the Old Order Amish Steering Committee—in order to remain a separate people.[1]

The Pressure to Organize

The genesis of an organization creates special opportunities for the social scientist, particularly when the organization in question emerges de novo from a relatively undifferentiated congeries of rural communities. Such milieus are rapidly disappearing into the realm of history. If the bureaucratization of the world is not complete, it has at least left few unrationalized enclaves.

Consequently, the appearance in 1966 of an embryonic bureaucracy known as the Old Order Amish Steering Committee merits examination. It provides an unusual opportunity to identify, in a contemporary setting, the environmental factors militating for initial adoption of formal organizational structure. A study of the evolution of the Steering Committee also confirms the pervasive character of the legal infrastructure and its decisive role both in initiating bureaucratization and in shaping the structure and process of existing organizations.

Laws, regulatory groups, and political systems were identified as discrete elements of organizational environments even by early proponents of what Aldrich and Marsden (1988:375) refer to as environmental contingency theory.[2] But it was another ten years before organizational theorists began a systematic explication of the impact of these elements. More recently the legal environment has been presented as being of paramount importance in relation to other environmental sectors: "Indeed, the state must be the *major* force affecting organizational formation in the twentieth century."[3] Perrow (1986:190) has come to see that "the power of the state to regulate and disburse entitlements is probably the single most important means of controlling an environment."

Study of the Steering Committee helps reveal one facet of the legal environment's primacy that has not been adequately appreciated. Its potency—what might plausibly be called its coerciveness—does not derive solely from its being backed by the power of the state. Nor does it depend on the substantive character of specific laws, e.g., that they may be unfair, oppressive, and intrusive. It derives rather from the pervasiveness of the legal infrastructure. Laws may be coercive in that they force collectivities that are subject to them to adapt bureaucratic structures if they are to survive, a consequence that is as unintentional as it is universal.

The evolution of the Steering Committee provides a telling confirmation of this pressure to bureaucratize not only because of its recency (and hence its accessibility to research) but also because Amish communities share a normative stance distinctly antithetical to organization.[4]

Amish Antipathy to Organization

The Old Order Amish stand out on the American cultural landscape like human outcroppings of especially unyielding material. One highly significant but seldom emphasized expression of their uniqueness is their rejection of formal organization. In a world where formal organizations have become necessarily ubiquitous, the Amish have been perhaps most unique in their ability to survive well into the twentieth century without employing the degree of formal organization routinely assumed to be a prerequisite for survival.[5] As with their rejection of certain types of technology, their rejection of formal organization was based on purposeful adherence to a set of ultimate values (see chapter 11). In this respect the Amish most closely approximate Weber's *wertrational* (value-rational) social action, a rational orientation to absolute values (Weber 1968).

Certainly the phrase "formal organization" is not part of Amish demonology, nor is it a term with which many Amish would be familiar. However, a brief inspection of some of the values fundamental to Amish culture reveals them to be profoundly antithetical to the establishment of formal organization. This normative stance derives from valuing:

1. an opposition to any ecclesiastical hierarchy beyond the local community,
2. a severing of all ties between the political and religious realms,
3. an untrained and unpaid clergy selected from within the community,
4. a separation from worldly (i.e., non-Amish) institutions to the extent possible, and
5. a glorification of simplicity.[6]

The value of simplicity is relevant to organizational structure because it has been translated into the use of technologies that do not require a high level of social differentiation. Adherence to all of these values explains much of the schismatic character of Amish history. More to the point for the present discussion, it explains their limited formal intercommunity and intercongregational association. To better understand the innovative character of the Steering Committee we need to look briefly at the context from which it emerged.

In the absence of any formal ecclesiastical hierarchy beyond the local community, possibilities for decision making outside of the church district (i.e., the congregation) are limited. Ministers and bishops of congregations connected by common church rules do meet on occasion to discuss appropriate positions toward new technologies, styles of dress, and institutions. One of the earliest recorded Amish conferences took place in Pennsylvania in 1809. The various articles of the resulting "discipline" adopted included, for example, an agreement that church members of the districts represented be prohibited from participating in jury service (Bender 1934).

A conference in 1865 addressed the draft issue, specifically the practice of exempting those who paid a commutation fee or provided a substitute (Bender 1946:223). Today the large Amish settlements in Lagrange County, Indiana, and Lancaster County, Pennsylvania, continue to hold annual and semiannual gatherings, respectively, of church officials. In other settlements such gatherings are held only when a problem arises that cannot be solved within the church district.[7]

Despite these occasional semiformal meetings, it would be injudicious to speak of the Amish as a single denomination. The Amish population is divided into numerous fellowships, all considered Old Order but differing in dress, level of technology considered appropriate, and other such issues. Members of a particular church district normally only will attend services in other districts if those districts are in fellowship with their own. The church district is the largest officially recognized administrative unit. The approximately nine hundred districts in the United States, and another seventeen in Canada (Raber 1993), contain about thirty to forty families each.

The highest religious official is the bishop, whose formal authority extends only to the families in his own district. This arrangement corresponds closely to the concept of congregational polity elaborated by Wood (1970). Informally, more senior bishops command greater respect at conferences. Likewise, the members of a church district, although totally autonomous in theory, will not lightly disregard the consensus of believers in other districts with which they are in fellowship. For example, a district's church discipline is determined nominally by its members alone, but in practice they will consider the disciplines of other districts in their fellowship.

As a result of this limited and uneven degree of formal coupling between districts, the establishment of a formally organized entity, speaking for all Amish communities in the United States, represents an unprecedented stratagem in Amish history.

Origins of the Steering Committee

The Amish, despite the bucolic surroundings with which they are usually associated, exist in an environment dominated by large-scale organizations. Separation from the world is necessarily imperfect. They rely on non-Amish banks, medical facilities, and corporations of all kinds for goods and services as well as for employment.[8] They pay income and property taxes, are subject to Department of Agriculture regulations, and must register with the Selective Service.

In 1966 an Amishman who had worked with Amish conscientious objectors (COs) was contacted by an official of the National Service Board for Religious Objectors, a private organization that counsels and aids COs. The official advised of possible changes in the draft laws and asked for a meeting with some Amish leaders. In the absence of any provision for selecting individuals for other than religious office, a group of bishops, many of whom had become involved with draft problems, called a meeting in Allen County, Indiana. Church leaders and laymen from at least four states attended, filling one of the local schoolhouses. At that time Amish draftees were almost routinely given CO status. Many of these young men would be assigned to two years of alternative service in urban hospitals, which was highly unsatisfactory to the Amish leadership: "Many boys go with good intentions but by having so much idle time, become involved with amusements, with the nurses or in other ways are led astray to the extent that when they could return home and become church members there are so many that no longer prefer to, or are in a position where they find they can hardly do so, with maybe a nurse of a different faith for a wife or similar circumstances" (Steering Committee 1972:1).

In fact, only about half of those assigned to hospital work returned to become members of Amish communities. Of those who did return, many did not remain Amish (Kinsinger 1988). The devastating consequences of this arrangement and the possibility of changes in the law that might cause the Amish to "lose what we already have" prompted an agreement to form "a committee to represent the Old Order Amish from all states as a group to Washington in matters that concern or hinder our Old Order Amish way of life" (Steering Committee 1972:4).

The month following the Indiana meeting a smaller group, almost equally divided between church leaders and lay members, met in Washington with the director of the National Service Board. At their hotel that evening the bishops caucused separately and emerged to announce that they had "now decided on a three man committee to represent the Amish for all States" (Kinsinger 1988:130). The three, all laymen, were designated as chairman, secretary, and treasurer of the newly named Old Order Amish Steering Committee. The committee was quickly endorsed at a meeting held in Holmes County, Ohio, by over one hundred representatives of Amish settlements in nine states.

In February 1967 the Steering Committee met with General Lewis B. Hershey, director of the Selective Service. For the first time Amish representatives spoke on behalf of virtually all Amish in the United States. They explained Amish objections to hospital work as alternative service and offered a plan, already approved at the Ohio meeting, for placing Amish COs who objected to public service on Amish-owned farms. The Amish plan was immediately accepted in principle (Steering Committee 1972).

The Institutionalization of the Steering Committee

Details of the farm plan were worked out by Hershey and the chairman of the Steering Committee,[9] but Hershey made it clear from the beginning that he was charging the committee with the responsibility of setting up and administering the program. This mandate soon included evaluating the sincerity of each applicant for a farm deferment. Within a week of their initial meeting with Hershey, church leaders and lay representatives met again, this time in Missouri, to approve "the form and guidelines for exempting the boys asking for farm deferments through the Steering Committee" (Steering Committee 1972:11). The language used in this excerpt from the committee minutes is significant. The Steering Committee had effectively usurped one function of the local draft boards, which until then had channeled any appeals for changes in an individual's Selective Service classification to the state appeals board.

The form developed by the Steering Committee, "Appeal to Old Order Amish Steering Committee," was to be filled out by the applicant in quadruplicate and forwarded to the chairman, who would consider the applicant's background and forward the appeal (at least initially through the National Service Board) to the Selective Service in Washington. A list, "Guidelines and Regulations Governing Appeals," was developed by the Steering Committee, and standard operating procedures evolved and were disseminated at annual meetings. The minutes of the first annual meeting, held in Pennsylvania in October 1967, make clear the pivotal position of the chairman: "The case has to be approved by the chairman of the Steering Committee before it is forwarded to D.C. . . . It was explained that General Hershey has agreed to accept the appeal if it is approved by the chairman of the Steering Committee" (Steering Committee 1972:19).

This meeting was attended by Amish from settlements in at least eleven states. At subsequent meetings the Steering Committee explained how Selective Service questionnaires should be filled out, advised representatives of changes in Selective Service procedures (e.g., elimination of certain categories of deferments and introduction of a lottery), and reiterated instructions to ensure a uniform Amish response to the draft, consistent with its agreement with Washington.

By the third annual meeting (1969) the chairman was able to report that no CO who had appealed through the Steering Committee had been assigned to hospital work. He also announced a more formal farm plan, already approved by General Hershey, under which privately owned Amish farms would be leased to the local church district for twenty-six months to facilitate the placement of COs for their two-year alternative service. For the period of the lease the former owner would in effect become the manager and be paid wages approximating his potential earnings as an owner. The arrangement caused a quantum leap in the volume of red tape.

Each placement required approval by the Steering Committee as well as submission to it of quarterly reports, on forms furnished by them, showing all income and expenses. Each lease had to be filled out in quintuplicate and three copies forwarded to the chairman for his approval and record. The Steering Committee also developed guidelines concerning the operation of the farm, addressing such issues as the amount of time off to be given the CO.

At this time the chairman was also requested by the Presidential Appeals Office of the Selective Service to interview Amish COs in various states who were being considered for prosecution (Steering Committee 1972). By 1971 the chairman was traveling over 26,000 miles on Steering Committee matters and was away from home the equivalent of two and one-half months of the year (Steering Committee 1972). These growing demands on the resources of one man, uncompensated for his time and attempting to run his own business, became overwhelming. At the fifth annual meeting the chairman offered a plan to strengthen and improve the Steering Committee. The proposed changes further bureaucratized the committee along classic Weberian lines by formalizing and intensifying its rudimentary degree of hierarchy, specialization, and reliance on rules and regulations.

The central elements of the proposal approved unanimously by the meeting included the following:

1. Creation of the position "State Director" for each state. The state director would function as an intermediary between the Steering Committee and representatives for each settlement. (In larger settlements with many church districts, there are several representatives.) He would handle minor problems, receive quarterly reports from church farms in his state, and

channel information between the Steering Committee and local representatives.

2. Creation of the position "Assistant to the Chairman." The assistant would actually be a vice-chairman, with authority to act as chairman in the latter's absence and to complete whatever tasks were assigned him by the chairman.

3. Detailed descriptions of (a) the duties of each officeholder, (b) the necessary qualifications for officeholders, and (c) standard operating procedures for the replacement of state directors and members of the Steering Committee.

4. A formal reiteration of the legitimate authority of the Steering Committee. "This Old Order Amish Steering Committee with its State Directors shall be considered the voice of the Old Order Amish Churches combined, throughout the United States and no other group or Committee shall infringe upon the Old Order Amish Churches or the Steering Committee" (Steering Committee 1972:56–64).

By the following year (1972) pressure from the Selective Service had eased. About one hundred COs were working on church farms, reaching the maximum number during the life of the program. But the Steering Committee had already begun to function as a point of articulation between the Amish communities and other government agencies. As a result of a meeting between the Steering Committee and officials of the Occupational Safety and Health Administration, all Old Order Amish were exempted from the requirement to wear hard hats when working as employees on construction jobs or in industry.[10] An agreement between the Steering Committee and the U.S. Department of State exempted the Amish from having to submit photographs of themselves when immigrating from Canada to the United States (Steering Committee 1972).

The annual meeting was now well institutionalized, scheduled a year in advance, and attended by growing numbers of community representatives as well as those merely interested in the proceedings. The 1972 meeting was attended by the 3-man Steering Committee, 11 state directors, 150 registrants, and "possibly others that did not register. Also fifty some women and a few boys" (Steering Committee 1972:71). The 1992 annual meeting was attended by the Steering Committee, 14 state directors representing 16 states (the relatively small Amish populations in Kentucky and Tennessee as well as Oklahoma and Kansas were combined under two directors), and over 400 registrants.

The functions of the Steering Committee also continued to expand. In response to a comment at the 1973 annual meeting questioning the continued need for the Steering Committee—"with the draft so quiet"—the chairman cited a host of issues being addressed by the committee, including changes in the milk cooling laws;[11] conflicts with state and local education officials;[12] the development of the Employers' Notice, a document requesting employers of Amish under the age of twenty-one to make out paychecks in the names of both parents and children;[13] and the Social Security issue, "which has been turned over to the Steering Committee." The consensus was clear: "The Steering Committee is needed as much or more than ever before. After this meeting there should not need again be further counsel as to whether the Steering Committee should be kept in force" (Steering Committee 1980:3).

A confirmation of this need can be found in the proliferating array of issues with which the Steering Committee has become involved. Almost all of these concerns have resulted from changes in state or federal laws, administrative procedures, or the introduction of new programs. Between 1973 and 1992 the Steering Committee investigated (and often made rulings concerning an appropriate Amish stance toward) Workers' Compensation, Federal Housing Administration loans, the Internal Revenue Service's Earned Income Credit program, Medicare, the Homestead Credit against income tax offered in several states, Individual Retirement Accounts, the Immigration Reform and Control Act of 1986, Soil Conservation Service programs, the use of state-subsidized immunization clinics, the Department of Agriculture's herd buy-out program, compulsory kindergarten, changes in Selective Service personnel and regulations, asbestos in schools, and the Gulf War.[14]

Social Security continued to be a troublesome issue for the Steering Committee. Despite an exemption granted in 1965 to self-employed Amish (and a broadening of that exemption in 1988), the need to deal with the Social Security agency continued. The Steering Committee served as an intermediary and a source of expertise. On several occasions the chairman reminded community representatives that at the time Amish adolescents "take church instruction to join church, then it should be explained to them that when they become church members they should . . . fill in their form 4029 Social Security exemption papers" (Steering Committee 1980:14). These forms were available from the committee representatives, who were instructed to "file copy C for future reference" (Steering Committee 1986:3). In cases where the exemption was disapproved, the chairman asked that it be sent to the Steering Committee, since "we should be able to have it approved" (Steering Committee 1980:34).

The committee also kept track of proposed legislation. In the case of a bill requiring children aged five or more to be assigned a Social Security number, the committee worked with two congressmen to add an amendment excusing those religiously opposed (Steering Committee 1986:75).

Another continuing concern of the Steering Committee, one demonstrating its increasingly institutionalized character, has been the Amish schools. In 1978 the committee issued a seventy-two-page pamphlet, "Guidelines in Regards to the Old Order Amish or Mennonite Parochial Schools," which included sections on creed, goal, school administration, duties of school board members, qualifications and duties of teachers, attendance policy, curriculum, and classroom rules. School-related topics are frequently discussed with the Steering Committee at annual meetings, with the committee often providing direction as new questions arise.

The institutionalization of the Steering Committee is further evidenced by the implicit acknowledgment by government officials of the committee's authority to represent the Amish communities. Rulings from the Occupational Safety and Health Administration and the Department of State have been addressed to the Steering Committee chairman. In 1979 the Senate requested a statement from the committee during a debate on proposed changes in Selective Service guidelines (Steering Committee 1980). That same year the chairman represented the Amish to a committee investigating the Three Mile Island accident.[15] In 1983 officials requesting assistance in controlling the rowdiness of some Amish youth wrote the chairman of the Steering Committee rather than church leaders (Steering Committee 1986). And contacts between the Steering Committee and members of Congress have become routine.

With its continued institutionalization, the Steering Committee has manifested in increasingly clear fashion most of the characteristics of bureaucracy outlined by Max Weber: division of labor, hierarchy, dependence on written documents, and development of general rules or standard operating procedures (Weber 1968). Two other characteristics have been less clearly expressed. The Steering Committee is not manned by full-time, paid officeholders. Committee members are only reimbursed for expenses, financed by periodic collections on a per member basis from all church districts that wish to contribute.

Weber's qualification with regard to the full-time character of officials is pertinent: "This too is only the product of a long development." The Steering Committee has been in existence less than thirty years. Its first chairman, an unusually articulate and effective individual, held his position until 1989. All three original members of the committee have been replaced according to the formal voting procedure it developed.

A final characteristic of bureaucracy—"Thorough training in a field of specialization"—is unlikely to emerge in other than on-the-job training. In part, the committee's first chairman was selected because the bishops meeting in Washington felt "they wouldn't be able to express themselves in English as well as they wanted to."[16] The chairman's facility with English was later augmented by other, more specialized knowledge. His familiarity with the world of congressional bills, subcommittees, and administrators, as well as his working relationship with members of Congress, further distinguished him from those who are dependent on the leadership of the Steering Committee for effective representation.

The Amish and the Iron Law of Oligarchy

The Amish face a classic dilemma. To paraphrase Michels (1962), they can escape the Scylla of unorganized ineffectiveness only by dashing themselves on the Charybdis of hierarchy.[17] For the Amish the hierarchy has proven to be relatively benign and certainly unobtrusive. Even so, the chairman of the Steering Committee has felt it necessary to issue several disclaimers essentially denying the hierarchical character of the organization. "Some people may think that the Committee is trying to run the churches but this should not be so. *The Committee is only the voice of the churches combined*."[18]

And, in a more tangible simile, "The Committee is like a wheel. The hub is like the various churches. . . . The spokes are like the State Directors connecting the hub with the rim, and the Committee is the rim holding all together, each useful in its place" (Steering Committee 1980:50).[19]

On another occasion the chairman deferred to the religious leadership. "The bishops are our highest human authority and the Steering Committee their servants" (Steering Committee 1980:3). This metaphor echoes that used by leaders at least as far back as Frederick the Great. The need for these denials of hierarchy might be symptomatic of the condition they deny.

An alternative interpretation of the significance of the iron law, offered by James Wood, is particularly relevant for the Amish case. Wood (1981:11) argues that even when an organization's policy (or, presumably in this case, the mere creation of the organization) contradicts the views of most of its members, the result is not necessarily goal displacement. He invokes the concept of organizational transcendence, "an organization's use of its name and other resources in actions not predictable from its members' attitudes toward those actions," thus allowing a distinction between transcendence that is illegitimate (i.e., oligarchy) and that which is not. Legitimate transcendence, based on the collective core values of the group, employs organizational structure as a means to protect values that are only precariously left to individuals. His analysis raises at least the possibility that the national Amish Steering Committee is not perforce subversive of Amish values.[20]

The significance of the Steering Committee for Amish life—the extent to which it represents innovative means in the service of traditional ends or a usurpation of those ends—is for now unknowable. What can be discerned is that the pressure to organize, the inevitable hierarchy, and even the disclaimers of the new Amish leadership, down to the image of leader as servant, are all part of a well-documented historical pattern,[21] recapitulated once more in the Steering Committee. Weber's (1968:973) observation regarding the technical superiority of bureaucratic organization or Michels' (1962:61) premise that "organization appears the only means for the creation of a collective will" do not require additional empirical support. What is of concern here is achieving an appreciation of what environmental factors finally created the need for a technically superior form of association and a collective will.

Discussion

An examination of the initial rationale for the formation of the Amish Steering Committee and the kinds of issues it has addressed provides an unambiguous indication of the source of stress in the environment. The Amish situation is similar in essential respects to that of the Taos pueblo described by Siegel (1970:11). Both are part of "a class of societies whose members attempt to establish and preserve a cultural identity in the face of what they feel are external threats to that identity." Both engage in defensive structuring in response to stress deriving largely from "constantly changing, imperfectly understood policies originating in Washington" (Siegel 1970:21).[22] Their defense, the formal designation of a central authority, is, echoing Weber and Michels, "The most economical and efficient means for coping with the problem" (Siegel 1970:30). Too much is at stake to allow significant local discretion.

A clear expression of this pressure toward hierarchy is found in the Steering Committee's argument that national standards be followed in all Amish schools. "It is the Committee's definite concern that one small group does not upset the general school system appreciated by many and approved by the United States Supreme Court" (Steering Committee 1980:42). The same rationale, offered several years later, leaves no doubt about what sector of the environment the Amish perceived as threatening: "Each community should have home rule and each community or state its home standards but all rules and standards should fit within the scope of the green guideline booklet so as to be protected as well as possible from legal action and the law" (Steering Committee 1986:4).

By controlling the pace of technological change within their own communities, the Amish were able to keep themselves, if not separate, at least at arm's length from the rest of society. As long as they had this control, formal organization was unnecessary. Weber (1968:224) saw this kind of connection when he identified the only exception to the universal pressure to bureaucratize as "those groups . . . who are still in possession of their own means of subsistence." The legal environment, however, is not amenable to control through self-discipline. The impact of statutes and regulations cannot be neutralized by retaining horsepower and kerosene lamps.

The continued rationalization of American society has meant the regulation and standardization of facets of American life that previously had not fallen under the purview of government. For the Amish the most relevant and threatening aspects of the rationalization of the public sector have been the centralization of school systems; introduction and later expansion of the Social Security system; a universal draft with provisions for conscientious objectors; and an ever finer net of regulations and standards dealing with agricultural production, insurance, taxation, and occupational safety and health. Their cumulative impact has been to create a legal environment so adverse to the perpetuation of Amish life that it has provoked the formation of a central authority to effectively represent and defend Amish interests.[23]

The history of the Steering Committee nicely illustrates Meyer and Brown's (1977:365–66) discussion of the origins of bureaucratization. They write, "In short, the process of bureaucratization begins with environmental pressures . . . and proceeds by developing rules to accommodate these pressures, elaborating organizational structures consistent with the rules and delegating authority as necessitated by structure."

The same conclusion is supported by the history of the various "Amish Aid" organizations. Like the Steering Committee, they evolved in response to environmental pressures, despite being nominally proscribed by doctrine. The idea of insurance is in principle an anathema to the Amish. Yet without it economic survival is jeopardized. Even if a family was willing to shoulder the risk of loss to fire, for example, without insurance it may be unable to secure financing needed for farm or business.[24] Many Amish groups have resolved this dilemma by the creation of their own risk-sharing plans.[25]

As early as the 1870s "Amish Aid plans" or "Amish Aid societies" were founded to issue fire and storm insurance policies. Beginning in the 1960s hospitalization plans generally known as "Church Aid" or "Hospital Aid" and liability plans ("Liability Aid") were added. Rising hospital costs and the growing possibility of liability suits, resulting primarily from buggy-automobile accidents, represented new environmental threats to which the Amish responded with new organizational formats.

These organizations are generally not acknowledged by the Amish as insurance companies even when the word "insurance" appears, as it sometimes does, in the titles or texts of their policies. But in their function, their procedures, and their organizational vocabulary these nascent bureaucracies replicate their more formalized commercial counterparts. Their directors, secretaries, treasurers, and appraisers may not be full-time, paid officeholders but they exemplify the specialization, hierarchy, and standard operating procedures of classic bureaucracy. They have had to develop financial reports of their activities, as well as rules and regulations detailing exclusions, limits of liability, deductibles, and the collection of premiums.

In their struggle against the legal and economic bureaucracies surrounding them, the Amish were compelled to adopt organizational structures that mirrored, on a less developed scale, those very bureaucracies.[26] In the case of the legal environment, whether or not the Amish are eventually exempted from a particular piece of legislation, the cumulative pervasiveness of legislation concerning all facets of their life requires a continuing bureaucratic response. A homogeneity of form is imposed on collectivities that are subject to this legislative web, including the Amish. The alternative, to eschew formal organization, is tantamount to collective suicide. As Weber (1968:224) argues,

"When those subject to bureaucratic control seek to escape the influence of the existing bureaucratic apparatus, this is normally possible only by creating an organization of their own which is equally subject to bureaucratization."

The influence of the legal environment, of course, extends well beyond providing an impetus for the creation of organizations and their subsequent bureaucratization. Established bureaucracies, from Exxon to the local Little League, must continually take into consideration and respond to the relevant government standards, codes, regulations, licensing requirements, and programs that comprise a given organization's legal environment. This pervasiveness has been only sporadically appreciated in the organizational literature.

The Amish, in their adherence to an alternative definition of what is valuable and what is appropriate, help throw into relief the omnipresent grid of assumptions and perceived inevitabilities that shape organizational behavior. The evolution of the Steering Committee also illuminates the uncompromising character of the legal environment. Even the relatively benign legal environment in which the Amish operate allows but two responses—bureaucratization or impotence.

In some settlements Amish women are increasingly involved in operating small businesses. These women are entering a retail fabric store operated by an Amish woman. (Photograph by Lucian Niemeyer).

13

Amish Women and the Feminist Conundrum

MARC A. OLSHAN AND KIMBERLY D. SCHMIDT[1]

Amish society is organized around preindustrial gender roles that for the most part have remained sheltered from the winds of feminism. At first glance Amish women appear to live under the domination of a male patriarchy legitimated by traditional religious teaching. Yet Amish women exhibit an unexpected self-confidence and strength. In this chapter Marc A. Olshan and Kimberly D. Schmidt explore this intriguing feminist conundrum and suggest that an understanding of gender roles in Amish society requires an understanding of their world view.

The Paradox of Strength and Submission

What are we to make of Amish women? Their acceptance of traditional gender roles, their overt submission to male authority, and their indifference to demands for the liberation of women would appear to put them squarely at odds with the objectives of feminism. Yet even the briefest contact with Amish women throws this conclusion into doubt. Their quiet self-confidence, strength and clarity of purpose, and unassuming self-respect are all attributes actively sought by feminists. These attributes are nourished by the high regard with which women are held in Amish society. The level of recognition they receive in their unabashedly patriarchal society is still being sought by feminists in the society around them.

Amish women certainly don't provide a model for contemporary feminists. But it would be a mistake, and a loss, to write them off as "little more than 'beasts of burden,' toiling long hours to care for a string of children" (Stoll 1977b:9). As Debra Kaufman (1991:3) points out in her study of adult Jewish women who chose to join traditional Orthodox groups, human thought and behavior "often express contradictory and ambivalent impulses. . . . [I]f we are to make sense of these women's motivations, choices, and 'born-again' attitudes, we must suspend preconceived judgments and assessments."

It would be tempting, for example, to view women's endorsement of their own subordinate status as an obvious instance of "false consciousness." But from what Olympian vantage point do contemporary analysts judge the beliefs of others? To characterize another's consciousness as "false" is an exercise in arrogance. That arrogance is compounded when the judgments made are not based on advances in either metaphysics or methodology, but merely on how closely the other's consciousness conforms to current assumptions of popular culture.

The subordinate status of women in Amish society is based on the belief that they are following "God's intended order between the sexes" (Stoll 1971:7). Such fundamentalism is typically rejected out of hand, if not ridiculed, as inconsistent with modern "truths." Apparently the current concern for diversity does not extend to those religious groups whose beliefs can be declared false (in a neat reversal of previous orthodoxy) merely on the basis of their biblical origins. But rejecting a spiritual framework because it is inconsistent with current conceptions of what is ideologically correct is less an expression of sophistication than of intolerance.

The argument that the situation of Amish women should be considered with an open mind is not based, however, solely on an appeal for toleration. It is based as well on the suspicion that there is something to be learned from how these women live their lives. Unfortunately scholarly work about Amish women is limited and Amish women themselves rarely speculate about their circumstances publicly.[2] Consequently what follows is less a description of Amish women's lives than a framework for appreciating the multifaceted nature of those lives.

Feminism and Amish Women

In *Plain and Simple: A Woman's Journey to the Amish*, author Sue Bender, a thoroughly modern woman with graduate degrees from Harvard and Berkeley, career demands, and feminist principles travels to two remote Amish communities and lives with Amish families for several months. There she undergoes feminist culture shock as she describes her astonishment at the contentment Amish women exhibit, even while performing menial tasks such as washing dishes and scrubbing floors (Bender 1989:44, 50, 76).

The Amish women Bender stayed with were consumed with household tasks. One of them, Becky, was mother to nine children. When Bender takes the children out to eat, Becky's husband, finally home alone with his wife for the first time in years, decides to do the dishes. For Becky, this was truly a special occasion. For many feminists, her life might look like a nightmare.

Amish women's lifestyle choices are limited by their religious community's standards. Amish women are valued for their domestic skills. The typical Amish woman spends her days in domestic pursuits, surrounded by children. The average number of live births per Amish family is seven (Hostetler 1993:99). One of the Amish woman's essential tasks is to teach sewing, gardening, cooking, canning, and housekeeping to the next generation of wives and mothers. Amish women engage in a lifestyle that many feminists have deemed oppressive.

Feminists, in contrast, value self-determination, education, and career options in addition to families and children. But as wide as the chasm between the two worlds of Sue and Becky seems to be, there are places where their worlds touch. Amish women's lives embody some of the values that feminists appreciate and work for in the rest of American society. The similarities between feminist ideology and Amish religious beliefs in regard to women warrant exploration. By broadly defining feminism and taking a closer look at Amish women's lives, we can begin to discern these similarities.

Often feminism is narrowly defined as women wanting to be equal with men and therefore devaluing all things traditionally associated with women's work. For example, rural life advocate Wendell Berry characterized feminists as demeaning household work: "Thus farm wives who help to run the kind of household economy that I have described are apt to be asked by feminists, and with great condescension, 'But what do you do?' By this they invariably mean that there is something better to do than to make one's marriage and household, and by better they invariably mean 'employment outside the home' " (Berry 1990:181). The Amish also hold to this view. They tend to think of "women's libbers" as those who denigrate traditional women's work and do not know their place. One Amishman wrote:

> Women in the world are no longer satisfied to be women. They are determined to be men. They dress like men. They demand the same jobs, the same pay, the same rights. The women's lib movement is actively seeking to break down any remaining distinctions between men and women in every area. . . . We plain people laugh at the foolishness of women who try to be men. To us women's lib is ridiculous. Yet, perhaps by small ways, by subtle and gradual degrees the attitudes and influences of women's lib are rubbing off on us and we may not even be aware of it. (Stoll 1977a:8)

Both Berry's and Stoll's criticisms are misguided. Not all feminists criticize traditional women's work. A more important point for many feminists is that in our society household work is not valued since those who do it are either underpaid or expected to perform the work for free.

The emphasis on "women trying to be men" or "trying to be equal with men" as the sole goal of feminism denies the history of feminism in this century and the complexity of women's movements of the past. Sara Evans (1979), writing about the women's movements of the 1960s, distinguishes between the women's equality movement and the women's liberation movement. The movement for equal rights came out of Betty Friedan's analysis, directed primarily at white middle- to upper-middle-class women. These educated women, secluded in the suburbs, had little outlet for their talents and ambitions. They wanted career opportunities and a chance to put their educations to work for them.

By contrast, the women's liberation movement stemmed from female students involved in the various "rights" movements of the day such as the Students for a Democratic Society and Student Non-Violent Coordinating Committee. These young women realized that men in their organizations, although involved in garnering civil rights for blacks and students, did not extend their liberal assumptions or causes to women. Women who started women's liberation wanted far more than equality with men and an end to discrimination against women. They wanted a world where women were accorded dignity and respect, and where the choices they made were valued and the work they accomplished, including housework, was recognized. In short, they wanted social transformation. Feminism is neither static nor monolithic but has evolved to include a number of issues. At its heart it is an ideology primarily committed to bettering the lives of women and children, but also of men.

Paradoxically, one response to the discontent felt by modern women is to "return" to patriarchal cultures where they feel fully valued as women. Kaufman (1991:10) describes the reasoning of women who elect to practice Orthodox Judaism:

> Adopting the stance that many values traditionally associated with women, such as mothering and the capacity for connectedness, are undervalued in society, these [newly Orthodox women] link the feminine and the female with sacred and spiritual meaning of life, turning their devalued status in the secular world into a high-status aspect that the Orthodox community confers. In the religious world, these women claim, the female and the family, and that which is associated with them, are seen as a positive source of value, not only for the self but for the community at large.[3]

The value placed on the family translates into greater participation by husbands in raising children, both in Orthodox and Amish households. And while both groups of women reject feminism, as Kaufman (1991:112) notes with regard to the Orthodox women: "focusing men's behavior on their roles as fathers and husbands resonates with issues long in feminist lexicon and history." One Amish father wrote how startled he was by the assumptions he found in Dr. Spock's *Baby and Childcare*. He noted that the author repeatedly addresses his advice to the mother, assuming she is the one training the child, making the decisions, and serving as the disciplinarian. "It gave me the impression that the father is the bread earner, but as a member of the family he just doesn't exist" (Stoll 1971:8).

Like feminists, Amish women are also misunderstood. In her journey, Bender found that Amish women's attitudes and worldviews are not as uniform as the clothing they wear. Sarah and Becky, for example, were Amish midwives. Becky took medical classes and the two women ran a birthing clinic using natural methods that many feminists, tired of the male domination of medical practices, might well envy. Amish businesswomen are becoming increasingly common since women's work has expanded to include cottage industries, now making a significant contribution to the Amish economy (see chapters 8 and 9).

The Amish Wife

The Amish wife is explicitly subordinate to her husband. Both men and women generally acknowledge that the woman is "the weaker vessel" and ought to be submissive toward her mate. The norm is based on several biblical injunctions: "The head of the woman is the man" (Corinthians 11:3); "But I suffer not a woman to teach, nor to usurp authority over the man, but to be in silence" (I Timothy 2:12); "To be discreet, chaste, keepers at home, good, obedient to their own husbands" (Titus 2:5); and "thy desire shall be to thy husband and he shall rule over thee" (Genesis 3:16).

For the Amish, however, submission does not denote exploitation or mistreatment. It means instead that areas of authority and responsibility are clearly defined and adhered to. An Amish author provides the following interpretation of the Amish perspective on equality between the sexes:

> It's not a question at all of whether or not women are as good as men. The Bible teaches very clearly that men and women are equal. . . . *But being equal in worth does not mean being the same in calling*. This is where modern women make their greatest mistake. Men are still men, women still women, no matter how equal. And each has been assigned separate and distinct roles by the great Creator.[4]
>
> Women are complaining today that they have been pushed back and cheated for generations. They are demanding education, careers, and leadership. They are making great efforts and sacrifices to reach their goal of being just like men. They are willing to do anything, be anything, except to be and do what God created them for—women. (Stoll 1977a:8)

The distinct roles of men and women are operational from birth. In fact birth announcements often identify the sex of the baby by future role rather than explicitly. For example, *Budget* letters included these items: "Born to Brother Mennos a little dishwasher named Katie," or "Enos Y's are the parents of a little woodchopper born last week." Children are incorporated into the family labor force at an early age. Boys of four or five will be assigned the job of hauling water and feed to livestock. Girls of the same age will help with the dishes and laundry in preparation for their adult duties.

The primary role of the Amish wife is to manage the household. In Amish society this is a full-time job and carries none of the stigma of repression and frustration that may be associated with being a housewife in contemporary American society. The economic importance of the wife's activities is acknowledged by her husband and the community at large.

In a household where income is typically limited, expenditures on food, clothing, medicine, and other domestic goods must also be reduced. The success of the Amish wife in limiting expenditures is indicated by low grocery bills and reduced energy consumption. "Even with large families, Amish housewives reported out-of-pocket grocery bills for food and non-food items on the range of $10 to $15 per week" (Stoltzfus 1973:202). This range is consistent with that mentioned by Amish in New York settlements in the late seventies. In a comparison of energy use in the household, "the average Amish family used 15,330 MCal per year, and the English families used 160,280 MCal" (Johnson et al. 1977:376). Although the figures in all instances are undoubtedly higher now, Amish expenditures will certainly continue to be low relative to those of the non-Amish population.

To achieve these results the Amish housewife must master numerous skills as well as learn how to efficiently manage her time and other resources. She is a seamstress, making most of her family's clothes. She is a butcher, processing dozens of chickens in the fall. In addition to being a cook for her family, she also typically puts up hundreds of jars for the winter larder. From the family garden, for which she is responsible, she may can tomatoes, pickles, beans, and sweet corn.[5] Numerous other vegetables will be grown and served in season. As with other areas for which she is responsible, the garden offers the Amish housewife opportunities for recognition as well as for hard work. "Gardens are watched with much interest by all members of the Amish community. For one thing, a good garden is a source of prestige for the women of the house. It is also much prized as a good place to teach growing children the value of work" (Mook and Hostetler 1957:24).

The Amish woman will probably take advantage of commercially grown strawberries and fruits when she can pick them herself at a reduced price. Peaches and pears are bought by the bushel, when the price is right, and canned at home. Occasionally the women and older children will earn some cash by picking apples if orchards are located nearby. And when particularly attractive sales are being held on dry goods, for example, the women will hire a van to take them even if the store is several hours journey away. Her role is physically, mentally, and emotionally demanding, yet it is apparently highly satisfying also.

From a feminist perspective one must ask: Do Amish women constitute an exploited resource or are they empowered by their work? On the surface there seems to be a conundrum. Amish society in spite of its anachronistic ways and domineering patriarchy, accords respect and dignity to women. Of one Amish woman, Bender (1989:76) wrote:

> Emma had a clear picture of the right way to be. It is true that she didn't get to choose it, and she certainly didn't question it, but freed from the

> necessity to make choices, her energy wasn't spent resisting or doubting her lot. She knew who she was as a woman. She knew that what she did mattered. The knowledge that her role in the family was necessary for its well-being permeated her life. . . . Her work was valued, she was valued. I never saw Emma or any other Amish woman look or say they were bored or lonesome. She wasn't sacrificing herself for the sake of her family. Making a commitment to marriage and family was seen as a worthy pursuit.

What might be characterized pejoratively as "women's work" in modern society is central to Amish culture and valued accordingly. The Amish housewife typically exhibits the calm assurance and quietly confident demeanor of one who knows she is doing an important job well. Nor is she at all obsequious in her relationship with her mate. While her husband is talking with a visitor she may be sitting nearby, apparently engrossed in shelling peas or some other household activity. However, when the unquestioned head of the household falters over a name or bit of information, he turns to his wife for help. And she, generally, is able to supply it. She may even interrupt when her husband has spoken in error or mispronounced a word and supply the correct information in a matter-of-fact tone that contains neither timidity nor censure.

Gertrude Huntington (1981:306) has suggested that Amish women are more involved in the family decision-making process than many modern women. The Amish woman is her husband's partner, not his handmaid: "The wife's relative position is illustrated by her position in church, where she has an equal vote but not an equal voice. Farms are generally in the name of both husband and wife. Important family decisions are made jointly. Unlike the 'corporation wife,' the Amish wife participates actively in any decision to move to a different locality."

The Amish woman's opinion is crucial to the decisions that affect her family. She exhibits a degree of self-control and confidence that might well be envied by her non-Amish, "liberated" counterpart. One expression of this paradox is the dress of Amish women. It might easily be characterized as stifling, unflattering, and restrictive. For most modern women that would be the case. But in the context of Amish culture "dress is a language" conveying commitment, humility, and modesty (Scott 1986:4).[6] The cape worn by Amish women and other plain groups distinguishes them from modern women by deliberately hiding the contours of the body. The comment of a nineteenth-century English woman on the Shaker woman's cape is richly evocative of the difference between the worldviews of Amish and modern women: "Certainly the most ingenious device ever contrived for concealing all personal advantage" (Quoted in Scott 1986:86).

The concealment of personal advantage is likely to strike contemporary women as an unnecessary and cruel imposition. It might be that, in part, for some Amish women as well. But that is not all it is. The self-effacement implicit in this concealment also contains a kind of freedom. This is the freedom invoked by Germaine Greer (1992:372) describing the serenity and power that come to older women with the realization "that everything is not about you":

> Only when a woman ceases the fretful struggle to *be* beautiful can she turn her gaze outward, find the beautiful and feed upon it. She can at last transcend the body that was what other people principally valued her for, and be set free both from their expectations and her own capitulation to them. It is quite impossible to explain to younger women that this new invisibility, like calm and indifference, is a desirable condition.

Greer's celebration of the freedom, serenity, and power of "invisibility" is no endorsement of the lifestyle of Amish women. There is, however, a clear correspondence between what she celebrates and what the Amish have always valued. Greer's analysis goes a long way toward making sense of the paradox of nominally submissive women exhibiting a degree of self-respect, self-confidence, and power usually associated with a different variety of liberation. In the relationship between the sexes, as in other areas, Amish culture provides valuable contrasts to our own society that may foster a clearer understanding of both ways of life.

Religion, Gender, and Productivity

How is it that Amish women are so highly regarded in spite of the rigid patriarchal character of their communities? As indicated in the previous section, the Amish wife's roles as manager and producer represent significant contributions to the family economy.[7] Hostetler (1993:15) observes that Amish women's work has a direct impact on the family's standard of living and leads to a higher status in the community.

Sociologist Richard A. Wright argues that when the household became a center of consumption rather than of production, women's work as consumers was devalued, ultimately giving rise to the women's movement. Wright (1977:55) contends that "the loss of a productive economic role is a more important factor producing modern feminism than is the existence of status differences between men and women." He cites the Amish as an example where definite status discrepancies exist between men and women yet where the housewife's economic importance is acknowledged and is a source of pride and self-respect. He claims that Amish women are still valued because their homes are rural centers of production. Thus, Wright argues, the explicitly subordinate status of Amish women does not generate discontent.

Wright, however, overlooks the many women's movements of the nineteenth century. Before 1960s feminism, numerous social movements within American society such as abolition, prohibition, and women's suffrage were funded and peopled by women, rural and urban. In fact historian Joan Jensen (1991:257) argues that feminism may have had its roots in the rural landscape:

> The Seneca Falls and West Chester women's conferences of 1848 and 1853 took place in rural areas and attracted rural women. The breeding grounds for early feminism may well have been the back country during rapid agricultural development. Early nineteenth-century feminists demanded legal, political, and occupational rights but still had qualms about dealing with relationships in the family. The fact that their movement was rural and family-based may help explain those qualms.

Rural areas were the first to vote for women's suffrage and historian Mary Jo Wagner (1988) argues that rural women were instrumental in the Grange and Populist movements of the late nineteenth century.[8] This history shows that rural, agrarian landscapes were capable of nurturing varieties of feminist activity well before its current expressions.

Additionally, contrary to Wright's assertion, productivity does not necessarily guarantee higher status, as underscored by anthropologist Deborah Fink's research on farm women in Nebraska between 1880 and 1940. Fink's rural women were overworked and undervalued and during times of economic stress they left the farm in record numbers (Fink 1992:128–30). Fink's research suggests that productivity and a rural landscape do not necessarily advance women's status. While Amish women's productivity is central to the maintenance and sustainability of the Amish community, an appreciation of women's economic contributions does not adequately explain their manifest self-confidence or the high regard with which they are held in the Amish community.

Community, Ritual, and Status

A more complete explanation of the respect accorded Amish women is found in the religious values and community ethics that set strict standards for male and female behavior. Religious beliefs touch Amish lives in the most basic of ways. Virtually everything, from the clothes they wear to modes of transportation and farming practices, is based on biblical interpretation, decided within church districts and enforced via church-based disciplinary mechanisms. Members join the church through adult baptism, thereby making a conscious choice to abide by the community standards either explicitly contained in the *Ordnung* or implied by it.

These community standards to a large extent protect members from deviance and violence. Amish beliefs demand that women submit to men and keep silent in public settings. But Amish religious values also limit male behavior. For example, aggression is constrained by a core belief in nonviolence. The centrality of the family sanctifies the roles of mother and wife and creates a supposition of commitment and permanence not widely found in the surrounding society.[9] Amish community standards are based on "gender constructions" that both inhibit and empower men and women in a complex pattern of rights and obligations.

The idea of gender constructions assumes a distinction between sex and gender. Notions of womanhood, femaleness, and appropriate relations between men and women are not the same in every culture. Instead, gender is formulated by social and cultural forces that are historically specific to time and place.[10] Feminist anthropologists have found, for example, that even in societies where women's work is distinct from that of men, as with the Amish, women are not necessarily considered inferior to men, nor is their work undervalued.[11] Likewise, although male dominance is virtually universal, its significance is not. Male dominance can assume a variety of expressions. It is shaped and channeled, ameliorated or magnified, by cultural definitions of what is socially acceptable in any given society.

Anthropologists have shown that one way of determining how gender constructions operate in a society is by analyzing the place of women within life rituals (Ortner and Whitehead 1981:1–3).[12] For example, in the Amish marriage ceremony one can clearly see the connections between community standards and gender constructions as well as the distinctive construction of male dominance in the context of Amish society.

Huntington's ethnographic study of an Amish community in Ohio found that families and individuals are supported by the community throughout their lives. The two most significant religious ceremonies in the Amish community, baptism and marriage, are also rites of passage into adulthood.[13] One cannot be married, however, without having first been baptized. The Amish do not marry nonbelievers. Instead they "Marry in the Lord."[14] They believe that if one follows God's will, one will choose the correct marriage partner. An Amish marriage, therefore, is ordained and blessed not only by the community but by a divine power.

"Marrying in the Lord" also means that the wife is to submit to her husband, but as Huntington points out, "Although she [the wife] is subject to her husband, she is also of one flesh with him and owes even as he does greater allegiance to God than to her spouse" (Huntington 1957:859). Huntington notes that if a husband violates church rules and is placed under the ban, the Amish wife will follow church censure and not talk to her husband. In this case, the wife's obligation to the community supplants her status as a wife. Both wife and husband are expected to uphold religious standards and to set an example for younger members of the community.

The Amish wedding ceremony is not simply a declaration of love and commitment between two persons. Instead, the Amish wedding incorporates the community in a number of ways. Amish weddings usually occur in the bride's home during the winter months after harvest when farm work is at a seasonal low. Thursday is a favorite day on which to hold weddings because it is considered a light day in the work week of the Amish community. Invited guests include church district members, relatives, and friends.

Stephen Scott's (1988:15) description of an Amish wedding notes how the opening sections of the wedding symbolize "the Amish beliefs about marriage: that it is a serious step involving not just the couple but the entire community." The bride is not, in a practice particularly abhorrent to feminists, "given away" like chattel from father to husband. Instead the young couple walks into the room together holding hands. Before the ceremony starts, however, the couple is ushered into a nearby room wherein they are asked a final time by a group of ministers whether they are ready for marital commitment.

During the ceremony the bride does not vow to "obey" her husband. Instead the bride is asked to "promise before the Lord and his church, that you will nevermore depart from him, but will care for him, cherish him, if bodily sickness comes to him, or in any circumstance which a Christian wife is responsible to care for, until the dear

God will again separate you from each other?" (Hostetler 1993:195–96). Grooms are asked the identical question and, based on Ephesians 5:25, admonished to "love your wife, as Christ also loved the church and gave himself up for it. . . ." Couples are not married by one elder. Instead, a few church ministers and the bishop take turns preaching and advising the young couple.

After the ceremony and following dinner the newly married couple sets up housekeeping with wedding gifts, usually household and farm items, and the bride's hope chest. Instead of a honeymoon the couple visits various relatives, sharing meals and sometimes staying overnight. In this manner, their entree into the community as a married couple is further recognized.

As the above description shows, even though women achieve status through marriage, their commitment to church teachings and to their church community is paramount. Although women are valued for their ability to work hard, they are further valued as integral members of the Amish community.

This is not to say that problems between the sexes do not exist in Amish life. A basic tenet of feminism is that men have been power brokers with little regard for women for too long. Amish men are also power brokers, but their religion and community standards may help keep the costs of male dominance down.[15] Noting how some Amishmen abuse their privilege, one Amish writer exhorted men to love, respect, and provide for their wives and children.

> . . . they [husbands] get the idea that their position of authority in the home gives them the right to be harsh, demanding, and unreasonable. The answer to this problem is *love*. . . . It is true that the Bible puts a lot of emphasis on how wives should obey, should submit, should be humble and faithful. And too often men forget that the Bible also says some things about the duty of husbands. . . . Let us remember that those who misuse the authority entrusted to them will someday have to account for their actions. (Stoll 1977b:8)

The author admonishes men to love their wives, but the need for his admonition implies that all might not be well within Amish households. Isaac Block, in a study of students at Mennonite colleges, found that in spite of their peace theology and supposedly protected community, 20 percent of female students experienced some form of violence. Furthermore, the perpetrators were known individuals such as family members or friends. In this case, a pacifist ideology and community did not protect women from physical and verbal abuse (Block 1992).

Since studies that analyze abuse and violence in Amish communities have not been done, it is impossible to know the extent to which Amish women face similar situations.[16]

It is also impossible, at this juncture, to know the extent to which Amish communities discriminate against women who are single, as limited anecdotal evidence indicates. Bender describes how Sarah, a single woman, was to sit with unmarried girls during church services until, in a minor act of self-assertion, she switched her apron color from white to black and joined the "wives" section in church, thus signifying her self-proclaimed entry into adulthood. Unmarried women are called *altmachen* ("old girls"). No matter what her age, the unmarried woman is not a *Frau* and she cannot obtain the same status as one who has married and produced children. This terminology, along with an observation that over the course of a few years a number of single Amish women in one community changed their church affiliation to Conservative Mennonite, caused one scholar to question whether single Amish women can find fulfillment within their communities.[17]

Only after Amish women jump through the hoops of matrimony and childbearing are they granted full respect and status as women. The distinction between "old girl" and "woman" is one more expression of strictly prescribed gender roles, and one more area where the voices of Amish women need to be heard if we are to understand their situation.

Different Worlds and Different Conclusions

The situation of Amish women cannot be understood only by invoking the gender inequalities that clearly exist. Gender inequalities may be universal but they "are hardly universal in their implications or their contents" (Rosaldo 1980:416). The same point is made by D. Kaufman (1991:68), whose observation on Orthodox Jewish women is equally applicable to the Amish:

> How is it possible to conclude that these women's lives are anything but oppressive and "alienated"? To account for women's commitment to patriarchal settings, some feminists have relied upon arguments that stress "false consciousness," or a powerlessness to change the conditions of their existence. What is missing in these portraits, however, is the understanding that women are often simultaneously victims and agents, subjects and objects. Theoretical categories cannot distinguish between an "authentic" and an "alienated" woman's experience. Vital

human experiences cannot be reduced to abstract orthodoxies—feminist or religious.

In the context of Amish society, for example, submission, humility, and self-effacement are virtues, to be actively striven for by men as well as women. According to one Amish minister: "Being a woman means there is one more level of subjection than being a man. That is all. It doesn't mean that a woman is thereby being degraded, cheated, or despised. It is simply a fact of life, like being born a girl in the first place" (Stoll 1971:8). It is not necessary to agree with this biblically-inspired interpretation to acknowledge that the concept of submission in Amish society carries a very different connotation than in the contemporary United States.

That feminism and the Amish woman's way of life can at least be partially reconciled is seen in Sue Bender's (1989:145) observation: "Their view of the world is different than mine, so they reached different conclusions about how to live. Their conclusions are not THE WAY, but one way—a way that works for them."

Amish women inevitably have a different worldview than feminists or "non-Amish" women. Many of the issues that are of paramount concern to feminists such as family abandonment, domestic violence, and poverty are simply not major problems for the vast majority of Amish women. Infants are born into a society that will care for them from cradle to grave. As women take care of their families, they are also cared for, enveloped in a loving network of friends and family from birth to death. One Amish woman related how, after an aunt died tragically, her family was supported by the community with daily visits and meals for over three months. The family was also helped with chores and other farm-related tasks for the same period (King 1992:21, 34). Amish women are respected for their roles as mothers, producers, and managers of the household. Whether or not they earn cash income, their contributions are acknowledged as critical to the economic survival of the family.

Finally, in Amish communities, religion both legitimizes and mitigates patriarchal authority. While women are to keep silent in the church and other public places, they are generally protected from the abuses often suffered by their non-Amish sisters, and their voices are heard and respected in private settings.[18] Feminists who deplore housework, childcare, and deference to men as necessarily constricting and demeaning will not understand or accept the choices of Amish women. Feminists who acknowledge the distinct premises of Amish culture, however, will understand the value of Amish women's work and perhaps even understand their decisions.

The stark images of women sledding raise questions about the significance of the Amish for modern society. (Photograph by Lucian Niemeyer).

14

Conclusion: What Good Are the Amish?

MARC A. OLSHAN

 *How should we view the Amish? Are they an irrelevant relic—a pre-Enlightenment society that stifles individual freedom and expression? Or have the Amish devised a morally superior way of life worthy of emulation? In this concluding essay, Marc A. Olshan suggests that neither view is helpful in thinking about the Amish contribution to our collective struggle with modernity. The Amish, suggests Olshan, are a light to the modern world to the extent that they teach us to have the courage to set limits on human behavior.*

Disparate Images

The Amish provoke mixed reactions. At one extreme the Amish way of life is seen as "a cage on human potential," a regressive existence that deliberately fetters individuality and imagination. According to this view, the Amish have sacrificed freedom in a blind submission to traditional social arrangements and the use of antique contrivances.[1] At the opposite extreme the Amish are seen as uncorrupted tillers of the soil, the most moral expression of what America is all about. According to this view, Amish aloofness has left them untainted by the pathologies of modern society. From organic farming enthusiasts to defenders of family values, the Amish are invoked as models for how the rest of us should live.

Implicit in both of these views is an image of the Amish as tenacious relics, pilgrims from the seventeenth century somehow stranded in the twentieth. The assumption of persistence and isolation is one expression of what has been called "Brigadoon thinking," after the fictional Scottish Highlands village miraculously isolated from the rest of the world (Carrier and Carrier 1987).

This mentality mistakenly equates the unfamiliar with the untouched and the unchanged. It fails to acknowledge that what is sometimes celebrated, sometimes derided, as traditional Amish culture is as much a product of the encroaching world as it is a reflection of the beliefs, values, and practices of an earlier, more pristine era.[2] Such Brigadoon thinking reduces the Amish to an interesting bit of living history that, fortunately or not depending on one's perspective, is incompatible with modern life. For example, the millions of tourists that flock to Lancaster County, Pennsylvania, and other Amish strongholds each year hope for little more than an entertaining glimpse of their imagined rural past.

A substantial academic literature challenges this viewpoint by acknowledging the processes of accommodation and negotiation that have always characterized Amish life.[3] Academics have been far more reluctant, however, to explicitly address the question of whether the Amish represent a moral benchmark for others, or a case of arrested moral development. Sociologists and anthropologists, for example, often reflexively shrink from such overtly normative judgments with the maxim that "science cannot tell anyone what he *should* do" (Weber 1949:54). There are, of course, good reasons for being circumspect in mixing value judgments with science. But analysis is rarely devoid of normative implications. In their descriptions and analysis of Amish life, social scientists have generally treated the Old Order with kid gloves. It is an understandable stance. Anyone who spends time with the Amish is likely to develop a respect for them. But the cumulative effect is a picture distorted by the frequent use of rose-colored glasses. This implicit endorsement of the Amish way of life is no less judgmental for being positive.

The positive character of much of the academic and popular literature on the Amish is curious given that many values central to the Amish are fundamentally inconsistent with the core values claimed by most Americans in general and by academics in particular. The Amish themselves are acutely aware of the gap between their views and those of "the world." One almost standard Amish response to outsiders' questions about Amish life is "What good is it for you to know?"[4] They may offer themselves as a light to the world but with little expectation that many will actually emulate their example. It follows that there is no need to debunk the Amish. Whatever modest claims they make for themselves are already free of false sentiment and pretension. But the way the Amish have often been presented to the world by others, whether inspired by sympathy or by the hope for bigger receipts at the turnstile, does need to be examined.[5]

To challenge widely held assumptions about the exemplary character of Amish life is not to argue that the Amish are without value or relevance. It is rather to argue that the value of the Amish for people living in a postindustrial society may lie elsewhere than in serving as a kind of primordial moral authority.

The Question of Values

Imagine flying over an Amish farmstead and being able to swoop down, pluck up an Amishman from his work, and carry him back to a typical American community. Shave off his beard, give him a contemporary haircut, and dress him in modern clothes. Then put him in front of an audience from that community and ask him about his attitudes toward other racial, ethnic, and religious groups, toward child rearing, toward education, or toward the proper role of women. Without the visual clues that seem to trigger an automatic exemption from judgment, I would guess that such an audience would find his views distasteful if not downright offensive.

The same people who crane their necks at a passing buggy would probably wince at the typical Amish birth announcement of "a little dishwasher" or "a little woodchopper." Consigning a human being to a narrowly fixed set of gender roles is not only inconsistent with the values claimed by most Americans. It is under many circumstances illegal. Likewise, the prevailing wisdom among Amish parents that it is necessary to "break the will" of the child around the age of two would probably outrage most American parents. They would no doubt have a similar reaction to the Amish practice of prohibiting education beyond the eighth grade, or limiting musical expression to slow hymns and Sunday night "singings," or emphasizing humility to the point of severely restricting creativity and personal development.

The same people who glorify the Amish defense of traditional values might be appalled at the comments of the Amish bishop who conceded that freedom of religion was a good thing but that it had been abused by groups like the Hare Krishna that weren't even religions. Despite a religious tradition that predates that of the Amish by several thousand years, in the eyes of many Amish the Hare Krishna don't qualify as a religion because they don't acknowledge the New Testament as the ultimate authority. Such ethnocentrism expressed by a neighbor or coworker would be ridiculed as the worst kind of provincialism. Likewise, Amish stereotyping of Jews and African-Americans would be dismissed as gauche coming from someone wearing a coat and tie. In their imperfections the Amish are certainly not unique, but how are we to reconcile our admiration for them with such intolerant attitudes?

The soft-edged versions of Amish life found in videos and popular photographic essays portray the Amish in bucolic farm scenes, close to nature, and in partnership with their farm animals. Such a portrayal ignores the fact that a clear majority of Amish no longer farm as their primary occupation. This Walt Disneyfied image also stands in contrast to a conversation I had recently with an Amish boy. We were discussing the danger of gas building up in silos when he told me that it really wasn't much of a problem. He said it was easy to find out if the air was bad: "Just send in a cat or something else that doesn't matter." This sentiment, or even the occasional arrests of Amish for animal abuse, are not particularly shocking. But neither are they particularly admirable.

What then is the basis for the deference with which the Amish are treated? Former president Bush's meeting with Amish and Mennonite leaders in a Lancaster schoolhouse in 1989 is instructive. He commended their communities for holding onto "traditional family values" and extolled them as role models for other Americans. Maybe more significant, however, was the White House's request that the hitching rails located behind the school be moved to the front. On the day of the visit the president was then able to walk past the newly moved rails, to which a horse and buggy had been duly attached, providing news photographers with a picturesque tableau of virtue by association.

The value of that association is illustrated in the use of Amish symbols to market everything from swimming pools to computer software. For example, Amish Software, Inc. features a photograph of a barefoot Amish boy in advertisements for its Amish utilities programs. "Amish Launch," "Amish Desk," "Amish File," and "Amish Memopad" have nothing to do with Amish culture either in their functions ("file directory viewing and manipulating") or their spirit ("run and switch between programs instantaneously"). But the value of the software and the integrity of its producers is implicitly claimed through the mere appropriation of the Amish name.

This blanket association of the Amish with everything good is also illustrated by the writer for a travel magazine who described going to an auction attended mostly by Amish. After the bidding he helped a group of Amishmen push a pickup out of the mud and was "rewarded with handshakes, smiles and a grateful 'Danke' or two. It was a scene I'll long remember" (Quickel 1991:E4). Suppose this journalist had come upon a band of honest, hardworking Episcopalians. Would his reaction to their handshakes and thank-yous have been as rhapsodic? Undoubtedly not, but the question is, why?

Part of the answer may be found in the relative lack of interest by journalists, tourists, and the general public in Mennonite groups, even those most closely related to the Amish. In their theology, values, and in much of their lifestyle, the most conservative Mennonites share with the Amish those moral attributes which the public presumably finds so appealing. On that basis, Old Order Mennonites, for example, would appear also to merit the almost reverential deference given to the Amish. But they lack the full panoply of archaic dress and technology that is the Amish hallmark. Tractors, even with steel-rimmed wheels, can't compete with the pastoral appeal of a team of horses. A woman in a storebought print dress, even if she wears a head covering, doesn't seem to inspire the feelings of approbation that well up at the sight of an Amishwoman in her traditional, homemade outfit. With fewer material trappings of righteousness, Mennonites are apparently associated with a more contemporary, and therefore less admirable, morality.

The Amish are more visibly reminiscent of an earlier, presumably more virtuous, era. Amish cultural accoutrements support the implicit claim that "We still are what you once were." Whether this lost world of rural virtue ever existed makes little difference. It serves as a conceptual Brigadoon of industrious, moral, community-minded people not yet infected with the virus of modernity. One reason for our attraction to the Amish is that we miss at least part of what we suspect we have lost. Even those who reject Amish life as stifling traditionalism might lament the loss of the warmth, solidarity, and security that are its corollaries. At least it is difficult to celebrate the cynicism, the violence, and the unremitting assault of social and technological change which characterize contemporary life. We might not miss all of what we have left behind but we admire the Amish for preserving what we imagine was the best of it. Such sentiments help explain the deference given to a people whose values have otherwise been thoroughly repudiated by a modern world.

Are the Amish then to be valued only as exotic remnants of an idealized past? Are they considered worthwhile only for the nostalgia they evoke? I once drove an Amish couple and their children to a city near the settlement where they lived. When we arrived they asked me to watch their youngest daughter while they took care of some business. She was a toddler and a beautiful one at that. But the extravagant smiles and sounds of admiration that were directed her way as we walked slowly along the sidewalk had more to do with her bonnet and miniature homemade coat than with any personal attributes. After all, toddlers, even beautiful ones, are a dime a dozen. This one was different. People were melting in their tracks because this was a little museum piece come alive.

This kind of reaction is less than a suitable basis for admiration. In a way it actually demeans the Amish since it belittles their very real accomplishments. The assumption that the Amish live in some isolated "Amishland," a neatly preserved bubble of the more moral past, is a denial of the very real struggle in which they are constantly engaged. Beyond that, it is not reasonable to expect that values consistent with sectarian, *Gemeinschaft*-like communities can also serve as moral guidelines for contemporary society. Our intellectual, moral, and sometimes even legal commitments to multiculturalism, feminism, rationalism, and the idea of personal growth are, for better or worse, thoroughly incompatible with Amish values. Our elevation of efficiency to the status of master-value also directly clashes with the Amish worldview. A pluralist society on the brink of the twenty-first century cannot call on a small group of Christian fundamentalists to provide moral leadership. The value of the Amish lies instead in their struggle to define for themselves the shape of their lives. In that struggle the Amish illuminate, and help us confront, a central dilemma of modernity.

Resisting an Anomic World

The freedom of modern society from traditional moral discipline has proved to be a mixed blessing. Its ambiguity has been a central theme for philosophers and social scientists since the Enlightenment. One well-examined negative consequence of this unprecedented freedom is the anomic character of contemporary life. Anomie is often defined as "normlessness," or more fully, as that situation where standards of behavior are weak, conflicting, or absent. But for Emile Durkheim, the sociologist most closely associated with the concept, anomie was a judgmental as well as a descriptive term. Durkheim's understanding of anomie had connotations of immorality, suffering, derangement, and sacrilege, all conditions that today's Amish readily recognize in the world around them. The result is a society without direction, suffering from a "morbid restlessness" and "insatiable appetites" that Durkheim saw as symptoms of "the malady of infiniteness" (Mestrovic and Brown 1985). The moral disorder of anomie is perfectly antithetical to the moral order (*Ordnung*) of the Amish.

The Amish Ordnung or church discipline consists of the generally unwritten guidelines that translate Amish principles and values into everyday behavior. It is a "blueprint for expected behavior" that puts clear limits on what is appropriate and what is necessary.[6] The act of adult baptism represents a commitment to live within the limits of the Ordnung. From that point on, each day spent as an Amish person reaffirms the decision to resist the world and remain Amish. To waver, to stop actively struggling, is to stop being Amish. As one Amishman put it: "The Christian life is a warfare." It is precisely in this Amish refusal to accept the assumptions, values, and definitions of the larger society that the relevance of the Amish for the rest of us may lie.

This rejection of outside authority gives the Amish a kind of freedom many Americans will never experience. The Amish have no use for self-improvement seminars, self-actualization workshops, or books on how to lose weight, run a marathon, or make love. In typically brusque Amish style, the guidelines for advertisers that appear in each issue of the Amish weekly newspaper *Die Botschaft* include this terse prohibition: "No books on positive thinking or how to get smart." In some ways the Amish are more liberated than those who feel compelled to excel at whatever the latest expert dictates, to conform to the latest fashion, or to ponder the legitimacy of every cause.

Outside authority is also implicitly rejected in the Amish exclusion of certain types of technologies. Automobiles, high-line electricity, and other innovations that might undermine community values are proscribed. The decision is not made out of ignorance or blind submission to tradition but in keeping with their own definition of what kind of life is appropriate. The Amish motivation for restricting technology is similar to that of the Greeks during their golden age of science. On the basis of their scientific work the Greeks could have developed a variety of new technologies. Their conscious decision not to do so "was the result, perfectly mastered and perfectly measured, of a certain conception of life" (Ellul 1964:29). The self-mastery of the Greeks and the Amish translates into a freedom from the dictates of circumstance or outside authority.

In contrast, the anomic absence of limits in modern society, rather than being an expression of radical freedom, appears to lead to a loss of self-control. One expression of that loss is evidenced in a great fear of missing out on whatever experience or product or opportunity others may be enjoying. The Amish don't seem to suffer from the combination of envy and impotence, the *ressentiment*, with which others pay for modernity. In fact, the most striking nontangible feature of Amish life is an absence of the chronic fear of losing that pervades American life. The Amish don't fear losing the race to accumulate and display the symbols of wealth. They don't fear losing all status in their community because of unemployment or failure to constantly advance in their work. They don't fear being discarded or treated with contempt in their old age. They don't fear death, at least not with the same sense of panic and ultimate failure with which death is typically regarded by their more rationalized contemporaries.[7] In Amish society even the threat of mortality is muted by the support of family, community, and a belief in immortality, so that "most individuals can face death confidently . . ." (Bryer 1979:260).

In their body language as well the Amish communicate a benign fearlessness. In their nonthreatening posture, their reserved manner, their slower and less expansive gestures, the Amish convey little of the territoriality and latent aggressiveness that often typify interactions in the society around them. Their assurance is not based on bravado but rather on the understanding that the concerns and pursuits of the world are after all irrelevant. In his characterization of Taoist thought, Thomas Merton (1965:11) could just as accurately be describing the Amish worldview: "a certain taste for simplicity, for humility, self-effacement, silence, and in general a refusal to take seriously the aggressivity, the ambition, the push, and the self-importance which one must display in order to get along in society."

One consequence of this refusal to let others define what is necessary and desirable is that the Amish have at least the potential to be successful. In the larger society the meaning of "success" has become either so bloated or so diffuse as to be unattainable. The "malady of infiniteness" makes each of us a Tantalus. Success is always just out of reach. One can never be secure enough, young enough, rich enough, skillful enough, fit enough, or attractive enough. One can never possess the latest of the unending stream of new products designed to make all that came before nothing more than an obsolete source of embarrassment. As Stoltzfus points out (1977:312–13):

> One of the characteristics of the cultural system of the American society is a kind of goal succession. The attainment of one level of economic and social reward triggers a higher level of aspiration and breeds dissatisfac-

> tion with past and current achievements. The money and status goals of Amish life result in different behaviors because they are bounded by finite cultural limits. . . . To the extent that such an economic and social system buffers the individual from limitless personal ambition and the discontent of impossible striving, it may operate as a kind of reward. The Amish dream is attainable for a much higher proportion of its dreamers than is the American dream.

The economic portion of the Amish dream is circumscribed by the values of humility, simplicity, and community. For the Amish, success is ultimately defined by living within the Ordnung and raising children who elect to become Amish. Neither of these objectives is easily achieved. But they at least have the potential for achievement. In this they differ from the fragmented and contradictory goals of career, family, and personal development that confront most Americans. The unlimited possibilities of an anomic society translate into a definition of success that is inevitably unreachable.

Amish values, Amish limits, and the Amish definition of success cannot be grafted onto American culture. It would be pointless to imitate their use of bonnets, buggies, and kerosene lamps. The value of the Amish lies, rather, in making clear the need for limits of some kind and in their insistence on defining for themselves the limits within which they will live. But anyone acknowledging that need must first face the challenge of establishing appropriate limits. The catch-22 we face is that selecting standards from the normative grab bag of a pluralist society requires some standard for selection. Answering the ageless question of how one ought to live is complicated by the modern presumption that cultural guidelines are relative, and to a degree arbitrary, rather than moral givens.

Among the Amish themselves, disagreements over where to draw the line have left a legacy of bitterness and fragmentation. There is no automatic consensus on whether to use haybalers, establish Sunday schools, or engage in evangelical activity. When a community cannot agree on a common Ordnung, the solution is often for one faction to move out, either joining another settlement or starting a new one of its own. The cumulative effect of these church divisions is the numerous Amish affiliations in the United States and Canada, each with its distinctive Ordnung. The task of defining appropriate limits has been formidable, even among the relatively small number of Amish, a people who share a common set of core understandings.

The task of defining limits for an entire nation composed of diverse groups with conflicting interests and agendas would be infinitely more difficult. In the attempt to "fill the hollow where God and community dwelt . . . what truth can a plural, post-modern civilization live by?" (Gardels 1991). Some have suggested that the answer may take the form of an amalgam of beliefs common to all religions or an ethic of environmental responsibility. To date there is scant evidence that such surrogates will be either attractive or influential. Appeals to ethnicity and nationalism have proven more seductive. The potential consequences of such appeals were demonstrated by the Nazi attempt to restore limits and meaning through the *volkisch* ideology of soul, soil, blood, and race. Part of the price of that "escape from freedom" (Fromm 1965) was an abdication of the very integrity and responsibility that are so central in refusing to let others define what is appropriate.

Even if we could agree on a kind of "national Ordnung" we would not be able to unilaterally control the character of our society. Just as the Amish are embedded in American society, so we are embedded in a global environment that establishes the context for our own struggle. To a significant degree our social, political, and economic institutions are shaped by the reality of international competition. The Amish have been similarly influenced by their environment. Economic and political forces beyond their control have driven them to develop new institutions, adopt new technologies, and enter nontraditional occupations. To survive they have had to accommodate to the forces of change but they have never surrendered to them. In their war against progress the Amish have occasionally retreated but always in good order and always with their awareness of the need for limits intact.

A Light to the Modern World

The Amish success in maintaining their identity is a tribute to the effectiveness of their struggle to define for themselves who they are, to define what is appropriate, and to insist on the need for limits despite a lack of control over exactly where those limits will be drawn. Even if circumstances make a national Ordnung unlikely, we might as individuals still consider the possibility of a "personal Ordnung." By not ceding authority to the legions of experts and advertisers, each claiming a role in defining success, we might partially free ourselves from their infinite demands. But unlike the Amish, we must first identify what might be the standard for an appropriate course of action. In a world gravid with cynicism and relativism this is no easy task.

As incisive a thinker as Wendell Berry admits to bewilderment when faced with picking a path through the complexities and ambiguities of contemporary social arrangements.[8] With regard to selectively rejecting some technologies and practices, for example, Berry (1990:195–96) writes:

> I am unsure where the line ought to be drawn, or how to draw it. But it is an intelligent question, worth losing some sleep over. I know how to draw the line only where it is easy to draw. It is easy—it is even a luxury—to deny oneself the use of a television set, and I zealously practice that form of self-denial. . . . I am better off without a computer. I joyfully deny myself a motorboat, a camping van, an off-road vehicle, and every other kind of recreational machinery. . . . It is plain to me that the line ought to be drawn without fail wherever it can be drawn easily. And it ought to be easy (though many do not find it so) to refuse to buy what one does not need.

Even this brief glimpse of one man's struggle to identify an appropriate standard makes it clear that the search will be difficult. As modest a touchstone as "need," Berry's criterion, is being constantly inflated by the ubiquitous appeals to consume that litter our airwaves, highways, and mailboxes.

For the Amish the appropriate standard is clear. No ideology or analysis can substitute for the word of God. Any attempt to extract something of value from Amish culture without acknowledging the validity of its religious foundation will strike the Amish as fundamentally flawed. For them there is no mystery about why Amish life is valuable. There is no need for analysis. They do nothing more than attempt to follow as closely as possible the precepts of the New Testament. They readily admit to faltering in this attempt. They confess to frequently disagreeing with one another over how to best conform to scripture. But whatever their shortcomings in this effort, its religious motivation is clear.

One Amish minister told of the bagful of letters he had accumulated from people asking about joining the Amish. He noted, however, that "They don't want to approach us through what means most to us—our commitment to Jesus Christ. Everything we do follows from this and our interpretation of it." Most of the curious lost interest when they received replies phrased in this kind of language.[9] It is ironic that in the realm of religion, the one area that many outsiders tend to ignore or even see as a drawback to an ecologically or economically commendable lifestyle, the Amish self-consciously offer themselves as a model for others. Without that religious foundation, no partial emulation of their culture makes sense to the Amish.

On this point the Amish and analysts of the Amish must disagree. There will inevitably be a gap between the way the Amish perceive themselves and the way they are perceived by others. To concede that the significance of the Amish can only be fully appreciated through Amish eyes is to abandon the modern world and the effort to live correctly in it. Some individuals have done just that by joining the Amish. It is a choice that requires tremendous strength of will and that is, in many respects, inspiring. But it is not an option for most individuals or for us as a society.

The Amish tend to be disparaged or admired for the wrong reasons. To see them as either caged by a blind submission to tradition or as an uncorrupted remnant of the moral past is to ignore the constant struggle in which they are engaged. It is precisely in this struggle to define an appropriate course of action, to insist on the need for limits, that the Amish provide an invaluable example for the rest of us. As a society we are unlikely to reach consensus on how to define moral behavior. Even as individuals we may fail to identify appropriate limits. But merely to insist that there are such things as appropriate behaviors, standards, and limits may be the most rational and at the same time the most noble act left to us.

The Amish stand as a promise of the autonomy, meaning, and humaneness that are possible when the limitlessness of an anomic world is resisted. They also stand as a reminder that the deliberate imposition of limits can have enormous costs. Beyond these two guideposts we must navigate the future on our own.

Appendix

Amish Migration Patterns: 1972–1992

DAVID LUTHY

Although the Amish are often portrayed as a people of stability, they are continually establishing new settlements to accommodate their growing population. Some of the new settlements thrive while others fail. Amish historian David Luthy charts the ebb and flow of Amish migrations in the two decades following the Supreme Court case that vindicated Amish education in 1972. Following a discussion of the migration patterns, Luthy provides a state by state listing of the Amish settlements in North America. The directory identifies the year of the settlement's founding as well as its number of congregations.

Patterns of Amish migration are shaped by a large variety of factors. Since the Amish are a rural people, and since their population nearly doubles every twenty years, the availability of reasonably priced land is of prime importance.[1] With land prices highest in the oldest, largest settlements, cheaper land in new areas is always being sought. For example, during the past few years Amish farmers who were faced with paying $7,000 to $10,000 an acre in Lancaster County, Pennsylvania, have migrated to Kentucky and Indiana where they paid $1,000 to $2,000 an acre. Is it any wonder that from 1972 through 1992 the number of settlements in North America increased more than twofold?

At the beginning of 1972 Amish families were living in 83 settlements in 16 U.S. states, 8 settlements in Ontario, 1 settlement in Honduras, and 1 in Paraguay.[2] The size of the settlements ranged from 1 congregation to as many as 68 congregations.[3] By 1992 the population had expanded to 227 settlements in the United States and Canada.

Besides the search for cheaper farmland, which is always a major motive for Amish migration, many other factors may influence the decision to move. People relocate for a variety of reasons and sometimes even opposite ones. The following reasons may encourage a move:

1. To establish a plainer (i.e. stricter) church discipline. For example, when the ministry in several congregations in Kansas in the 1930s allowed members to farm with tractors rather than horses, some families relocated to where a more traditional *Ordnung* would be kept.
2. To establish a more liberal church discipline. Some Amishmen may feel that to continue farming they need more modern equipment, such as milking machines. If the ministry disagrees, some families may move elsewhere and obtain ministerial assistance from a like-minded bishop.
3. To escape church tensions and conflicts. Sometimes, if a congregation cannot reach agreement on issues, from the use of particular farming implements to clothing regulations, the settlement may disband, with some families moving to a more liberal community and some to a more traditional one.
4. To improve teenage behavior and practices. For example, since the larger settlements have hundreds of teenagers, it is more difficult for those settlements to control such practices as the drinking of alcoholic beverages. As a result, some families move to smaller settlements, which often (but not always) have better control of their teenagers.
5. To avoid urban sprawl and the regulations it imposes on rural people. Cities such as Canton, Ohio, and Dover, Delaware, have put pressure on the Amish to leave because real estate developers purchase Amish farms and inflate land prices. Of course, with residential developments come stricter building codes and zoning laws, which Amish farmers feel are in conflict with their way of life.
6. To revert to farming from a nonagrarian occupation. For example, many Amishmen in Lagrange County, Indiana, work in trailer factories. Originally their idea was to earn extra cash with which to buy a farm. But faced with rising land prices in their community, some are migrating to Wisconsin, where land sells for half the price.

7. To better oneself financially. Some Amish farmers have settled in areas where land is less expensive, but the weather is unpredictable. Since they cannot make a living in that area, they may move to another more profitable one.

Until 1972 a primary reason for migration was to avoid the enforcement of school attendance laws by local officials. This happened especially in the three most densely Amish-populated states: Pennsylvania, Ohio, and Indiana. Because Amish parents did not want their children to attend large consolidated elementary schools or high schools, they looked for states with more lenient school laws. In 1940, in opposition to school consolidation in Lancaster County, families moved to neighboring Maryland, where they founded a settlement in St. Marys County. Soon after World War II the Amish in Indiana and Ohio focused their attention on Missouri, where nine settlements were founded from 1947 to 1971.

At the same time that Amish families were moving to Missouri, some were migrating to Wisconsin. It was not known for lenient school laws and contained only one Amish settlement. However, between 1960 and 1970 six new settlements sprang up there. Undoubtedly the farmers were attracted to Wisconsin because of its highly rural character and its reputation as the nation's "Dairy State." Since dairy farming was a main source of income for the Amish, it seemed like the logical place for them to settle.

Perhaps the Amish were a little naive in moving to Wisconsin, for they were soon in conflict with state officials concerning school attendance laws. The officials decided to legally force the Amish to send their children to high school until their sixteenth birthday. This resulted in the now historic *Wisconsin v. Yoder* case, which eventually was decided by the United States Supreme Court in 1972. The court ruled in favor of the Amish, stating that no state could require Amish children to attend school beyond the eighth grade because it violated their religious beliefs.[4]

The Supreme Court's ruling resulted in many more Amish migrating to Wisconsin, so that by the end of 1992 the number of settlements in that state had increased from seven to twenty-seven. They also moved into other states where previously they had only sparsely settled, having also feared the enforcement of school attendance laws. For example, Michigan and New York, adjacent to the three states with the largest concentration of Amish (Pennsylvania, Ohio, and Indiana), have experienced remarkable growth. Michigan went from five settlements in 1971 to twenty-three in 1992. New York's growth has been even more spectacular, going from one settlement in 1971 to fifteen in 1992.

The Supreme Court's ruling did not, however, open the door for Amish migration quite as widely as some people thought. When several families from Ohio settled near Pawnee City, Nebraska, in 1977, they were immediately confronted with a school problem with a new twist. The officials demanded that they employ a certified, college-trained teacher at their tiny rural school. When the Amish continued to operate their school without a certified teacher, the officials prepared to take legal action. Headlines such as "Nebraska's Amish Find Old Problems Remain" began appearing in Nebraska newspapers and soon in other U.S. newspapers as well.[5]

The crisis in Nebraska was moving to what looked like another test case for the U.S. Supreme Court when the conflict suddenly evaporated. Rather than face litigation, the five families at Pawnee City quietly left the state, resettling in Ohio, Missouri, and Wisconsin. Their brief but memorable attempt to settle in Nebraska lasted from 1977 to 1982.[6]

Another earlier reason for Amish migration was to avoid the U.S. military draft, which continued for many years after the end of World War II. A number of families moved to Canada, where there was no postwar draft, founding seven settlements in Ontario from 1953 to 1962. Cheaper land prices and the fact that their teenage sons would not be required to serve in the I-W program of alternative service in large city hospitals appealed to the migrants. However, with the removal of the U.S. draft in the 1970s, Amish migration to Ontario decreased considerably.

Another situation that not only stopped some Amish farmers from moving to Ontario but actually caused some to return to the United States, developed in 1977 when the Ontario Milk Marketing Board ruled that all milk must be mechanically cooled in bulk tanks. Ever fearful of governmental regulations and cautious about changes in their traditional farming practices, many Amish viewed the ruling as a threat to their way of life. No new settlements have been founded in Ontario since that ruling. Several have decreased in size and two have become extinct.[7]

At the end of 1992 there were 220 settlements in 22 U.S. states and 7 settlements in Ontario. That the Amish are spreading into new areas is best illustrated by the fact that of the 227 settlements existing in December 1992, 63 percent or 144 were founded since 1971 as shown in table A.1.

TABLE A.1.
Amish Settlements in North America in 1992

Period founded	*Settlements*
1700s	3
1800–1887	15
1888–1908	3
1909–1929	9
1930–1950	8
1951–1971	45
1972–1992	144
Total	227

The list of settlements in table A.1 does not include the more than one hundred settlements that were founded at various times but that later became extinct. Since new settlements are generally founded by individual families desiring to move elsewhere rather than as a well-organized, church-sanctioned migration, many settlements do not take root. Even those that survive for a time can become extinct for a variety of reasons: (1) unproductive land for farming; (2) years of unfavorable weather for crop production; (3) inability to attract or retain resident ministers; (4) inferior church leadership; (5) internal disunity; (6) unforeseen government regulations; (7) failure to attract enough families; and (8) attracting families who often migrate and will move again.

Taking into consideration only the most recent time period of 1972–1992, we see in table A.2 that eighteen settlements were founded and expired in these two decades.

Naturally the question arises as to how many families constitute a settlement. As a rule of thumb there must be at least three families initially or at least one minister and one additional family. Such tiny settlements either grow larger or soon become extinct. For example, the settlement at Pulaski, Tennessee, which had only one minister and one other resident family, had a very short-lived history from 1982 to 1984. Several other extinct settlements listed in table A.2 were only slightly larger. None of them at any one time contained more than sixteen families. Even older settlements can die. For example, by 1992 the

TABLE A.2.
Amish Settlements That Were Founded and Expired Between 1972 and 1992

Homer, Michigan, 1975–1989	Springville, Tennessee, 1978–1983
McRae, Arkansas, 1975–1987	Maywood, Missouri, 1980–1989
DeGraff, Ohio, 1976–1977	Dundee, New York, 1981–1988
Trout Run, Pennsylvania, 1976–1991	Flemingsburg, Kentucky, 1981–1985
Andover, Ohio, 1976–1990	Beaver Springs, Pennsylvania, 1982–1992
Watsontown, Pennsylvania, 1977–1992	Pulaski, Tennessee, 1982–1984
Albion, Michigan, 1977–1981	Piketon, Ohio, 1984–1989
English, Indiana, 1977–1990	Puxico, Missouri, 1989–1991
Pawnee City, Nebraska, 1977–1982	Reed City, Michigan, 1983–1992

group at Plain City, Ohio, which was founded in 1896 and at one time had three congregations, had dwindled to less than a dozen families and was without a resident minister.

The Amish who have settled in Texas present an unusual situation. None of them own their own land. Because of the economic recession of the 1980s, some migrated there to work as tenant farmers on huge non-Amish-owned dairy and chicken farms. The Texas settlements fluctuate in size and geographic distribution depending on where the people can find jobs. One Amishman is known to have relocated within the state at least six times during a five-year period.[8] As 1992 ended there were three small settlements in Texas.

Another unusual settlement is situated at Pinecraft, Florida. Originally founded in 1927 on muck land for vegetable farming, it has developed primarily into a retirement community. It has the distinction of being the only Amish community without a horse and buggy.[9] The residents rely on bicycles, tricycles (for the elderly), taxis, and public transportation.

Occasionally a new settlement begins where an earlier one existed but failed. Amish families settled in 1989 near Bremen in Fairfield County, Ohio, where a settlement had existed from 1834 to 1880. When families moved in 1989 to Homer, Michigan, it was the third settlement at that location, the earlier two lasting from 1940 to 1950 and from 1975 to 1989.

Several mailing addresses have two distinct, non-fellowshipping settlements.[10] Since Amish society is divided into a number of subgroups or affiliations, each with a different Ordnung, this is possible. Salem, Indiana, for example, has separate settlements that began in 1972 and 1981. Gladwin, Michigan, has settlements founded in 1979 and 1982.

Some settlements grow slowly, such as the very plain group living at Paoli, Indiana. Families located there in 1956, but a second congregation was not formed until thirty-five years later in 1991. Some settlements, however, grow rapidly such as the one at Munfordville, Kentucky. It was founded in 1989 and had three congregations two years later. The household heads in that particular community are a good example of Amishmen leaving jobs in factories in an old settlement (Geauga County, Ohio, founded in 1886) to return to farming in a new community where land is less expensive.

States that have experienced a dramatic increase in the number of settlements established since 1971 are Missouri, with 10, Kentucky, 11, New York, 14, Michigan, 18, Ohio, 20, Wisconsin, 20, and Pennsylvania, 23. Concerning the frequency with which settlements were being founded in Wisconsin (twelve during 1988–1992), an Ontario correspondent to the weekly Amish newspaper *Die Botschaft* commented: "I heard say every time it rains, a new settlement springs up in Wisconsin."[11] And a Wisconsin correspondent to another Amish newspaper, *The Budget*, stated: "It appears the state of Michigan and the state of Wisconsin are trying to outdo each other in starting new settlements."[12]

Because of the influx of millions of tourists, residential sprawl, and escalating land prices in Lancaster County, Pennsylvania, some families are migrating elsewhere. A dozen daughter settlements have sprung up since 1967 in distant valleys of Pennsylvania. In recent years, however, attention has focused more on out-of-state areas. In 1989 families from Lancaster County began a settlement at Hopkinsville, Kentucky, and in 1991 one at Rockville, Indiana.

The migration out of Pennsylvania by Lancaster County families prompted some interesting comments by correspondents writing in *Die Botschaft*:

> An acute case of Kentucky fever has broken out in the Pequea [an area in Lancaster County]. Just last week several of the church folks made the 16 hour, $200 trek to the Land of Canaan. They came back with glowing reports: tobacco as high as our corn, corn as high as a man on

a horse, ears as long as a man's forearm, great gobs of land for sale at generation ago prices, and no sewers, no zoning, no permits, 160 day school terms, and no tourists.[13]

A load from this area travelled last week to Indiana in search of greener grass, or maybe I should say cheaper grass.[14]

Indiana sounds pretty interesting to Bennie and Fannie and their family. But, oh dear, that's just another case where we'll probably end up saying "Good-bye, it's been nice knowing you!" After all it's hard to get my man 20 miles down the road. At least it'll be 600 miles closer to Kentucky and a nice stopping off place on your way to Kentucky. That should help, as I've heard tell if you're so tired from sitting that you can't hardly make it anymore, then you are only halfway to Kentucky![15]

Many tourists, much traffic in Lancaster County. I guess if you grew up with it, you would be used to it. While there we heard that some from Lancaster are starting a new settlement in western Indiana, though I don't know what town.[16]

During 1972–1992 there were 162 settlements founded (including the 18 that also expired during that period), an average of nearly 8 each year. Of the 227 settlements in 1992, Pennsylvania had the most with 44, followed by Ohio with 33, Wisconsin with 27, and Michigan with 23. The number of congregations in 1992 totaled 930—an increase of 563 from the 367 existing in 1971. Table A.3 shows the distribution of settlements and congregations by state and province in 1992.[17]

As can readily be seen in table A.3, Ohio has fewer settlements than Pennsylvania but more congregations. Pennsylvania, however, contains the three oldest settlements and the only ones that were established in the eighteenth century: Lancaster County founded ca. 1760, Somerset County ca. 1772, and Mifflin County in 1791.

During 1972–1992 the Amish migrated north, south, east, and west within the United States. The northernmost settlement began in 1975 at Rexford, Montana; it also was the westernmost settlement until 1992, when a daughter settlement was started at Libby, Montana. The easternmost settlement began in 1974 at Norfolk, New York, close to the St. Lawrence River and the Canadian border. The families who settled in 1982 near Gonzales, Texas, live nearly as far south as those residing at Pinecraft, Florida.

Just as Amish forebears in the eighteenth and nineteenth centuries thought it was necessary to leave Europe for North America, so today

TABLE A.3.
Amish Settlements and Congregations by State and Province in 1992

State/province	Settlements	Congregations
Ohio	33	258
Pennsylvania	44	221
Indiana	16	166
Wisconsin	27	53
Michigan	23	39
Missouri	15	32
New York	15	30
Iowa	7	25
Illinois	3	21
Kentucky	12	21
Ontario	7	17
Minnesota	5	9
Delaware	1	8
Maryland	2	6
Tennessee	3	6
Kansas	3	5
Oklahoma	2	4
Texas	3	3
Montana	2	2
Florida	1	1
Georgia	1	1
North Carolina	1	1
Virginia	1	1
Total	227	930

descendants are meandering across the continent searching for locations where they can practice their faith and unique way of life. As the twenty-first century approaches, one cannot help but wonder where the next Amish settlements will be established.

A directory of all the Amish settlements in North America in 1992 appears in table A.4. The settlements are listed by state and province. The year of founding as well as the number of congregations (church districts) in 1992 is included.

TABLE A.4.
A Directory of Amish Settlements in North America (1992)

Settlement	*Year founded*	*Congregations*
Delaware		
Dover/Hartly (Kent County)	1915	8
Florida		
Pinecraft (Sarasota County)	1927	1
Georgia		
Vidalia (Toombs County)	1990	1
Illinois		
Arthur/Arcola (Douglas-Moultrie Counties)	1864	19
Mt. Vernon (Jefferson County)	1987	1
Ava (Jackson County)	1991	1
Indiana		
Nappanee (Marshall-Kosciusko Counties)	1839	24
Elkhart-Lagrange Counties	1841	78
Kokomo (Howard-Miami Counties)	1848	2
Berne/Monroe (Adams County)	1850	25
Grabill/New Haven (Allen County)	1852	11
Montgomery (Daviess County)	1868	12
Paoli (Orange County)	1956	2
Hamilton (Steuben County)	1964	2
Milroy (Rush County)	1969	3

TABLE A.4.
Continued

Settlement	Year founded	Congregations
Salem (Washington County)	1972	1
South Whitley (Whitley County)	1974	1
Salem (Washington County) Swiss	1981	1
Vevay (Switzerland County)	1987	1
Rockville (Parke County)	1991	1
Williamsburg (Wayne County)	1992	1
Worthington (Greene County)	1992	1
Iowa		
Kalona (Johnson-Washington Counties)	1846	8
Hazelton (Buchanan County)	1914	6
Milton (Van Buren County)	1969	3
Bloomfield (Davis County)	1971	4
McIntire (Mitchell County)	1975	2
Edgewood (Delaware County)	1986	1
Chariton (Lucas County)	1992	1
Kansas		
Haven/Yoder (Reno County)	1883	2
Hutchinson (Reno County)	1883	1
Garnett (Anderson County)	1903	2
Kentucky		
Guthrie (Todd County)	1958	3
Crofton (Christian County)	1972	1
Marion (Crittenden County)	1977	3
Dunnville (Casey County)	1978	1
Glasgow (Barren County)	1982	2
Park City (Barren County)	1984	2
Upton/Sonora (Hardin County)	1986	1
Gradyville/Columbia (Adair County)	1986	2
Munfordville (Hart County)	1989	3
Hopkinsville (Christian County)	1989	1
Springfield (Washington County)	1990	1
Three Springs (Hart County)	1991	1

TABLE A.4.
Continued

Settlement	Year founded	Congregations
Maryland		
Oakland (Garrett County)	1850	1
Mechanicsville (St. Marys County)	1940	5
Michigan		
Centreville (St. Joseph County)	1910	6
Camden (Hillsdale County)	1956	2
California (Branch County)	1960	2
Mio (Oscoda County)	1970	2
Bronson (Branch County)	1971	1
Greenville (Montcalm County)	1973	1
Quincy (Branch County)	1977	2
Charlotte (Eaton County)	1977	2
Hale (Iosco County)	1978	1
Gladwin (Gladwin County) Swartzentruber	1979	2
Reading (Branch-Hillsdale Counties)	1979	2
Clare (Clare County)	1981	2
Ludington (Mason County)	1981	1
Rosebush (Isabella County)	1981	1
Gladwin (Gladwin County)	1982	2
Stanwood (Mecosta County)	1982	2
Blanchard (Isabella County)	1983	1
Marlette (Sanilac County)	1987	2
Ovid (Clinton County)	1987	1
Homer (Calhoun County)	1989	1
Evart (Osceola County)	1989	1
Fremont (Newaygo County)	1990	1
Coral (Montcalm County)	1991	1
Minnesota		
Wadena (Wadena County)	1972	1
Bertha (Todd County)	1973	1
Harmony (Fillmore County)	1974	4
Utica (Winona County)	1975	2
Pine City (Pine County)	1984	1

TABLE A.4.
Continued

Settlement	Year founded	Congregations
Missouri		
Bowling Green (Pike County)	1947	3
Jamesport (Daviess County)	1953	6
Clark (Audrain-Randolph Counties)	1954	6
Anabel (Macon County)	1957	1
Seymour (Webster County)	1968	5
Windsor (Henry County)	1975	2
LaPlata (Macon County)	1976	1
Dixon (Pulaski County)	1980	1
Prairie Home (Cooper County)	1980	1
Kahoka (Clark County)	1985	1
Canton (Lewis County)	1986	1
Humansville (Polk County)	1987	1
Milan (Sullivan County)	1990	1
Carrollton (Carroll County)	1990	1
Verona (Lawrence County)	1990	1
Montana		
Rexford (Lincoln County)	1975	1
Libby (Lincoln County)	1992	1
New York		
Conewango Valley (Cattaraugus County)	1949	9
Norfolk (St. Lawrence County)	1974	1
Heuvelton (St. Lawrence County)	1975	4
Dewittville (Chautauqua County)	1976	1
Clymer (Chautauqua County)	1976	3
Clyde (Wayne County)	1979	1
Newport (Herkimer County)	1979	1
Prattsburg (Steuben County)	1980	1
Romulus (Seneca County)	1981	1
Friendship/Belfast (Allegany County)	1982	2
Woodhull/Jasper (Steuben County)	1983	2
Fort Plain (Montgomery County)	1986	1
Albion (Orleans County)	1986	1

TABLE A.4.
Continued

Settlement	Year founded	Congregations
Fillmore (Allegany County)	1988	1
Addison (Steuben County)	1991	1
North Carolina		
Union Grove (Yadkin County)	1985	1
Ohio		
Holmes-Wayne-Tuscarawas Counties	1808	143
Geauga-Trumbull Counties	1886	54
Plain City (Madison County)	1896	1
Hartville (Stark County)	1905	2
Hicksville (Defiance County)	1914	1
Lodi/Homerville (Medina County)	1952	7
Kenton (Hardin County)	1953	4
Ashland (Ashland County)	1954	6
Lakeville (Holmes County)	1962	3
Danville (Knox County)	1964	3
Newcomerstown/Port Washington (Tuscarawas County)	1969	2
Utica/Martinsburg (Licking County)	1970	1
Marietta (Washington County)	1970	1
Fredericktown (Knox County)	1972	7
Belle Center (Logan County)	1974	3
Kinsman (Trumbull County)	1975	2
West Union (Adams County)	1976	2
Salesville (Gurnsey County)	1977	1
Chesterhill (Morgan County)	1978	1
Carrollton (Carroll County)	1981	1
Shiloh (Richland County)	1983	1
Mt. Vernon (Knox County)	1986	1
Lewisville (Monroe County)	1987	1
Bladensburg (Knox County)	1987	1
Jeromesville (Ashland County)	1987	1
Circleville (Pickaway County)	1988	1
Bremen (Fairfield County)	1989	1
Brinkhaven (Knox County)	1990	1

TABLE A.4.
Continued

Settlement	Year founded	Congregations
Somerset (Perry County)	1990	1
Loudenville (Ashland County)	1991	1
Dorset (Ashtabula County)	1991	1
Leesburg (Highland County)	1991	1
Andover (Ashtabula County)	1992	1
Oklahoma		
Chouteau (Mayes County)	1910	3
Clarita (Coal County)	1978	1
Ontario		
Milverton/Millbank (Perth County)	1824	5
Aylmer (Elgin County)	1953	3
Norwich (Oxford County)	1954	2
Chesley (Grey County)	1954	2
Lakeside/St. Marys (Oxford County)	1958	1
Mt. Elgin (Oxford County)	1962	2
Lucknow (Bruce County)	1973	2
Pennsylvania		
Lancaster-Chester Counties	ca. 1760	103
Meyersdale/Springs (Somerset County)	ca. 1772	4
Belleville/Reedsville (Mifflin County)	1791	17
New Wilmington (Lawrence County)	1847	12
Enon Valley (Lawrence County)	1924	1
Atlantic (Crawford County)	1924	3
Myerstown (Lebanon County)	1941	3
Mercer (Mercer County)	1942	3
Mifflintown (Juniata County)	1950	4
Aaronsburg (Centre County)	1950	2
Winfield (Union County)	1959	1
Smicksburg (Indiana County)	1962	11
Gettysburg (Adams County)	1964	1
McClure (Snyder County)	1965	1
Spartansburg (Crawford County)	1966	8

TABLE A.4.
Continued

Settlement	Year founded	Congregations
LeRaysville (Bradford County)	1966	1
Rebersburg (Centre County)	1967	3
Dry Run (Franklin County) Path Valley	1968	3
Lewisburg (Union County)	1968	1
Conneautville (Crawford County)	1969	1
Sugargrove (Warren County)	1969	3
Newburg (Franklin County)	1971	3
Guys Mills (Crawford County)	1972	3
Troutville (Clearfield County)	1972	3
Townville (Crawford County)	1972	1
Loganton (Clinton County)	1972	2
Tionesta/Fryburg (Forest County)	1972	1
Howard (Centre County) Nittany Valley	1973	2
Danville (Montour County)	1974	2
Turbotville (Montour County)	1974	1
Delta (York County)	1975	1
Loysville (Perry County)	1975	1
Montgomery (Lycoming County)	1976	1
Gratz (Dauphin County) Lykens Valley	1978	3
Pocahontas (Somerset County)	1980	1
Union City/Cambridge Springs (Erie County)	1983	1
Clintonville (Venango County)	1983	2
Jersey Shore (Lycoming County) Nippenose Valley	1985	1
Linesville (Crawford County)	1985	1
Saegertown (Crawford County)	1988	1
Tyrone (Blair County)	1988	1
Fredonia (Mercer County)	1990	1
Shanksville (Somerset County)	1992	1
Ulysses (Potter County)	1992	1
Tennessee		
Ethridge (Lawrence County)	1944	4
Huntingdon (Carroll County)	1975	1
Nunnelly (Hickman County)	1982	1

TABLE A.4.
Continued

Settlement	*Year founded*	*Congregations*
Texas		
Gonzales (Gonzales County)	1982	1
Stephenville (Erath County)	1983	1
Pickton/Como (Hopkins County)	1987	1
Virginia		
Burkes Garden (Tazewell County)	1990	1
Wisconsin		
Medford (Taylor County)	1925	3
Blair (Trempealeau County)	1960	2
New Glarus (Green County)	1964	1
Amherst (Portage County)	1966	3
Cashton (Vernon County)	1966	8
Wilton (Monroe County)	1969	4
Spencer (Marathon County)	1970	2
Chetek (Barron County)	1974	1
Greenwood (Clark County)	1975	1
Evansville (Rock County)	1975	1
Pardeeville/Kingston (Columbia County)	1977	3
Augusta (Eau Claire County)	1978	4
Granton (Clark County)	1981	3
Wautoma (Waushara County)	1983	2
Hillsboro (Vernon County)	1985	3
Bonduel (Shawano County)	1987	1
LaValle (Sauk County)	1988	1
Loganville (Sauk County)	1988	1
Loyal (Clark County)	1989	1
Oconto (Oconto County)	1990	1
Readstown (Vernon County)	1990	1
Athens (Marathon County)	1990	1
Mondovi (Buffalo County)	1991	1
New Holstein (Calumet County)	1992	1
Unity (Clark County)	1992	1
Viroqua (Vernon County)	1992	1
Blue River (Grant County)	1992	1

NOTES

Chapter 1. The Struggle to Be Separate

1. Hershberger's (1985) booklet, *A Struggle to Be Separate*, traces the history of the Amish parochial school movement in Ohio.

2. An early and classic Anabaptist articulation of a sharp separation from the world is found in the Schleitheim statement of 1527, translated and reprinted in Yoder (1973).

3. The story of the persecution is recorded in the twelve-hundred-page *Martyrs Mirror*, which is often found in Amish homes and referenced sometimes in Amish sermons (Braght 1951).

4. Introductions to the history of the Anabaptists can be found in Dyck (1993), Weaver (1987), and in the five volume *Mennonite Encyclopedia* (1956).

5. Nolt (1992) provides a helpful introductory history of the Amish. For a recent translation of the letters of correspondence surrounding the controversy of the Amish schism, see Roth (1993). Hostetler (1993) has written a helpful account of the division.

6. The Old Order label for the Amish emerged in the last half of the nineteenth century when progressive subgroups of Amish adopted more modern practices and began calling themselves Amish-Mennonites and eventually joined the Mennonite church. This story is chronicled by Yoder (1991). The more conservative mainline Amish groups soon became known as the Old Order Amish. Between 1965 and 1975 several clusters of Amish became more progressive in their use of technology and more expressive in their religious experience and language. These more progressively inclined groups eventually became known as New Order Amish. Their largest concentration is in the Holmes County area of Ohio.

7. Hostetler (1993) provides a general introduction to Amish life based on ethnographic studies of the three largest settlements in Ohio, Pennsylvania, and Indiana. For a social history of the Lancaster settlement and an introduction to Amish culture and social organization, see Kraybill (1989).

8. District size varies numerically somewhat depending on whether it is a recently formed district and whether it is located in an old settlement or a newer one. In general, districts in newer settlements tend to be somewhat smaller numerically than those in the older, more established settlements. The Holmes County, Ohio, settlement has 145 persons per district on the average (1988 *Ohio Amish Directory, Holmes County and Vicinity*). In Lancaster the average is 163 (Kraybill 1989:263) and the Elkhart-Lagrange settlement in Indiana averages 165 persons (Miller 1988). Given the smaller districts in the many

newer settlements, 150 persons per district across the nation is a reasonable estimate.

9. Kraybill (1989:109–10) describes the "lot" process that is used to select persons for leadership. In most settlements each bishop is responsible for one church district; however, in the Lancaster settlement most bishops have oversight of two districts.

10. Other biblical passages cited in support of separation from the world include John 17:14; I Peter 2:9; James 4:4; and I John 2:15, 16.

11. This is not a formal argument that the Amish have made in so many words, but this is the argument that emerges from their collective experience over the years. Every distinctive culture in one way or another has fashioned an argument about the appropriate social and moral arrangements that lead to a satisfying life.

12. Family size varies a bit from settlement to settlement and between traditional farming families and those in nonfarm occupations. The average number of children per family reported by most studies ranges from six to eight, with seven being the most common.

13. In a recent paper Meyers (1991a) conducted an in-depth analysis of defection patterns in the Elkhart-Lagrange settlement. His estimates of retention in the Elkhart-Lagrange settlement are based on data provided in the *Indiana Amish Directory, Lagrange and Elkhart Counties* (Miller 1988). The estimates for Lancaster, provided by Kraybill (1989:14), are based on a sample of twenty church districts conducted in 1986.

14. The retention data for the Holmes County settlement are derived from the 1988 *Ohio Amish Directory, Holmes County and Vicinity*. Data were compiled on all of the New Order congregations and on all of the districts affiliated with the Andy Weaver group. A sample of one-third of the districts was used to generate the estimates for the Old Order group.

15. The 1988 Directory for the Elkhart-Lagrange settlement provides a summary of occupations that yields the following breakdown: factory workers = 34 percent; farmers = 33 percent; a combination of factory and farming = 8 percent; miscellaneous shops and other occupations = 25 percent. Both this summary and Meyers' (1991b:315) tabulation suggest that only about one-third of the household heads in this large settlement are farming.

16. This tabulation was provided by the Sanitary Engineering Department of Geauga County, Ohio, and summarized in a memo to Uria R. Byler, dated 3 August 1977. A copy of the memo is located in the Heritage Historical Library, Alymer, Ontario. Foster (1984b:8) reports similar percentages for this settlement based on its 1973 and 1982 directories. He found 28 percent were farming in 1973 and 31 percent in 1982.

17. These numbers, derived from the settlements' directories, are reported by Kreps et al. (1992:14). My own tabulation of the occupational data in the 1988 Ohio directory, broken down by affiliation, showed the following percentages involved in farming: Andy Weaver group = 46 percent, Old Order group = 36 percent, and New Order = 35 percent. These findings are discussed in more detail in chapter 4.

18. Martineau and MacQueen (1977) reported that 66 percent of the Lancaster Amish were farming. In a sample of twenty church districts a decade later, Kraybill (1989) found that 67 percent were involved in agriculture. Using data from the settlement's 1988 directory, Dorsten (1992) determined that the number farming had dropped to 53 percent. The proportion who are farming varies considerably from district to district depending on their location in the county.

19. These included the infamous *Wisconsin v. Yoder* (1972), *United States v. Lee* (1982), and *Minnesota v. Hershberger* (1990). The court ruled in favor of the Amish in the first case and against them in the second case, which involved Social Security payments by an Amish employer. The third case, concerning the use of slow-moving vehicle signs, was returned to the Minnesota Supreme Court. All of these cases are described in detail in Kraybill (1993a).

Chapter 2. The Amish Encounter with Modernity

1. A competing explanation to this hypothesis is the fact that some of the smaller, more rural Amish settlements are also newer. These are sometimes made up of families who want to maintain a more traditional Ordnung and have sought more rural isolated areas where they can continue in farming. Consequently a self-selection factor may complicate what otherwise appears to be an inverse relationship between urbanization and traditional Amish practices.

2. See Berger (1974:21) and Berger et al. (1973:177) for a discussion of this argument.

3. As Berger (1977) and Kraybill (1990a) have shown, the various features of modernity are highly interrelated and not easily separated into discrete categories for causal analysis.

4. Another example of emergent bureaucracy is the recent formation of an Amish credit union in the Lagrange settlement of Indiana. The newly formed organization lends money to members of the Amish church for the purchase of real estate.

5. Bellah et al. (1985) and Berger et al. (1973) both make a compelling argument about the separation that accompanies industrialization.

Chapter 3. War Against Progress: Coping with Social Change

1. I am indebted to Marc Olshan for the notion of a "war against progress." It may sound oxymoronic to talk about the pacifist Amish engaged in a war, but they do view life as a spiritual warfare whose outcome will have eternal consequences for their community. It may be more fitting to talk about a war against the "spirit" of progress, for the Amish are not opposed to progress per se; they are interested rather in thwarting the spirit of progress that her-

alds individualism, novelty, progress at any cost, and technological advances that rupture human communities.

2. For a discussion of the struggle with the telephone see Kraybill (1989) as well as chapter 6 of this volume, by Diane Zimmerman Umble.

3. For an extended discussion of the various patterns of electrical usage consult Kraybill (1989:50–164) and Scott and Pellman (1990).

4. Scott and Pellman (1990:9) estimate that about 97 percent of the Amish use motorized washing machines.

5. For an introduction to the many confrontations between the Amish and the state in the twentieth century, see the collection of essays edited by Kraybill (1993a).

6. For an extended discussion of this controversy, see Zook (1993).

7. Many affiliations permit members to eat in public restaurants during the day while on the job, but frown on families eating out for convenience or pleasure.

Chapter 4. Plotting Social Change Across Four Affiliations

1. The data reported in this chapter are based on personal observation and discussion with Amish informants in the Holmes County, Ohio, settlement in August 1992 and May 1993. I am grateful to all those who generously shared their time and ideas with me. I especially thank Leroy Beachy, Levi Miller, George Kreps, and three members of the Amish community for reading an earlier draft of this chapter and providing helpful suggestions. Although I refer to the settlement as "Holmes County," it spills into four contiguous counties—Wayne, Stark, Tuscarawas, and Coshocton.

2. This estimate of the number of districts is based on the 1965 edition of the *Ohio Amish Directory, Holmes County and Vicinity* and the 1993 *Address and Business Directory for Holmes County and Vicinity* [Amish] as well as Raber's (1993) *Almanac* and local informants. The estimates include the major affiliations and Swartzentrubers as well as small break-off groups, but do not include the more progressive Beachey Amish, who drive cars.

3. There have been surprisingly few studies conducted on the Holmes County settlement. Huntington's (1957) dissertation is the basic and most comprehensive study of the settlement. Many of the observations reported in Schreiber's (1962) book come from this area but his work is not a systematic social description of the settlement. Sparse historical information on the settlement is provided in the various Ohio Amish directories for Holmes County and vicinity (1965, 1973, 1981, 1988) as well as in Kaufman and Beachy (1991) and Miller (1977). Miller (1992) provides a brief and popular introduction to all the Anabaptist-related groups in the Holmes County area as well as a fictional account based on the settlement (Miller 1989). A communication-oriented dissertation by Olsen (1989) focused on the New Order affiliation. Kreps et al. (1992) discuss changing occupational roles in the Holmes County area.

4. This is the time period for the emergence of the "Old Order" label given

by Holmes County historian Leroy Beachy, who grew up in the Old Order Amish church. Personal interview, 31 May 1993.

5. The so-called strict Meidung has often been a focus of church controversy and division. Those who support a "softer" Meidung are inclined to lift the shunning if a member joins another Amish or Mennonite congregation and is in "good standing" with the new congregation. One Amishman noted that "many times when 'strict shunning' is given as the apparent reason for a division, there's often a personality conflict below the surface."

6. This is no longer the case today. Typically a boy who buys a car cannot stay at home.

7. Because of their strict interpretation of shunning, the Andy Weaver group was "in fellowship" (affiliated) with the Amish in the Lancaster settlement. This has become somewhat ironic in recent years because the Andy Weavers, who are more conservative than the Old Orders in Holmes County, are affiliated with the much more progressive Lancaster Amish.

8. Amish minister David A. Miller of Oklahoma stirred up the Holmes County Amish community in 1950 with fervent revivalist preaching that was out of character with traditional Amish views. He quickly became an unwelcome guest in many Old Order Amish communities and his congregation in Oklahoma eventually affiliated with the Beachey Amish Fellowship (Yoder 1987:80). In 1957 Mennonite evangelist George R. Brunk II brought his tent campaign to Holmes County and again promoted assurance of salvation and personal Bible study, all of which threatened Old Order leaders and encouraged some Amish youth and progressive-minded leaders to become critical of Old Order practices.

9. Elmer S. Yoder (1987) describes the formation of the Beachy Amish Mennonite Fellowship churches in the twentieth century. He gives special attention to the Holmes County area and reports that by 1985 there were twenty-one congregations in this affiliation in the state of Ohio.

10. The group preferred and used the name Amish Brotherhood at the time of their origin but the term New Order Amish—in contrast with Old Order—has gradually emerged as their recognized name over the years. See Elmer S. Yoder (1987:80) for a brief discussion of the evolution of the name. Other New Order congregations have also emerged in several other states including Illinois, Indiana, Kentucky, Michigan, New York, North Carolina, and Pennsylvania, as well as in other areas of Ohio.

11. Bed courtship, sometimes called "bundling," refers to the practice of unmarried young people sleeping together or at least spending part of an evening together in bed. The New Orders felt that this practice led to immorality and fornication and they strongly opposed it. For an essay outlining the New Order opposition to bed courtship, see *Treatise* (n.d.). Although no publication date or author is listed in the pamphlet, the author, a New Order minister, wrote it in 1980–81.

12. Entitled *Christlicher Ordnung* or *Christian Doctrine*, the Ordnung is organized around twenty-one points and printed in pamphlet form in English. The most formal articulation of New Order belief and doctrine is *The Truth in Word*

and Work, a seventy-five-page booklet that summarizes the thinking of the church on thirty-one beliefs including Satan, Singing, the Non-Use of Force, and the Holy Kiss, as well as Excommunication and the Ban (*Truth* 1983).

13. Although one or two of the New Order districts do not hold Sunday school, the majority of them do.

14. In all fairness, it must be noted that many Old Order young people also work in English-speaking environments.

15. At the time of this writing rubber panties were starting to come into use among the Swartzentrubers.

16. For an extended discussion of the threat of the car as well as the symbolic significance of the carriage, see Kraybill (1989:73–78, 165–71). Scott (1981) has written the most complete description of the various styles of Amish carriages.

17. The Swartzentrubers' refusal to display the slow-moving vehicle emblem was reviewed by the U.S. Supreme Court in a case that originated in Minnesota. For a discussion of the story, see Zook (1993). At the time of this writing the state of Ohio was considering legislation that would require the emblem, as well as flashing lights, on all carriages.

18. Scott and Pellman (1990) provide a description of household technology in other Amish settlements.

19. For an extended discussion of the Amish fear and acceptance of the tractor in the Lancaster settlement, see Kraybill (1989:171–77).

20. It is not completely clear why the engine was permitted on the sprayer. It is difficult to obtain adequate water pressure with a wheel-driven pump. The need for weed and insect control apparently overwhelmed the reluctance to break an old taboo and the fear that the use of one implement with an engine would lead to others.

21. My tabulation of the occupational data reported in the 1988 *Ohio Amish Directory, Holmes County and Vicinity* shows that 39 percent of the males are involved in full-time farming. This estimate is based on a full enumeration of the Andy Weaver and New Order districts and a one-third, systematic sample of the Old Order districts. If part-time farmers are included, the percentage of farmers in the settlement is 43, which is what Kreps et al. (1992:14) also report. None of these estimates includes the Swartzentruber districts, which are excluded from the directory. The percentage of Swartzentrubers in farming is much higher than in the other groups.

22. These are listed by type of business in the 1993 *Address and Business Directory of Holmes County and Vicinity* [Amish].

23. The Swartzentrubers have had some problems with young people literally running away from home. In some cases they return and join the church, but some do not return. Some persons think that this is why the Swartzentrubers do not permit their young people to study geography even in Amish parochial schools. One Swartzentruber student is reported to have said that, "They don't want us to study geography so we won't know where to go." Other observers doubt that this is the reason for the taboo on geography.

24. The use of "high" and "low" and moving "up" and "down" to de-

scribe intergroup relationships is somewhat problematic and indeed suggests an ethnocentric bias on the part of observers who talk about traditional Amish moving "up" to "higher" churches that are more likely to be closer to the sympathies of the observer or analyst. There are, however, good reasons for using the terms low and high to describe mobility from more traditional Anabaptist groups to more progressive ones. The Amish themselves frequently distinguish between churches with a low (traditional) Ordnung and those with a higher (less restrictive) Ordnung. Consequently they also talk about "low" and "high" churches.

The use of "low" and "high" also has a substantive meaning in Anabaptist culture. The virtues of humility, self-denial, meekness, and lowliness are esteemed in traditional Anabaptist groups. All of these virtues, the essence of Gelassenheit, symbolize the subjection of the individual to the community. Churches that tolerate greater individualism and arrogant and proud behavior are viewed as "high" churches. Moreover a greater use of the English language—the currency of the dominant society—also symbolizes upward social mobility to "high" society in the eyes of traditionalists. Thus, for all these reasons it is appropriate to describe the shift to a more progressive group as a move "up." Driedger (1977) has used the term "ladder" to describe the stratification of Anabaptist groups. I prefer the metaphor of escalator because it suggests that although there are steps between the groups they are all—even the most conservative—moving upward as they gradually accept new innovations. Redekop (1989:38) makes a brief reference to an "escalator" to liberalism in describing the same phenomenon.

Chapter 5. Persistence and Change in Amish Education

1. This chapter is a revision of a major lecture given at the international conference, Three Hundred Years Of Persistence And Change: Amish Society 1693–1993, held at the Young Center for the Study of Anabaptist and Pietist Groups, Elizabethtown College, 22–25 July 1993.

2. *Blackboard Bulletin*, February 1960, reprinted in the *Challenge of the Child* (Stoll 1967:120–22). The author contended that, "There is a world of difference between refusing to co-operate on matters of no religious significance, and refusing to compromise in our religious beliefs."

3. J. F. S. "Unser Kinder in der Zwangschulen," *Herold der Wahrheit*, 1 June 1952:332.

4. Simons (1956:950), *The Challenge of the Child: Selections from* The Blackboard Bulletin, *1957–1963*, Stoll (1964:22–24), and Stoll (1967:49–52).

5. See Huntington (1957:439–42), a study of an Old Order Amish community in Ohio, for an illustration of Amish parents precipitating the removal of a public school teacher.

6. *The Budget*, 18 January 1951:1.

7. Ibid.

8. Ibid., 15 January 1954:6.

9. An Amish authored history of the Ohio parochial school movement is titled *A Struggle to Be Separate* (Hershberger 1985).

10. Riddle (1910:44). He also observed that "as school directors the Amish have been found to be among the most progressive in the country." In the 1950s the most conservative Amish still rejected teaching geography.

11. *Budget*, 23 December 1954:1, and 17 January 1955:4. For a detailed discussion of the Amish school controversy in central Ohio in the mid-1950s, see Huntington (1957:465–95), Hershberger (1985), Buchanan (1967), and Meyers (1993:87–108).

12. *Guidelines* (1981:42), Hostetler and Huntington (1992:40–41), Kraybill (1989:128–29), Meyers (1993:92), and Hostetler (1993:261–64).

13. Pennsylvania still has a functioning vocational school program, but vocational classes have been discontinued in Ohio and Indiana and were never started in most other states.

14. *Wisconsin v. Yoder* (1972). This case is mentioned in virtually every discussion of Amish education published after 1972. See Albert N. Keim (1975).

15. Consensus on starting a school was relatively easy to achieve in townships where the Amish were having trouble, but in areas where public schooling was going relatively smoothly it was more difficult.

16. For more information concerning the Iowa case, see Erickson (1966:82–87, 102–103; 1968:36–44, and 1969:15–59); Hughes (1969:7–14); Meyers (1993:87–108); and Rodgers (1969).

17. The figures for all of the data come from the *Blackboard Bulletin*. Because reporting is voluntary the figures are only approximate. Sometimes they have been modified by knowledgeable people, sometimes arbitrary assumptions are made, such as that schools that do not report the number students are generally assumed to have twenty pupils and schools that do not report the number of teachers are assumed to have one teacher. The data from which the pre-1956 figures were determined were compiled by Ira Stoll from the *Blackboard Bulletin*, reprinted in Stoll (1967:116). The date of founding of eight schools was unknown. Table 5.1 was adapted and expanded from the *Blackboard Bulletin*, October 1987:23. By counting the schools reporting in the various issues of the *Blackboard Bulletin*, and by using the above estimate for nonreporting schools, Karen Yoder determined the number of schools to be: 1965—150, 1970—303, 1975—399, 1980—490, 1985—595, 1990—722, and 1994—846. The preface to *School Bells Ringing* (Byler 1969) stated that there were 60 Amish schools in 1958 and 230 in 1968.

18. Numbers vary slightly depending on one's source and one's definition of when a school is founded: when classes begin, when a building is erected, when it reports to *Blackboard Bulletin*, etc.

19. Hostetler and Huntington (1992:5).

20. Hostetler and Huntington (1992:59–60) and Fishman (1988:79).

21. Occasionally non-Amish teachers are hired. They are expected to be of good character but are not complete role models and of course are not obedient to the Ordnung.

22. For example Byler (1969), Miller (n.d.), and the series of books for grades 2–8, *Helping with English*, compiled by Ohio Teachers Committee, re-

vised 1988. An early example of an activity book was Jonas Nisley's, *Children's Read, Write, Color, Book* (1965). It was a hand-duplicated, 320-page, loose leaf book of pictures, sayings, news items, and educational selections, sold to parents and teachers.

23. There were about twenty-one teachers in 1951, a figure that had more than doubled, to about fifty-one, by 1957. The history of the *Blackboard Bulletin* was compiled from interviews with Joseph Stoll by the author.

24. This was published by Pathway and widely distributed among the Amish. It was also published in Keim (1975:16–42).

Chapter 6. Amish on the Line: The Telephone Debates

1. This schism is described in detail by Kraybill (1989:141–46) and by Umble (1991a:ch.5).

2. The theoretical framework for this approach to the study of communication technologies is rooted in the cultural study of communication articulated by James Carey (1989) and applied to the telephone by Carolyn Marvin (1988 and 1989). The discussion of boundaries and rituals is rooted in the symbolic anthropology of Cohen (1985) and Turner (1982). For a more detailed description of the role of rituals in managing communication in Amish society, see Umble (1991a and 1991b).

3. For extensive descriptions of Amish worship practices, see Hostetler's (1993) anthropological study, chapter 7, and Kraybill's (1989) sociological perspective, chapter 5.

4. The Old Order Mennonites also experienced conflicts over the telephone. In 1907, the Pennsylvania Old Order Mennonites crafted a compromise that allowed lay people to own telephones but prohibited clergy from doing so. In Iowa, the telephone troubles were debated, in part, with respect to the dilemma of telephone stock ownership. Many rural telephone companies were organized as cooperatives. In order to subscribe to a telephone, one had to buy stock in the company. Iowa Amish were prohibited from owning stock, so local companies made an exception and allowed them to simply rent a telephone instrument. For more on the Old Order Mennonite troubles, see Umble (1991a) and Hoover (1982). The Iowa struggles are described by Atwood (1984) and M. Gingerich (1986).

5. The strict application of shunning had long been a contentious issue in the Pennsylvania settlement. The debate became especially painful when Old Order Amish minister Moses Hartz and his wife, Magdalena, were excommunicated, in part for refusing to shun their son in 1894. Dissatisfaction over the handling of this incident festered for years and colored subsequent discussions of the issue (Kraybill 1989:141–43). The strict application of shunning was also a point of disagreement in the Ohio and Illinois Amish settlements (Nolt 1992:204–207).

6. *Ephrata Review*, 6 November 1914:9.

7. Kraybill (1989:149), his emphasis.

Chapter 7. The Origin and Growth of Amish Tourism

1. This chapter is to a large extent based on often anonymous articles and brochures of the tourist industry. See also Buck (1978) and Kraybill (1989) for other perspectives on the Lancaster tourist industry.

2. For more details on this story, see Kraybill (1989:122–23).

3. "Printing Record of *Rosanna of the Amish* "(Yoder 1940), prepared by Paul M. Schrock, Mennonite Publishing House, February 1994.

4. The Bureau was originally formed in 1957 as the "Visitors Bureau" of the Lancaster Chamber of Commerce. Ten years later it became a separate organization, which by 1978 represented approximately 350 tourist-related businesses and attractions (Loose 1978:204).

5. "Film on Lancaster County Produced for Bicentennial," *Mennonite Weekly Review*, 19 February 1976:6.

6. David Luthy, personal interview with Roy Weaver, founder and owner of Dutch Haven, 9 November 1984.

7. "Lancaster County Amish are Subjects of New Broadway Musical Comedy," *The Budget*, 10 March 1955:1,6.

8. Letter dated 17 January 1978 from Betty Goodman to David Luthy.

9. For comment on Wilson's candid photos, cf. Prusha 1986:1.

10. Jim Carney, "Berlin's Amish Lure Travelers," *Akron Beacon Journal*, 25 June 1989:A1.

11. Joe Ionne, "The Selling of the Amish," *The Columbus Dispatch Sunday Magazine*, 10 June 1979.

12. Paul Locher, "Look What Tourism's Done for the Amish," *The Daily Record*, 30 May 1989.

13. Kathy Barks, "On Auction Day Shipshewana Gets Lively," *The Goshen News*, 23 August 1977.

14. O. Vernon Miller, "Shipshewana, Indiana," *The Budget*, 1 February 1989:16.

15. O. Vernon Miller, "Shipshewana, Indiana," *The Budget*, 11 April 1990:12.

Chapter 8. Amish Cottage Industries as Trojan Horse

1. An earlier version of this chapter appeared as "The Opening of Amish Society: Cottage Industry as Trojan Horse," in *Human Organization* 50/4 (1991): 378–84.

2. There is no single, formally organized group known as the Old Order Amish. The term encompasses many relatively diverse and autonomous churches. The terms Old Order Amish, Old Order, and Amish will be used synonymously here to refer to this diversity of groups.

3. See, for example, *Who Are The Amish?* (n.d.).

4. See Hostetler (1993) and Kraybill (1989).

5. The figure is based on a tabulation of the districts listed in *The New American Almanac*, which is updated each year (see Raber 1993).

6. The first Amish settlement in New York, founded in 1949, remains the largest, with nine church districts. In 1974 two additional settlements were established, and between 1976 and 1992 another thirteen. One settlement was recently disbanded, its members leaving for other states.

7. This diversity exists within as well as among families. Cottage industry, wage labor, and agriculture are not mutually exclusive choices. The majority of New York Amish families have members engaged in various combinations of all three. The relative importance of any activity will depend on the number of family members engaged in each, the time of year, and local economic conditions. It can be said with certainty, however, that the contribution of cottage industry is far greater than it has ever been.

8. The accuracy of these evaluations is less important than the fact that they are widely and sincerely held and thus real in their consequences.

9. For a history and analysis of *Wisconsin v. Yoder* see Keim (1975).

10. Stoll in Eric Bender, "Cottage Industries Help Amish Change With Times," *London Free Press*, 21 March 1981:B2.

11. Both Hostetler (1993) and Kraybill (1989) argue that Amish cottage industry serves to reduce interactions with non-Amish. For Amish customers in the largest settlements this may be true. For example, in Lancaster County, "Today's Amish can purchase most of their everyday supplies and services from Amish proprietors" (Kraybill 1989:214). But when a significant percentage of the Amish population is *selling* goods and services to the public, the argument for reduced interaction is vitiated. For another perspective on the significance of cottage industry see Foster (1984b).

12. In their descriptions of Amish life, social scientists have generally treated the Old Order with kid gloves. It is an understandable stance. Anyone who spends time with the Amish is likely to develop a respect for what they are attempting and accomplishing. At the same time the cumulative effect has been a picture somewhat distorted by the frequent use of rose-colored glasses.

13. Ed Klimuska, "He's Got So Many Phones In There . . . ," *Lancaster New Era*, 20 October 1990:A14.

14. Jennifer Stoffel, "Fresh From Ohio's Amish Ovens," *The New York Times*, 10 June 1990:6V.

15. Jennifer Stoffel, "Fresh From Ohio's Amish Ovens," *The New York Times*, 10 June 1990:6V.

16. W. Thompson Holland, "Experts See Amish Shift From Farming to Cottage Industries," *Lancaster Intelligencer Journal*, 2 January 1990:B-1.

17. In a similar vein Edmund Wilson (1972:34), paraphrasing Michelet, writes of the merchant that "he leads the most miserable existence of all, compelled to be servile to his customers. . . ."

18. See, for example, Cohen (1970) and Mayer (1979).

Chapter 9. The Rise of Microenterprises

1. The Pequea district formed about 1790 and became a permanent district of the settlement. Other districts in Lancaster County likely began before 1790 but did not survive. The Conestoga district near the boundaries of Lancaster and Berks County had formed in the Conestoga Valley about 1760.

2. Some Amish persons did begin working in local factories when several mobile home factories were built near the Amish community. By the early seventies nearly one hundred Amishmen were working in these factories, but the economic slump in the midseventies forced layoffs and the closing of some of the plants, which increased suspicion of factory work among the Amish community.

3. The exact percentage of adult men who are farming is unknown and varies considerably from church district to church district. In a sample of twenty church districts in 1987, 64 percent of the adult men were farming. The 1988 *Directory* reported 53 percent of the men as farmers (Dorsten 1992). The percentage farming has dropped in subsequent years and is likely below 50 percent.

4. This project was made possible in part by a grant from the Center for Rural Pennsylvania, a legislative agency of the Pennsylvania General Assembly, under a subcontract from the Pennsylvania State University. Professors Steven Smith and Jill Findeis, at the Pennsylvania State University, served as codirectors of the project. The Young Center of Elizabethtown College was subcontracted to conduct the field work. Interviews were conducted in the spring of 1993 but reflected business activity for the calendar year of 1992. A representative sample of 13 church districts was selected from the Lancaster settlement. All the households and enterprises in the 13 districts of the sample were enumerated. Interviews were conducted with 114 owners of the 118 enterprises that were identified in the sample, yielding a cooperation rate of 97 percent. Interviewers included Martin Franke, Lester Hoover, Steven M. Nolt, and Jerold Stahly. We are grateful for their fine help and assistance with the project. Steven M. Nolt coordinated the field work and also conducted 35 in-depth interviews beyond those in the sample.

5. Within the sample of 13 church districts, which had 118 enterprises, we found no cases of bankruptcy and little evidence of failure.

6. Self-employed Amish persons and those working for Amish employers are exempt from Social Security. However, those working for non-Amish employers are required to pay Social Security—even though many of them do not collect its benefits.

7. The study, consisting of face-to-face interviews with two hundred visitors to Lancaster County, was conducted by Jéan Paul Benowitz in May 1993 at the Mennonite Information Center. Visitors to the Center were asked a variety of questions about their perceptions of Amish products.

8. Many entrepreneurs were once day laborers themselves. Day laborers have limited financial means but are not necessarily locked into that class or hindered from becoming small business owners as a result.

Chapter 10. Lunch Pails and Factories

1. A few families live across the southern border of Lagrange County in northern Noble County.

2. The data for this table were taken from a dissertation (Juberg 1966) and three community directories (Cross and Gingerich 1970), (Gingerich 1980), and (Miller 1988).

3. For a discussion of migration see Luthy (1992) and Hostetler (1993).

4. For more information on the dynamics of retention and defection in this settlement, see Meyers (forthcoming).

5. This basic theological premise, that the world is divided into a sacred and eternal realm and an earthly arena that is ephemeral, is taken directly from the sixteenth-century forebears of the Amish, the Anabaptists. It is at the heart of Amish culture and is a perspective that shapes many areas of their life. For a description of the application of a two-kingdom theology in the area of education, see Meyers (1993).

6. Alfred Albrecht, personal correspondence, 16 September 1991.

7. The pattern in other settlements is more hierarchical. See Kraybill (1989: 82–86) for a discussion of the ministers' meetings in Lancaster County, Pennsylvania.

8. *Die Blatte* (7 May 1992):14.

9. For a discussion of the rationale behind the testing of the boundaries of the Amish community see Hostetler (1993) and Kraybill (1989).

10. Statistical significance was determined by Cramer's $V=.07$, $P>.05$.

Chapter 11. Modernity, the Folk Society, and the Old Order Amish

1. The original version of this chapter appeared in *Rural Sociology* 46/2 (1981): 297–309.

2. Just how untenable are such quasi-psychological explanations was clearly demonstrated by White (1969).

3. Berger (1974:21), emphasis in the original.

4. "Tractors Never Foal," *Wall Street Journal*, 1 May 1946:66.

5. "Amishmen Battle to Keep Life Drab," *New York Times*, 15 August 1937: II,2.

6. The vast majority of Amish school-age children are now enrolled in Amish parochial schools.

7. See Olshan and Hall (1991) for an analysis of the justification for these plans.

8. Dick Snyder, "Amish Undisturbed by the War Shortages, Have Always Done Without Autos and Such," *New York Times*, 12 April 1942:I,10.

9. See, for example, *New York Times*, 6 December 1973:4 and 16 March 1974:64.

Chapter 12. Homespun Bureaucracy

1. An earlier version of this chapter appeared as "The Old Order Amish Steering Committee: A Case Study in Organizational Evolution," in *Social Forces* 69 (1990): 603–16.

2. See, e.g., Schein 1965:89; Stinchcombe 1965:142; Thompson 1967:28.

3. Aldrich 1979:164; emphasis in original.

4. The terms "Amish" and "Old Order Amish" are used synonymously in this chapter.

5. The question of Amish adaptation and survival has been frequently addressed (see, e.g., Stoltzfus 1973; Lewis 1976b; Ericksen et al. 1980; Hostetler 1977, 1984; Kraybill 1989). This literature has not, however, explicitly addressed the absence of formal organization as a discrete factor.

6. The list is not meant to be comprehensive. For an overview of Amish culture and its Anabaptist origins, see Hostetler (1993).

7. David Luthy, personal communication, 18 April 1979.

8. For example, in the largest Old Order Amish settlement—the Holmes County, Ohio, area—less than one-half of all Amishmen are now engaged in farming. Almost one-quarter are employed as factory workers or laborers (Troyer & Willoughby 1984). A similar trend is evidenced in Lancaster County, Pennsylvania (Martineau & MacQueen 1977).

9. Andrew S. Kinsinger, interview 17 July 1989, Gordonville, Pa.

10. Official correspondence of George C. Guenther, Assistant Secretary of Labor, to A. S. Kinsinger, 30 May 1972 and 14 June 1972, Washington, D.C.

11. Proposed laws in Indiana and Missouri requiring that milk be cooled to 50 degrees instead of 60 degrees would have forced the Amish to use mechanical coolers or to sell their dairy herds.

12. The Steering Committee was not directly involved in the 1972 U.S. Supreme Court ruling exempting Amish children from compulsory attendance beyond the eighth grade. The case nonetheless demonstrates the efficacy of organization. The Amish effort was funded by the National Committee for Amish Religious Freedom, a group organized on behalf of the Amish. Despite the ruling, other areas of conflict, such as the qualifications of teachers, continued to exist (for a history of the issues, see Keim 1975). Also, some local education officials, especially in areas being newly settled by Amish, seemed unaware of the court's decision and had to be educated about it.

13. The document cited both the Bible and Chief Justice Burger in legitimizing the practice of not paying minors directly. It claimed to "serve as a *fair* and *legal* notice; parent shall have full authority to collect any wages paid direct to the minor child by employer" (Steering Committee 1980:5; emphasis in original).

14. Steering Committee 1980, 1986, 1989, 1992.

15. "Some Amish Missed News of Nuclear Plant Accident," *Ithaca Journal* 8 August 1979:2.

16. Andrew S. Kinsinger, interview 17 July 1989, Gordonville, Pa.

17. This frequently cited metaphor perpetuates Michels' misreading of

Homer. Despite the unlikeliness of dashing oneself against a whirlpool, the image seems to have served well in evoking the concept of a dilemma.

18. Steering Committee 1972:58; emphasis in original.

19. The image of the organization as a wheel, with its graphic denial of hierarchy, was also invoked by the Industrial Workers of the World. Their circular organizational chart, the "Wheel of Fortune," was intended to convey the idea of rule by the rank and file. It was adapted at the 1905 founding convention (Dubofsky 1969).

20. Wood's explication provides a useful (and neatly symmetrical) counterpoint to Perrow's (1986:170) assertion that "Michels' insight has . . . blinded us all." According to Perrow, Michels showed how leaders are induced unwittingly, without malice, and inevitably to compromise original goals. Michels thus neglected the possibility that leaders may in fact be malicious, corrupt, and uncommitted to organizational values in the first place. Wood raises the opposite possibility, that organizational values may be well served by a committed leadership despite the evolution of hierarchy.

21. Although interpretations of the causes and significance of this pattern vary, the universal diffusion of bureaucratic forms is undisputed. For one example of the literature documenting the history of bureaucracy, see Jacoby (1973).

22. Hostetler (1977) acknowledges Siegel's thesis but does not mention the Steering Committee as an expression of defensive structuring. Hostetler's (1977:360) conclusion that "defensive structuring does not adequately explain the existence of the Amish" is indisputable in light of the history of the Amish to 1966. Yet it does not acknowledge that, since then, the Amish themselves have recognized the need for a new adaptive strategy.

23. Amish communities in Canada constitute a quasi-control group for their U.S. brethren. The absence of military conscription and a generally more tolerant administrative approach have meant a much less stressful environment for the Canadian Amish. They have not felt compelled to organize formally.

24. The original impetus for at least one plan was that, "The banks wanted something that . . . could be used as security to obtain mortgages on farm loans" (Wagler 1966:250).

25. Some Amish affiliations have rejected all such institutionalized risk-sharing and rely strictly on free will offerings to help cover losses. For a discussion of these divergent viewpoints see Olshan and Hall (1991).

26. Although the Amish are not mentioned, their use of bureaucratic structures is an example of antagonistic acculturation, one expression of which is "the adaption of new means in order to support existing ends" (Devereux and Loeb 1943:139). Another example is that of the reorganization of the U.S. Army "along German lines" (Devereux and Loeb 1943:141).

Chapter 13. Amish Women and the Feminist Conundrum

1. Authors are listed in alphabetical order and share authorship equally.

2. One exception is Alma Hershberger's (1992) *Amish Women*. Other potential exceptions are the female scribes for *Die Botschaft* and *The Budget*. In these cases, however, the writers limit themselves almost entirely to the more or less neutral reporting of daily events.

3. In a second study of women who had opted for Orthodox Judaism, Lynn Davidman (1991:194) reaches the same conclusion: Women found orthodoxy "appealing precisely because it offered a conception of femininity in which women's roles as wives and mothers were honored and seen as central. . . ."

4. Stoll 1977b:9; emphasis in the original.

5. For typical levels of production in Lancaster County see Ericksen and Klein (1981).

6. The same could be said of hair. In a recent study of hair loss Bodo and Baba (1992:28) found that Amish women who were losing their hair "did not seem to be as concerned about attractiveness as they were about being different."

7. Reschly and Jellison's (1993) analysis of Amish households in Lancaster County, Pennsylvania, in the 1930s confirms the significance of this contribution for that time period as well.

8. See also Bettie Gay (1981: 309) and Donald Marti (1984: 247–61).

9. The importance of the family is indicated by the fact that the size of Amish church districts is defined by the number of families rather than the number of individual members.

10. This section relies on the analysis presented in Joan W. Scott (1986). For discussions of gender as a culturally bound construction see M. Z. Rosaldo (1980) and Sherry B. Ortner and Harriet Whitehead (1981).

11. See Peggy Reeves Sanday (1981) on how gender inequalities are not necessarily related to separate female and male work responsibilities.

12. For example, Sherry B. Ortner's study of Polynesians found that their society values kinship ties: "where prestige is importantly maintained and augmented through the enlargement of descent lines, kinswomen—sisters and daughters—appear as particularly valuable beings . . . and . . . are thus treated with rather contradictory forms of respect" (Ortner and Whitehead 1981:5). The Amish also highly value kinship networks and perhaps Ortner's work can point the way for further research.

13. In her study of an Old Order Amish community, Huntington (1957: 815n52) observed that it is "really not until the birth of his[/her] first child that [the individual] is considered a full adult."

14. Huntington 1957:857–59 and Scott 1988:15.

15. Jane M. Pederson (1993) discovered how a Norwegian community banded together to lynch a man who was terrorizing his family and the community. The Amish eschew such violence. But Amish community norms may have the same impact in limiting male aggression.

16. Violence against women is not unknown in Amish society as one di-

vorce case shows. The Amishwoman was granted a divorce "on the ground of extreme cruelty" after the court found that her husband had physically abused her on several occasions (*Byler v. Byler* 1981).

17. Karen Yoder, telephone conversation, 19 July 1993.

18. See Kraybill (1989), Hostetler (1993), and Huntington (1957) for a discussion of the role of women.

Chapter 14. What Good Are the Amish?

1. Brad Gillespie, "Amish Lifestyle a Cage on Human Potential," *Rochester Democrat and Chronicle*, 11 January 1985:4A.

2. Carrier and Carrier (1987:271) make this point with regard to the presumed survival of traditional Melanesian culture.

3. See, for example, Hostetler (1993), Hostetler and Huntington (1992), Kraybill (1989), and Yoder (1991).

4. See, for example, Miller (1943:58).

5. Buck (1978:224) refers to the "managed curiosity status" of the Amish accorded them by entrepreneurs of tourist attractions.

6. See Kraybill's discussion of the Ordnung in chapter 1.

7. The relationship between envy, fear, and death is strikingly made in John H. Snow's (1971) "Fear of Death and the Need to Accumulate."

8. Berry (1977 and 1982) explicitly addresses the relevance of the Amish elsewhere.

9. Jim Nagel, "Amish Will Be Driving Cars Within 40 Years, Mennonite Predicts," *Kitchener-Waterloo Record*, 11 March 1978.

Appendix. Amish Migration Patterns: 1972–1992

1. The Amish population increases so rapidly because the Amish do not as a rule practice artificial birth control. Completed families have an average of about seven children.

2. The seventeen states having Amish settlements at the beginning of 1972 were Delaware (1), Florida (1), Illinois (1), Indiana (10), Iowa (3), Kansas (3), Kentucky (1), Maryland (2), Michigan (5), Missouri (9), New York (1), Ohio (12), Oklahoma (1), Pennsylvania (23), Tennessee (2), Virginia (1), and Wisconsin (7).

3. The settlement, having sixty-eight congregations at the end of 1971, stretched across three Ohio counties: Wayne, Holmes, and Tuscarawas.

4. "The Amish School Decision: full text of the U.S. Supreme Court's decision in *Wisconsin v. Yoder*, together with dissenting and concurring opinions and footnotes," printed by Capitol Church Publishers, Washington, D.C., n.d. [1972].

5. Frank Santiago, "Nebraska's Amish Find Old Problems Remain," *World-Herald*, February 1978:1, 6.

6. "Amish Families Abandon Nebraska Colony," *Mennonite Weekly Review*, 15 April 1982.

7. An exception to this is the community at Aylmer, Ontario, which allowed dairy farmers to have bulk tanks powered by diesel motors. That settlement has grown considerably since the 1977 ruling.

8. This statement is verified by this particular Amishman's subscriber card at Pathway Publishers (the Amish publishing house) at Aylmer, Ontario.

9. Various communities that use the name "Amish-Mennonite" allow the ownership of automobiles. This study of migration deals only with the Amish who do not permit automobile ownership, including both Old Order Amish and New Order Amish.

10. Although the Old Order Amish and the New Order Amish travel by horse and buggy, there are many differences of church discipline (Ordnung) between them so that at least seven subgroups exist that do not exchange ministers at their services. In earlier chapters the word *affiliation* was used to refer to these subgroups.

11. Amanda Yoder, "St. Marys, Ontario," *Die Botschaft*, 11 July 1990:18.

12. E. S. Miller, "Kingston, Wisconsin," *The Budget*, 7 February 1990:11.

13. *Die Botschaft*, 7 August 1991:18.

14. *Die Botschaft*, 3 July 1991:36.

15. *Die Botschaft*, 17 July 1991:22.

16. *Die Botschaft*, 14 August 1991:23.

17. The listing of settlements and congregations in 1992 was compiled primarily from information appearing in the 1993 *Almanac* (Raber 1993). However, since the deadline for the 1993 edition was actually June 1992, that edition does not contain any data for 1993 as the date on the cover implies. Additional information not appearing in the *Almanac* was obtained from settlement files in the Heritage Historical Library, Aylmer, Ontario.

BIBLIOGRAPHY

Address and Business Directory of Holmes County and Vicinity [Amish]
1993 Millersburg, Ohio: Mast Printing.

Aldrich, Howard E.
1979 *Organizations and Environments.* Englewood Cliffs, N.J.: Prentice-Hall.

Aldrich, Howard E., and Peter V. Marsden
1988 "Environments and Organizations." In *Handbook of Sociology,* edited by Neil J. Smelser. Newbury Park, Calif.: Sage Publications.

Amish Directory of the Lancaster County Family: 1988
1989 Gordonville, Pa.: Pequea Publishers.

"Amish Hayride Tours"
1975 *Tuscarawas County Visitors Handbook* 7(3):11.

Amish Health Aid Plan [for Geauga County, Ohio]
n.d.

Appel, Mrs. T. Roberts, and Mrs. Calvin N. Wenrich
1933 *Old Pennsylvania Recipes.* Lancaster, Pa.: Privately printed.

"Are All Things Lawful?"
n.d. Aylmer, Ont.: Pathway Publishers.

Atwood, Roy Alden
1984 "Telephone and its Cultural Meanings in Southeastern Iowa, 1900–1917." Ph.D. diss., University of Iowa.

August, Evelyn
1977 "Indiana's Amish Country." *Michigan Living Motor News* (July): 30–31, 39.

Aurand, A. Monroe, Jr.
1938 *Little Known Facts About the Amish and Mennonites.* Harrisburg, Pa.: Aurand Press.
1942 *Where to Dine in the Penna. "Dutch" Region.* Harrisburg, Pa.: Aurand Press.

Bachman, Calvin George
1961 *The Old Order Amish of Lancaster County.* Vol. 60. Norristown, Pa.: The Pennsylvania German Society.

Beiler, Benjamin K.
1988 (ed.) *Old Order Shop and Service Directory*. Gordonville, Pa.: Pequea Publishers.

Beiler, Joseph F.
1977 (ed.) *Old Order Shop and Service Directory*. Gordonville, Pa.: Pequea Publishers.
1986 "Forward." In *Amish and Amish-Mennonite Genealogies*, compiled by Hugh F. Gingerich and Rachel W. Kreider. Gordonville, Pa.: Pequea Publishers.

Beiler, Lydia F.
1964 "Our Teachers' Meetings." In *Challenge of the Child* (mimeographed), 58.

Bellah, Robert N., R. Madsen, W. M. Sullivan, A. Swidler, and S. M. Tipton
1985 *Habits of the Heart*. Berkeley and Los Angeles: University of California Press.

Bender, Harold S.
1934 "Some Early American Amish Mennonite Disciplines." *Mennonite Quarterly Review* 8:90–97.
1946 "An Amish Bishop's Conference Epistle of 1865." *Mennonite Quarterly Review* 20:222–29.

Bender, Sue
1989 *Plain and Simple: A Woman's Journey to the Amish*. San Francisco: Harper Collins Publishers.

Berger, Peter L.
1974 *Pyramids of Sacrifice*. New York: Basic Books.
1977 *Facing Up to Modernity*. New York: Basic Books.

Berger, Peter L., Brigitte Berger, and Hansfried Kellner
1973 *The Homeless Mind: Modernization and Consciousness*. New York: Random House.

Berry, Wendell
1977 *The Unsettling of America*. New York: Avon.
1982 "The Amish Way." *Country Journal* (February): 45–50.
1990 *What Are People For?* San Francisco: North Point Press.

"Beyond the Bonnets and Buggies"
1980 *Family Life* (May): 7–8.

Blackboard Bulletin
1957– Aylmer, Ont.: Pathway Publishers.

Blakely, Paul L.
1937 "Rebecca of Honeybrook Farm." *America* (18 December): 245–46.

Blatt, Die
1992 Shipshewana, Ind.: Pleasant Ridge Printers.

Block, Issac
1992 "Domestic Abuse: A Case Study." In *Peace Theology and Violence Against Women*, edited by Elizabeth G. Yoder. Occasional papers no. 16. Elkhart, Ind.: Institute of Mennonite Studies.

Bodo, Dawn, and Marietta Baba
1992 "Hair Routes: An Anthropological Look at Hair and Hair Loss in Diverse American Cultures." Unpublished study, Wayne State University.

Botschaft, Die
1975– Lancaster, Pa.: Brookshire Publications and Printing.

Bourjaily, Vance
1980 "The Amish Farmer." *Esquire* (October): 92–99.

Braght, Thieleman J. van
1951 (comp.) *The Bloody Theatre; or, Martyrs Mirror*. Scottdale, Pa.: Mennonite Publishing House. Originally published in Dutch (Dordrecht, 1660).

Bryer, Kathleen B.
1979 "The Amish Way of Death: A Study of Family Support Systems." *American Psychologist* 34 (March): 255–61.

Buchanan, Frederick S.
1967 "The Old Paths: A Study of the Amish Response to Public Schooling in Ohio." Ph.D. diss., Ohio State University.

Buck, Roy
1978 "Boundary Maintenance Revisited: Tourist Experience in an Old Order Amish Community." *Rural Sociology* 43:221–34.

Budget, The
1890– Sugarcreek, Ohio: Sugarcreek Budget Publishers, Inc.

Byler, Uria R.
1969 *School Bells Ringing*. Aylmer, Ont.: Pathway Publishers.
1985 *As I Remember It*. Middlefield, Ohio: Elizabeth Byler.

Carey, James
1989 *Communication As Culture: Essays on Media and Society*. Boston: Unwin Hyman.

Carrier, Achsah H., and James G. Carrier
1987 "Brigadoon, or; Musical Comedy and the Persistence of Tradition in Melanesian Ethnography." *Oceania* 57:271–93.

Chalkdust
1991 . Aylmer, Ont.: Pathway Publishers.

"Choice of Two Evils"
1976 *Family Life* (February): 10–13.

"Christdag Among the Amish"
1985 *The Economist* (21 December): 23.

Coachmen Industries
1964 Unpublished document. Author unknown.

Cohen, Anthony P.
1985 *The Symbolic Construction of Community*. New York: Travistock Publications.

Cohen, Arthur A.
1970 *A People Apart: Hasidism in America*. New York: E. P. Dutton & Co.

Cronk, Sandra
1981 "Gelassenheit: The Rites of the Redemptive Process in Old Order Amish and Old Order Mennonite Communities." *Mennonite Quarterly Review* 55(1): 5–44.

Cross, Harold E.
1976 "Population Studies and the Old Order Amish." *Nature* 262 (1 July): 17–20.

Cross, Harold E., and Eli E. Gingerich
1970 *Indiana Amish Directory*. Baltimore: The Johns Hopkins University Press.

Davidman, Lynn
1991 *Tradition in a Rootless World: Women Turn to Orthodox Judaism*. Berkeley: University of California Press.

De Angeli, Marguerite
1936 *Henner's Lydia*. Garden City, N.Y.: Doubleday Company.
1944 *Yonie Wondernose*. Garden City, N.Y.: Doubleday, Doran and Company.

Devereux, George, and Edwin M. Loeb
1943 "Antagonistic Acculturation." *American Sociological Review* 8:133–47.

Dorsten, Linda
1992 "Direct and Indirect Effects on Infant Mortality in a Traditional Religious-Ethnic Population." Revision of a paper presented at the North Central Sociological Association Annual Meetings in Ft. Wayne, Ind., April 26.

Driedger, Leo
1977 "The Anabaptist Identification Ladder: Plain Urban Continuity in Diversity." *Mennonite Quarterly Review* 51:278–91.

Dubofsky, Melvyn
1969 *We Shall Be All: A History of the Industrial Workers of the World.* Chicago: Quadrangle Books.

Durkheim, Emile
1984 *The Division of Labor in Society*, translated by W. D. Halls. New York: The Free Press.

Dyck, Cornelius J.
1993 *An Introduction to Mennonite History.* Third edition. Scottdale, Pa.: Herald Press.

Elkhart County Chamber of Commerce
1966 *Amish.* Goshen, Ind.: Chamber of Commerce.

Ellul, Jacques
1964 *The Technological Society.* New York: Knopf.

Ephrata Review, The
1914– Ephrata, Pa.: The Ephrata Review, Inc.

Ericksen, Eugene P., Julia A. Ericksen, and John A. Hostetler
1980 "The Cultivation of the Soil as a Moral Directive: Population Growth, Family Ties, and the Maintenance of Community Among the Old Order Amish." *Rural Sociology* 45(1):49–68.

Ericksen, Julia, and Gary Klein
1981 "Women's Roles and Family Production Among the Old Order Amish." *Rural Sociology* 46:282–96.

Erickson, Donald A.
1966 "The Plain People vs. the Common Schools." *Saturday Review* (19 November): 82–87, 102–103.
1968 "The 'Plain People' and American Democracy." *Commentary* 45 (January):36–44.
1969 "Showdown at an Amish Schoolhouse: A Description and Analysis of the Iowa Controversy." In *Public Controls for Non-Public Schools,* edited by Donald A. Erickson. Chicago and London: The University of Chicago Press.

Evans, Sara M.
1979 *Personal Politics: The Roots of Women's Liberation in the Civil Rights Movement and the New Left.* New York: Knopf.

Family Life
1968– Aylmer, Ont.: Pathway Publishers.

Fink, Deborah
1992 *Agrarian Women: Wives and Mothers in Rural Nebraska, 1880–1940*. Chapel Hill: The University of North Carolina Press.

Fischer, Claude S.
1992 *America Calling: A Social History of the Telephone to 1940*. Berkeley: University of California Press.

Fisher, Gideon L.
1978 *Farm Life and Its Changes*. Gordonville, Pa.: Pequea Publishers.

Fishman, Andrea
1988 *Amish Literacy: What and How It Means*. Portsmouth, N.H.: Heinemann Educational Books.

Foster, Thomas W.
1984a "Occupational Differentiation and Change in an Ohio Amish Settlement." *Ohio Journal of Science* 84(3):74–81.
1984b "Separation and Survival in Amish Society." *Sociological Focus* 17(1):1–15.

Friedan, Betty
1983 *The Feminine Mystique*. New York: W. W. Norton & Company.

Fromm, Erich
1965 *Escape from Freedom*. New York: Avon Books.

Fuller, Raymond Tifft
1935 "Domain of Abundance." *Travel* (November): 15–17.

Gardels, Nathan
1991 "The Last Modern Century." *New Perspective Quarterly* 8:2–3.

Gay, Bettie
1981 "The Influence of Women in the Alliance." In *The Farmers' Alliance History and Agricultural Digest*, edited by Nelson A. Dunning. Washington, D.C.: Alliance Publishing Co.

Getz, Jane C.
1946 "The Economic Organization and Practices of the Old Order Amish of Lancaster County, Pennsylvania." *Mennonite Quarterly Review* 20:53–80, 20:98–127.

Gingerich, Eli E.
1980 *Indiana Amish Directory*. Middlebury, Ind.

Gingerich, Hugh F., and Rachel W. Kreider
1986 (comps.) *Amish and Amish-Mennonite Genealogies*. Gordonville, Pa.: Pequea Publishers.

Gingerich, Melvin
1986 *The Mennonites in Iowa City*. State Historical Society of Iowa.

Glick, Aaron S.
1987 "Pequea Amish Mennonite Church Twenty-Fifth Anniversary." Unpublished manuscript.

Glick, Nettie
1933 *Historical Sketch of Walnut Creek, Ohio, Amish Mennonite Church.* Sugarcreek, Ohio: Mennonite Publishing House.

Goffman, Erving
1967 *Interaction Ritual*. Garden City, N.Y.: Anchor Books.

Goodman, Betty
n.d. *There's No Place Like Holmes*. Cleveland, Ohio: Mrs. Ray Goodman.

Goshen, The First 150 Years: Goshen, Indiana, 1831–1981
1981 Goshen, Ind.: News Printing Co.

Goulder, Grace
1957 "Ohio Scenes and Citizens: Goulder Tour No. 3." *Cleveland Plain Dealer Pictorial Magazine* (23 June): 16–17.

Greer, Germaine
1992 *The Change: Women, Aging and the Menopause*. New York: Knopf.

Gross, Leonard
1980 *The Golden Years of the Hutterites*. Scottdale, Pa.: Herald Press.

Guidelines In Regards to the Old Order Amish Or Mennonite Parochial Schools
1981 Fourth printing. Gordonville, Pa.: Gordonville Print Shop.

Gutkind, Peter C. W.
1952 "Secularization Versus the Christian Community: The Problems of an Old Order House Amish Family of Northern Indiana." Master's thesis, University of Chicago.

Hark, Ann
1938 *Hex Marks the Spot*. New York: J. B. Lippincott Co.
1943 *The Story of the Pennsylvania Dutch*. New York: Harper and Brothers.
1952 *Blue Hills and Shoofly Pie*. New York: J. B. Lippincott Co.

Helm, Ruth
1956 *Wonderful Good Neighbors*. New York: J. B. Lippincott Co.

Herald der Wahrheit
1912– A monthly periodical published by conservative Amish Mennonites and the Old Order Amish.

Hershberger, Alma
1992 *Amish Women*. Danville, Ohio: Art of Amish Taste.

Hershberger, Noah L.
1985 *A Struggle to Be Separate: A History of the Ohio Amish Parochial School Movement*. Orrville, Ohio: Noah L. Hershberger.

Hildreth, Joseph S., and Charles S. Rice
1955 *Such Friendly People*. Radnor, Pa.: Chilton Co.

Hoover, Amos B.
1982 (ed.) *The Jonas Martin Era*. Denver, Pa.: published by the editor, Muddy Creek Farm Library.

Hoover, Helene M., and Kenneth H. Hoover
1979 *Concepts and Methodologies in the Family: An Instructor's Resource Handbook*. Boston, Mass.: Allyn and Bacon.

Hostetler, John A.
1952 *Amish Life*. Scottdale, Pa.: Herald Press.
1977 "Amish Survival." *Mennonite Quarterly Review* 51:352–61.
1982 *The Amish*. Scottdale, Pa.: Herald Press.
1984 "Silence and Survival Strategies Among the New and Old Order Amish." In *Internal and External Perspectives on Amish and Mennonite Life*, edited by Werner Enninger. Vol. 1. Essen: Unipress.
1993 *Amish Society*. Fourth edition. Baltimore: The Johns Hopkins University Press.

Hostetler, John A., and Gertrude E. Huntington
1971 *Children in Amish Society: Socialization and Community Education*. New York: Holt, Rinehart and Winston.
1992 *Amish Children: Education in the Family, School, and Community*. Fort Worth, Tex.: Harcourt Brace Jovanovich.

Hughes, Harold E.
1969 "The Amish School Controversy in Iowa; the View From the Governor's Office." In *Public Controls for Nonpublic Schools*, edited by Donald A. Erickson. Chicago and London: The University of Chicago Press.

Huntington, Gertrude Enders
1957 "Dove at the Window: A Study of an Old Order Amish Community in Ohio." Ph.D. diss., Yale University.
1981 "The Amish Family." In *Ethnic Families in America*, edited by Charles H. Mindel, Robert W. Habenstein, and Roosevelt Wright, Jr. New York: Elsevier.
1993 "Ideology, History and Agriculture: Examples from Contemporary North America." *Culture and Agriculture* 45/46 (Winter/Spring): 21–25.

"In the Heart of Amish Country"
1975 *Tuscarawas County Visitors Handbook* 7(3):11.

Jacoby, Henry
1973 *The Bureaucratization of the World*. Berkeley: University of California Press.

Jefferson, Thomas
1894 *The Writings of Thomas Jefferson*. New York: G. P. Putnam Sons.

Jensen, Joan
1991 *Promise to the Land: Essays on Rural Women*. Albuquerque, N.M.: University of New Mexico Press.

Johnson, Warren A., Victor Stoltzfus, and Peter Craumer
1977 "Energy Conservation in Amish Agriculture." *Science* 198:373–78.

Juberg, Richard C.
1966 "Selection in the ABO Rhesus, and MNSs Blood Group Polymorphisms in an Amish Isolate of Northern Indiana in 1966." Ph.D. diss., University of Michigan.

Kaufman, Alma
1961 *Meet Your Amish Neighbors*. Wooster, Ohio: Flair Travel Consultants.

Kaufman, Debra Renee
1991 *Rachel's Daughters: Newly Orthodox Jewish Women*. New Brunswick: Rutgers University Press.

Kaufman, Stanley A., and Leroy Beachy
1991 *Amish in Eastern Ohio*. Walnut Creek, Ohio: German Culture Museum.

Kay's Pennsylvania Dutch Cook Book of Fine Old Recipes
1934 Lancaster, Pa.: Kay Jewelry Company.

Keene, Carolyn
1955 *The Witch Tree Symbol*. New York: Grosset & Dunlap.

Keim, Albert
1975 (ed.) *Compulsory Education and the Amish: The Right Not to be Modern*. Boston, Mass.: Beacon Press.

Kephart, William M., and William W. Zellner
1991 *Extraordinary Groups*. New York: St. Martin's Press.

Ketchum, Richard M.
1979 "Letter from the Country." *Country Journal* 6 (July): 18–19.

King, Emma
1992 *Joys, Sorrows, and Shadows: A True Story of the Heartaches Following the Murder of a Loved One*. Lancaster, Pa.: Privately published.

Kingston, Joseph T.
1953 *The Amish Story*. Lancaster, Pa.: Intelligencer Journal.

Kinsinger, Susan
1988 (comp.) *Family and History of Lydia Beachey's Descendants, 1889–1989*. Gordonville, Pa.: Gordonville Print Shop.

Kollmorgan, Walter M.
1942 "Culture of a Contemporary Rural Community: The Old Order Amish of Lancaster County, Pennsylvania." Rural Life Studies, 4. Washington, D.C.: USDA, Bureau of Agricultural Economics.

Kraybill, Donald B.
1989 *The Riddle of Amish Culture*. Baltimore: The Johns Hopkins University Press.
1990a "Modernity and Modernization." *Anabaptist-Mennonite Identities in Ferment*. Occasional papers no. 14, pp 91–101. Elkhart, Ind.: Institute of Mennonite Studies.
1990b *The Puzzles of Amish Life*. Intercourse, Pa.: Good Books.
1993a (ed.) *The Amish and the State*. Baltimore: The Johns Hopkins University Press.
1993b "The Riddle of Amish Culture." Paper presented to the International Conference on the Amish Tricentennial, France, 20–22 August.

Kreps, George M., Martha W. Kreps, and Joseph Donnermeyer
1992 *The Shifting Occupational Roles of the Amish in Ohio*. Paper presented at the 55th annual meeting of the Rural Sociological Society, Pennsylvania State University.

Kurowski, Jeff
1990 "Shipshewana: Marketing the Amish." *Indiana Business* (May): 65–66, 68–70.

Lapp, Christ S.
1991 (ed.) "Minutes of the Book Society Meetings, 1957–1990." In *Pennsylvania School History, 1690–1990*, 521–26. Compiled and published by Christ S. Lapp, Gordonville, Pa.

Lapp, John K.
1986 "Remarks of By-Gone Days: A Few Remarks of Old Times." Pamphlet. Gordonville, Pa.: Gordonville Print Shop.

Lenski, Lois
1963 *Shoo-Fly Girl*. New York: J. B. Lippincott Co.

Lerner, Daniel
1968 "Modernization: Social Aspects." In David Sills (ed.), *Encyclopedia of the Social Sciences*, vol. 10, pp. 386–95. New York: Macmillan and Free Press.

Levy, Marion J., Jr.
1972 *Modernization: Latecomers and Survivors*. New York: Basic Books.
1986 "Modernization Exhumed." *Journal of Developing Studies* 2:1–11.

Lewis, Russell E.
1976a "Continuity and Change Among the Old Order Amish: A Case

Study of Amish Kinship." Paper presented at World Congress of Rural Sociology, Torun, Poland.

1976b "Controlled Acculturation Revisited: An Examination of Differential Acculturation and Assimilation Between the Hutterian Brethren and the Old Order Amish." *International Review of Modern Sociology* 6:75–83.

Loose, John Ward Willson

1978 *The Heritage of Lancaster*. Woodland Hills, Ca.: Windsor Publications.

Luthy, David

1981 "The Blue Gate Legend." *Family Life* (May): 19–20.

1992 "Amish Settlements Across America: 1991." *Family Life* (April): 19–24.

Marti, Donald

1984 "Sisters of the Grange: Rural Feminism in the Late Nineteenth Century." *Agricultural History* 58:247–61.

Martin, Helen R.

1905 *Sabina, A Story of the Amish*. New York: The Century Co.

Martineau, William H., and Rhonda Sayres MacQueen

1977 "Occupational Differentiation Among the Old Order Amish." *Rural Sociology* 42(3):383–97.

Marvin, Carolyn

1988 *When Old Technologies Were New*. New York: Oxford Press.

1989 "Experts, Black Boxes and Artifacts: New Allegories for the History of Electric Media." In *Rethinking Communication Volume 2: Paradigm Exemplars*, edited by Brenda Dervin and Larry Grossberg. London: Sage.

Mayer, Egon

1979 *From Suburb to Shtetl: The Jews of Boro Park*. Philadelphia: Temple University Press.

McConnachie, Brian, and Russ Heath

1976 "Amish in Space." *The Best of National Lampoon* 5: n.p.

"Menno-Hof Visitors Total Tops 32,000 Since May"

1989 *Mennonite Weekly Review* (5 January).

Mennonite Encyclopedia, The

1956–1990 Five vols. Scottdale, Pa.: Mennonite Publishing House; Hillsboro, Kans.: Mennonite Brethren Publishing House; Newton, Kans.: Mennonite Publication Office. Vol. 5 printed in 1990.

Mennonite Weekly Review, The
1920– Newton, Kans.: Herald Publishing Co.

Mennonite Yearbook, The
1992 Scottdale, Pa.: Mennonite Publishing House.

Merton, Thomas
1965 *The Way of Chuang Tzu*. New York: New Directions.

Mestrovic, Stjepan G., and Helene M. Brown
1985 "Durkheim's Concept of Anomie As *Dérèglement*." *Social Problems* 33:81–99.

Meyer, Marshal W., and M. Craig Brown
1977 "The Process of Bureaucratization." *American Journal of Sociology* 83:364–85.

Meyer, Marshall W., William Stevenson, and Stephen Webster
1985 *Limits to Bureaucratic Growth*. New York: Walter de Gruyter.

Meyers, Thomas J.
1983 "Stress and the Amish Community in Transition." Ph.D. diss., Boston University.
1991a "Factors Affecting the Decision to Leave the Old Order Amish." Paper presented at the American Anthropological Association Meeting, 24 November, Chicago, Ill.
1991b "Population Growth and Its Consequences in the Elkhart-Lagrange Old Order Amish Settlement." *Mennonite Quarterly Review* 65 (3):308–21.
1993 "Education and Schooling." In *The Amish and the State*, edited by Donald B. Kraybill. Baltimore: The Johns Hopkins University Press.
F.C. "The Old Order Amish: To Remain in the Faith or to Leave." *Mennonite Quarterly Review*, forthcoming.

Michels, Robert
1962 (1911). *Political Parties; A Sociological Study of the Oligarchical Tendencies of Modern Democracy*. New York: Collier Books.

Milhouse, Katherine
1940 *Lovina*. New York: Charles Scribner's Sons.

Miller, Betty
1977 *Amish Pioneers of The Walnut Creek Valley*. Wooster, Ohio: Atkinson Printing.

Miller, D. Paul
1978 "Amish Technology." Illinois Sociological Association Annual Meeting, 27–28 October.
1980 *The Illinois Amish*. Gordonville, Pa.: Pequea Publishers.

Miller, E. Jane
1943 "The Origin, Development, and Trends of the Dress of the Plain People of Lancaster County, Pennsylvania." Unpublished M.S. thesis, Cornell University.

Miller, Edna Mae
n.d. *The Teacher's Helper*. Arthur, Ill.: Echo.

Miller, Elva, and Betty Miller
1973 *Mrs. Miller's Amish Cook Book*. Millersburg, Ohio: Elva and Betty Miller.

Miller, Jerry E.
1988 *Indiana Amish Directory, Lagrange and Elkhart Counties*. Middlebury, Ind.: Jerry E. Miller.

Miller, Levi
1989 *Ben's Wayne*. Intercourse, Pa.: Good Books.
1992 *Our People: The Amish and Mennonites of Ohio*. Revised edition. Scottdale, Pa.: Herald Press.

Miller, Ora E.
1983 *Down Home Shoppers Guide*. Millersburg, Ohio: Miller Designs.

Mook, Maurice, and John Hostetler
1957 "The Amish and Their Land." *Landscape* 6:21–29.

Nagle, James
1978 "Amish Will Be Driving Cars Within 40 Years, Mennonite Predicts." *Kitchner-Waterloo Record*, Kitchner, Ont., March 11.

Newswanger, Kiehl, and Christian Newswanger
1954 *Amishland*. New York: Hastings House.

Nolt, Steven M.
1992 *A History of the Amish*. Intercourse, Pa.: Good Books.

Ohio Amish Directory, Holmes County and Vicinity
1965–1991 1965, 1973, 1981, 1988, and 1991 supplement. Millersburg, Ohio: Ohio Amish Directory, Inc.

Ohio Department of Economic and Community Development
1979 "Ohio's Amish Country." *Travel Ohio* (insert).

Olsen, Patricia Marie
1989 *The Light on the Hill: An Organizational Culture Study of an Amish Redemptive Community*. Ph.D. diss., Bowling Green State University.

Olshan, Marc A.
1981 "Modernity, the Folk Society, and the Old Order Amish." *Rural Sociology* 46:297–309.

1990 "The Old Order Amish Steering Committee: A Case Study in Organizational Evolution." *Social Forces* 69:603–16.

1991 "The Opening of Amish Society: Cottage Industry as Trojan Horse." *Human Organization* 50:378–84.

1992 "Social Change Among North American Amish." Presentation to the World Congress for Rural Sociology and the International Rural Sociology Association, 11–16 August, University Park, Pa.

1993 "The National Steering Committee." In *The Amish and the State*, edited by Donald B. Kraybill. Baltimore: The Johns Hopkins University Press.

Olshan, Marc A., and William M. Hall

1991 "The Old Order Amish, Social Change, and the Deviance Process." Paper presented to American Anthropological Association, Chicago, Ill., 21–24 November.

"Only One Step"

1985 *Family Life* (May): 12–18.

Ortmayer, Roger

1947 "The Amish and Tractors." *Mennonite Life* 2 (January): 43.

Ortner, Sherry B., and Harriet Whitehead

1981 *Sexual Meanings: The Cultural Construction of Gender and Sexuality*. Cambridge, England: Cambridge University Press.

Pederson, Jane M.

1993 "Gender, Justice, and a Wisconsin Lynching, 1889–1890." *Agricultural History* 67:65–82.

Penrod, John

1978 *Indiana: A Pictorial Adventure*. Berrien Center, Mich.: Penrod/Hiawatha Card Co.

Perrow, Charles

1986 *Complex Organizations: A Critical Essay*. New York: Random House.

Prusha, John

1978 "His Candid Photos Offer True Pictures of Amish Cultures." *Market Basket* (18 October): 1.

Questions and Answers on the Christian Life, 1001

1992 Aylmer, Ont.: Pathway Publishers. Based on Daniel Kauffman, revised and enlarged recently by Amish bishops, ministers, and other brethren.

Quickel, Stephen W.

1991 "Amish Country Almanac." *Travel and Leisure* 21:E1-E4.

Raber, Benjamin J.
1993 (ed.) *The New American Almanac*. Gordonville, Pa.: Gordonville Print Shop.

Redekop, Calvin W.
1989 *Mennonite Society*. Baltimore: The Johns Hopkins University Press.

Redfield, Robert
1947 "The Folk Society." *American Journal of Sociology* 52 (January): 293–308.
1953 *The Primitive World and Its Transformations*. Ithaca, N.Y.: Cornell University Press.
1960 *The Little Community and Peasant Society and Culture*. Chicago: University of Chicago Press.

Regulations and Guidelines for Old Order Amish Liability Aid
1973 Gordonville, Pa.: Gordonville Print Shop.

Reschly, Steven D., and Katherine Jellison
1993 "Production Patterns, Consumption Strategies, and Gender Relations in Amish and Non-Amish Farm Households in Lancaster County, Pennsylvania 1935–1936." *Agricultural History* 67:134–62.

Rich, Elaine Sommers
1975 "Thinking With." *Mennonite Weekly Review* (25 March): 11.

Riddle, William
1910 *Cherished Memories of Old Lancaster-Town and Shire*. Lancaster, Pa.: Intelligencer Printing House.

Rodgers, Harrell R., Jr.
1969 *Community Conflict, Public Opinion and the Law: The Amish Dispute in Iowa*. Columbus, Ohio: Charles Merrill Publishing Co.

Rosaldo, M. Z.
1980 "The Use and Abuse of Anthropology: Reflections on Feminism and Crosscultural Understanding." *Signs: Journal of Women in Culture and Society* 5(3):389–417.

Roth, John
1993 (trans. and ed.) *Letters of the Amish Division: A Sourcebook*. Goshen, Ind.: Mennonite Historical Society.

"Sam Buys a Farm"
1972 *Family Life* (July): 13–14.

Sanday, Peggy Reeves
1981 *Female Power and Male Dominance: On the Origins of Sexual Inequality*. Cambridge, England: Cambridge University Press.

Schein, Edgar H.
1965 *Organizational Psychology*. Englewood Cliffs, N.J.: Prentice Hall.

"School Directory: Old Order Amish, 1978–1979"
1978 *Blackboard Bulletin* (December): 11–21.

"School Directory, 1993–1994"
1993 *Blackboard Bulletin* (November): 9–25.

Schoolteachers' Signposts
1985 Teachers' Aid Series. East Earl, Pa.: Schoolaid.

Schreiber, William I.
1962 *Our Amish Neighbors*. Chicago: University of Chicago Press.

Schwartz, Hillel
1973 "Early Anabaptist Ideas About the Nature of Children." *Mennonite Quarterly Review* 47 (April): 102–14.

Scott, Joan W.
1986 "Gender: A Useful Category of Historical Analysis." *American History Review* 5:1053–75.

Scott, Stephen
1981 *Plain Buggies: Amish, Mennonite, and Brethren Horse-Drawn Transportation*. Intercourse, Pa.: Good Books.
1986 *Why Do They Dress That Way*? Intercourse, Pa.: Good Books.
1988 *The Amish Wedding and Other Special Occasions of the Old Order Communities*. Intercourse, Pa.: Good Books.

Scott, Stephen, and Kenneth Pellman
1990 *Living Without Electricity*. Intercourse, Pa.: Good Books.

Seyfert, Ella Maie
1939 *Little Amish Schoolhouse*. New York: Thomas Y. Crowell.
1942 *Amish Moving Day*. New York: Thomas Y. Crowell

Shenk, John B., and Charles S. Rice
1947 *Meet the Amish*. New Brunswick, N.J.: Rutgers University Press.

Shipshewana Flea Market & Area Visitors' Guide
1984 Lagrange, Ind.: Lagrange Publishing Co.

Shoemaker, Alfred L.
1951 *3 Myths About the Pennsylvania Dutch Country*. Lancaster, Pa.: Pennsylvania Dutch Folklore Center of Franklin and Marshall College.
1953a *My Off Is All*. Lancaster, Pa.: Pennsylvania Dutch Folklore Center of Franklin and Marshall College.
1953b *Hex, No!* Lancaster, Pa.: Pennsylvania Dutch Folklore Center of Franklin and Marshall College.

1954 *A Peek at the Amish*. Lancaster, Pa.: Pennsylvania Dutch Folklore Center of Franklin and Marshall College.

1959 "Zinn's Modern Diner." *Amish and Pennsylvania Dutch Tourist Guide*. Kutztown, Pa.: The Pennsylvania Folklife Society.

Siegel, Bernard J.

1970 "Defensive Structuring and Environmental Stress." *American Journal of Sociology* 76 (July): 11–32.

Simons, Menno

1956 *The Complete Writings of Menno Simons*, translated by Leonard Verduin, and edited by John C. Wenger. Scottdale, Pa.: Herald Press.

Snow, John H.

1971 "Fear of Death and the Need to Accumulate." In *Ecology: Crisis and New Vision*, edited by Richard E. Sherrel. Richmond, Va.: John Knox Press.

Sorensen, Virginia

1955 *Plain Girl*. New York: Harcourt, Brace & World.

Spock, Benjamin

1976 *Baby and Child Care*. New York: Hawthorn/Dutton.

Steering Committee, Old Order Amish

1966–1992 *Minutes of Old Order Amish Steering Committee*. Vols. 1–5. Gordonville, Pa.: Gordonville Print Shop.

Steinfeldt, Berenice

1937 *The Amish of Lancaster County*. Lancaster, Pa.: Arthur G. Steinfeldt.

Steinmeier, Dorothy E.

1967 "Overlooked Indiana." *Travel* (June): 30.

Stinchcombe, Arthur L.

1965 "Social Structure and Organizations." In *Handbook of Organizations*, edited by James G. March. Chicago: Rand McNally.

Stoll, Elmo

1977a "Views and Values: Women's Lib and the Amish." *Family Life* (February): 7–8.

1977b "Views and Values: Daughters of Sarah." *Family Life* (March): 8–10.

1977c "Views and Values: Heirs Together." *Family Life* (April): 8–9.

1990 "The Cash Economy." *Family Life* (June): 7–8.

Stoll, Elmo, and Mark Stoll

1980 *Pioneer Catalogue of Country Living*. Toronto: Personal Library Publishers.

Stoll, Joseph
1964 (ed.) *The Challenge of the Child: Selections from the Blackboard Bulletin 1952–1963*. Aylmer, Ont.: Pathway Publishers.
1965 *Who Shall Educate Our Children*. Aylmer, Ont.: Pathway Publishers.
1967 (ed.) *The Challenge of the Child: Selections from the Blackboard Bulletin 1957–1966*. Aylmer, Ont.: Pathway Publishers.
1971 "Fireside Chats: Men and Women." *Family Life* (October): 7–9.

Stoltzfus, Victor
1973 "Amish Agriculture: Adaptive Strategies for Economic Survival of Community Life." *Rural Sociology* 38 (Summer): 196–206.
1977 "Reward and Sanction: The Adaptive Continuity of Amish Life." *Mennonite Quarterly Review* 51:308–18.

Teacher Talk: 35 Articles for the Blackboard Bulletin 1967–72
1974 Aylmer, Ont.: Pathway Publishers.

Tips For Teachers: Articles from the Blackboard Bulletin
1970, 1991 Aylmer, Ont.: Pathway Publishers.

Thomas, Bill
1968 "Ohio's Amish Country." *Travel* (April): 52–53, 62–63.

Thompson, James D.
1967 *Organizations in Action*. New York: McGraw-Hill.

Thompson, Lillian
1935 "A Critical Biography of Mrs. Helen R. Martin." Master's thesis, English Department, The Pennsylvania State College.

Tortora, Vincent R.
1958 *The Amish Folk of Pennsylvania Dutch Country*. Lancaster, Pa.: Photo Arts Press.

"Tourist Count Sets Record"
1979 *Supplement to the Ephrata Review* (2 August): 6.

Tourist Guide Through the Dutch Country
1954 Lancaster, Pa.: Pennsylvania Dutch Folklore Center of Franklin and Marshall College.

Treatise on Courtship
n.d. Sugarcreek, Ohio: Schlabach Printers.

Troyer, Henry, and Lee Willoughby
1984 "Changing Occupational Patterns in the Holmes County Ohio Amish Community." In *Internal and External Perspectives on Amish and Mennonite Life*, edited by W. Enninger. Essen: Unipress.

Truth in Word and Work, The
1983 Baltic, Ohio: Amish Brotherhood Publications.

Turner, Victor
1982 *From Ritual to Theatre*. New York: Performing Arts Journal Publications.

Umble, Diane Zimmerman
1991a "The Coming of the Telephone to Plain Country: A Study of Amish and Mennonite Resistance in Lancaster County, Pennsylvania at the Turn of the Century." Ph.D. diss., University of Pennsylvania.
1991b "Religion as a Cultural Determinant of Technology Adoption: The Case of Plain People and the Telephone." A paper presented at the Forty-first Annual Conference of the International Communication Association, Chicago, Ill.

U.S. Census
1979, 1992 Statistical Abstract of the United States: Washington, D.C.

Wagler, David
1966 *The Mighty Whirlwind*. Aylmer, Ont.: Pathway Publishers.
1968 "History and Change of the Amish of Reno County, Kansas." Unpublished term paper, Bethel College, North Newton, Kansas.
1990 "The Curious Tourist." *Family Life* (October): 17–18.

Wagner, Mary Jo
1988 " 'Helping Papa and Mamma Sing the People's Songs': Children in the Populist Party." In *Women in Farming: Changing Roles, Changing Structures*, edited by Wava G. Haney and Jane B. Knowles. Boulder, Co.: Westview Press.

Weaver, J. Denny
1987 *Becoming Anabaptist: The Origin and Significance of Sixteenth-Century Anabaptism*. Scottdale, Pa.: Herald Press.

Weber, Max
1949 *Max Weber on the Methodology of the Social Sciences*. Glencoe, Ill.: The Free Press.
1968 *Economy and Society*, edited by Guenther Roth and Claus Wittich. New York: Bedminster Press.

Welcome to Shipshewana
1977 Lagrange, Ind.: Lagrange Publishing.

White, Leslie
1969 *The Science of Culture*. New York: Farrar, Straus and Giroux.

Who Are The Amish?
n.d. Aylmer, Ont.: Pathway Publishers.

Wilson, Edmund
1972 *To the Finland Station*. New York: Farrar, Straus and Giroux.

Wilson, Fred J.
1975 "Welcome to Ohio's Amishland." Brochure. Massillon, Ohio: Grace and Fred Wilson.
1976 *A Vistor's Guide to Ohio's Amish Country*. Berlin, Ohio: Berlin Printing Co.

Wolf, Charlotte
1990 "Relative Advantage." *Symbolic Interaction* 13(1):37–61.

Wood, James R.
1970 "Authority and Controversial Policy: The Churches and Civil Rights." *American Sociological Review* 35:1057–69.
1981 *Leadership in Voluntary Organizations: The Controversy Over Social Action in Protestant Churches*. New Brunswick, N.J.: Rutgers University Press.

Wright, Richard A.
1977 "A Comparative Analysis of Economic Roles Within the Family: Amish and Contemporary American Women." *International Journal of Sociology and the Family* 7:55–60.

Yoder, Elmer S.
1987 *The Beachy Amish Mennonite Fellowship Churches*. Sugarcreek, Ohio: Schlabach Printers.

Yoder, John H.
1973 (trans. and ed.) *The Legacy of Michael Sattler*. Scottdale, Pa.: Herald Press.

Yoder, Joseph W.
1940 *Rosanna of the Amish*. Huntington, Pa.: The Yoder Publishing Co. Published by Herald Press, Scottdale, Pa., since 1960.

Yoder, Paton
1991 *Tradition & Transition: Amish Mennonites and Old Order Amish 1800–1900*. Scottdale, Pa.: Herald Press.

Yutzy, Daniel
1961 "The Changing Amish: An Intergenerational Study." Columbus, Ohio: Unpublished Master's thesis, Ohio State University.

Zehner, Olive G.
1955 "Dutch by the Ton." *The Dutchman* (Summer): 7–9.

Zook, Lee
1993 "Slow-Moving Vehicles." In *The Amish and the State*, edited by Donald B. Kraybill. Baltimore: The Johns Hopkins University Press.

CONTRIBUTORS

GERTRUDE ENDERS HUNTINGTON received her Ph.D. in social science from Yale. Her three-volume dissertation on the Amish of Ohio has received wide acclaim. Co-author of *Amish Children* (Harcourt Brace Jovanovich, 1993) she has conducted fieldwork and written widely on many Amish communities in addition to teaching at the University of Michigan.

DONALD B. KRAYBILL received his Ph.D. degree from Temple University. He is the author of *The Riddle of Amish Culture* (1989) and editor of *The Amish and the State* (1993), both published by The Johns Hopkins University Press, as well as many other books and articles on Anabaptist groups. Kraybill is professor of sociology at Elizabethtown College (Pa.) where he also directs the Young Center for the Study of Anabaptist and Pietist Groups.

DAVID LUTHY is director of Heritage Historical Library, which is part of Pathway Publishers, the Amish publishing house at Aylmer, Ontario.

THOMAS J. MEYERS taught in an Amish school in Indiana before receiving his Ph.D. in sociology at Boston University. His dissertation, as well as a variety of journal articles, deals with social change among the Amish. He is professor of sociology at Goshen College (Ind.).

STEVEN M. NOLT is the author of *A History of the Amish*. He has also published a number of historical articles on a variety of Amish and Mennonite groups.

MARC A. OLSHAN is professor of sociology at Alfred University, Alfred, N.Y. He received his Ph.D. in the sociology of development from Cornell University, where he wrote his dissertation on the Old Order Amish. His work in Amish communities, in Israel, and in Cuba focuses on social change.

KIMBERLY D. SCHMIDT is a Ph.D. candidate in American History at the State University of New York at Binghamton, where she received an American Association of University Women Dissertation Year Fellowship. Her dissertation focuses on Mennonite women in the twentieth century.

DIANE ZIMMERMAN UMBLE received her Ph.D. in communication from the University of Pennsylvania. Her dissertation and many of her articles have dealt with the resistance of Old Order communities to the telephone. She is assistant professor of communication at Millersville University (Pa.).

INDEX

UNIVERSITY PRESS OF NEW ENGLAND publishes books under its own imprint and is the publisher for Brandeis University Press, Brown University Press, University of Connecticut, Dartmouth College, Middlebury College Press, University of New Hampshire, University of Rhode Island, Tufts University, University of Vermont, Wesleyan University Press, and Salzburg Seminar.

Library of Congress Cataloging-in-Publication Data

The Amish struggle with modernity / edited by Donald B. Kraybill and Marc A. Olshan.
p. cm.
Includes bibliographical references and index.
ISBN 0-87451-683-8. — ISBN 0-87451-684-6 (pbk.)
1. Amish—Doctrines. 2. Amish—Social life and customs.
I. Kraybill, Donald B. II. Olshan, Marc Alan, 1945– .
BX8129.A6A47 1994
289.7'3—dc20 94-13668
∞